GW00634531

GUIDE TO THE

DEPARTMENT OF MANUSCRIPTS AND RECORDS

THE NATIONAL LIBRARY OF WALES

GUIDE TO THE
DEPARTMENT OF MANUSCRIPTS
AND RECORDS

THE NATIONAL LIBRARY OF WALES

LLYFRGELL GENEDLAETHOL CYMRU
NATIONAL LIBRARY OF WALES

ABERYSTWYTH

1996

First reprint: 1996

The cataloguing record for this book is available from the British Library.

ISBN: 0-907158-80-3

Printed at the press of the National Library of Wales, Aberystwyth.

CONTENTS

FOREWORD

When the National Library of Wales came into being in 1909, it was fortunate to be presented with the magnificent collections of manuscripts owned by Sir John Williams, the Library's first President. Over the years it acquired further extensive collections of manuscripts, descriptions of which have been published in the *Handlist of Manuscripts in the National Library of Wales* (1940-).

From an early date, the Library also collected *records* or, to use a more all-inclusive term *archives*, comprising public records (such as the records of the Courts of Great Sessions), ecclesiastical records, including those of the Church in Wales and the Calvinistic Methodist Archives, deeds and documents of landed estates, and the papers of national organisations and of prominent Welsh men and women. The curatorial department which was entrusted with the custody of these collections was the Department of Manuscripts and Records.

Although the Department's archival collections have been described in the Library's *Annual Report* and a large proportion of them have been listed and indexed, no all-embracing published guide to them has been available hitherto. This volume fills that gap. Though a section is devoted to the Department's *manuscript* collection, it is on the *records* - the second half of the Department's title - that this guide mostly concentrates.

In mountaineering terms, guides give invaluable advice to the climber on which is the most favourable route to the summit, what crevices may be encountered on the way and what points of reference can ensure that the climber is on the right track. However the climber still has to do the climbing and in the same way, the reader wishing to traverse the plethora of collections held by the Department will still need to search its lists and indexes, though this guide will prove an indispensable companion on the journey.

Many members of the Department contributed to this volume: Nia Henson, who laid the foundation of Appendix I, Tudor Barnes, Mary Davies, Philip Wyn Davies and Glyn Parry. Robert Davies gave advice about maps. The main hand however has been that of Daniel Huws, who planned and edited the Guide and wrote a large part of the text, completing the work after his retirement as Keeper in 1992. The Library's debt to him is boundless.

Gwyn Jenkins
Keeper of Manuscripts and Records

vii

ABBREVIATIONS

AR	*Annual Report* of the National Library of Wales
BL	British Library
co.	county
cos	counties
d.	died
NLWJ	*National Library of Wales Journal*
PRO	Public Record Office
RMWL	*Report on Manuscripts in the Welsh Language* (Royal Commission on Historical Manuscripts, London, 1898-1910)
RO	Record Office
UW, Aberystwyth	University of Wales, Aberystwyth (formerly University College of Wales)
UW, Bangor	University of Wales, Bangor (formerly University College of North Wales, Bangor)
UW, Cardiff	University of Wales, Cardiff (formerly University College of South Wales and Monmouthshire)
UW, Swansea	University of Wales, Swansea (formerly University College of Wales, Swansea)
@	See explanation on p.45

INTRODUCTION

The Department of Manuscripts and Records came into being with the foundation of the Library in 1909. A user's guide more substantial than the current series of departmental pamphlets is overdue. This Guide appears when the Department is on the threshold of large-scale automation of its information systems. Its successor will reflect a very different world.

Hitherto the convenient surveys of the holdings of the Department have been chapter VIII of William Davies, *A History of the National Library of Wales* (Aberystwyth, 1936), also issued as an offprint, E. D. Jones, 'The Department of Manuscripts and Records', *The National Library of Wales Journal*, 5 (1947), pp.96-120, and *Encyclopedia of Library and Information Science* ed. Allen Kent (New York/Basel, 1968-   ), vol. 41, pp.356-60. All these accounts give some details about the history of the Department which are not repeated in this Guide. The *List of unpublished catalogues, handlists and schedules in the National Library of Wales* (Aberystwyth, 1934) is subsumed in the appendix to this Guide.

The raw material for a fuller guide to the Department than the present one is available in print in the *Annual Report* of the Library. The appendixes to these Reports include over 1500 pages listing in considerable detail the annual accessions to the Department. Prior to the end of the Second World War some minor accessions and even a few major ones were not included in the Reports. Since the late 1940s all substantial accessions have been described in the Reports, albeit briefly, very briefly since 1980, with the exception of three categories, two of them very small, the third larger: (i) a small proportion of material which is under embargo, excluded either at the request of the donor or depositor or at the Librarian's discretion, (ii) material omitted by oversight and (iii) from all Reports from 1948 to 1981, the archives of the Presbyterian Church of Wales, the Calvinistic Methodist Archives. Annual reports on accessions of the third category will for this period be found only in *The Journal of the Calvinistic Methodist Historical Society*[1]. The appendixes to the *Annual Report* cover, therefore, all but a very small fraction of the material held in the Department and include most of the information

1. *Cylchgrawn Cymdeithas Hanes y Methodistiaid Calfinaidd*, from 1977 *Cylchgrawn Hanes y Methodistiaid Calfinaidd*.

1

which would be provided by a Guide; but all in a very undigested state. There is in the catalogue room of the Department a card index to all personal names which are contained in the descriptions of accessions to the Department in the *Annual Report*. Many of the entries in this index are repeated in other indexes (see below, pp. 14-16) but it has value as an index of last resort. There is no corresponding index to subjects and places mentioned in the *Annual Report* (but see below, p.14).

The Guide aims to describe summarily the main holdings of the Department and to indicate what is available by way of catalogues, lists and indexes at the end of March 1994. All lists, both printed and typescript, in which archives and collections in the Department are described are listed in Appendix I to the Guide. A complete set of lists is available on the shelves of the reading room. Most of them are available in the National Register of Archives in London and, those produced up to 1985, on microfiche in the *National Inventory of Documentary Sources in the United Kingdom* published by Chadwyck-Healey. Copies of lists, as appropriate to their contents, are also distributed to Welsh county record offices and to other libraries and record offices. The Guide offers an introduction to all material which has been listed or catalogued and to the main archives or collections for which no list is yet available. For the fullest survey available in print of the Department's holdings the searcher will still have to resort to the *Annual Report*. The Guide should be of value as a key to the Reports.

The Department is unusual among manuscript departments of national libraries in having also been from the beginning a department 'of records'. The founders of the National Library acknowledged the absence of a record office for Wales. There is still no such record office; the dual function of the Department is deep-rooted. The title implies a distinction between 'Manuscripts' and 'Records'. It is a distinction which could more easily be made in earlier centuries, between 'codices' or 'manuscript books' on the one hand and 'records' or 'archives' on the other. Today the distinction is often unclear. 'Manuscripts' may often constitute part of an archive, while the *disiecta membra* of archives often come to be treated as 'manuscripts', as indeed has long been the case, witness much archival material in the Cotton, Harley and Hengwrt collections. Despite its unsatisfactory nature the distinction, applied at times somewhat arbitrarily, accounts for some major divisions of

2

material in the Department. This will become apparent in what follows.

The reader more familiar with record offices than libraries needs to be aware of the two other curatorial departments in the National Library and their resources: the Department of Printed Books and the Department of Pictures and Maps (formerly the Department of Maps, Prints and Drawings). The former department holds much printed ephemera which might be sought among archives. The latter has custody of most manuscript and other maps which are integral to archives held in the Department of Manuscripts and Records, not to mention manuscript maps acquired separately; it also holds the main photographic and audio-visual collections. For further detail on map collections see below, pp.15, 28 and 46.

In order to make full use of the finding aids of the Department -- the catalogues, schedules and lists on the one hand and the corresponding indexes on the other -- a searcher needs to be aware of the possible channels taken by manuscripts or archives when they were received by the Department. Accession is by gift or bequest, by purchase or by deposit ('indefinite loan'). Each accession is registered and given an accession number, a number for internal use only; the accession is then channelled into one of the classes shown in the diagram below:

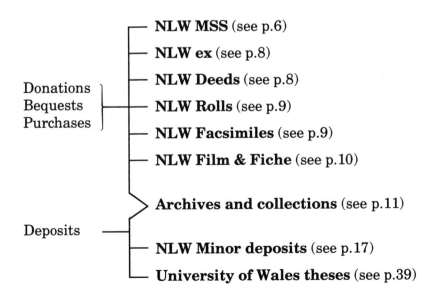

Donations / Bequests / Purchases
- **NLW MSS** (see p.6)
- **NLW ex** (see p.8)
- **NLW Deeds** (see p.8)
- **NLW Rolls** (see p.9)
- **NLW Facsimiles** (see p.9)
- **NLW Film & Fiche** (see p.10)

Deposits
- **Archives and collections** (see p.11)
- **NLW Minor deposits** (see p.17)
- **University of Wales theses** (see p.39)

Each of the classes shown on the right hand side of the diagram will be explained in turn. First, however, it is appropriate to introduce under the heading *Manuscript Collections* a number of closed collections of manuscripts which are of special status and importance, the main foundation collections of the Department.

MANUSCRIPT COLLECTIONS

The preamble to the charter of incorporation of the National Library of Wales granted in 1907 names a number of owners of collections of manuscripts who had signified their intention of giving their collections to the Library. The acquisitions of the Department in the early years were dominated by these and a number of other manuscript collections of high importance which came to the Library by gift or purchase. Indeed, it is no exaggeration to say that in any list of the most valuable manuscripts by which pre-1800 Welsh literature survived, well over half would be found to have come into the National Library during the first decade of its existence, largely as the result of remarkable generosity on the part of benefactors. Foremost among the foundation collections are the Hengwrt-Peniarth MSS.

A brief history of the Hengwrt-Peniarth manuscripts, which since their re-numbering by J. Gwenogvryn Evans have been known as the **Peniarth** manuscripts, will be found in the Library's *Handlist of Manuscripts in the National Library of Wales* (Aberystwyth, 1940-), vol. I, pp.iii-xxiii. The Welsh language manuscripts in the collection (MSS 1-327 and 533-9) had been catalogued in detail while they were at Peniarth by J. Gwenogvryn Evans for the Royal Commission on Historical Manuscripts in his invaluable *Report on Manuscripts in the Welsh Language* (London, 1898-1910, referred to henceforth as *RMWL)*. This remains the standard catalogue. Peniarth MSS 328-532, generally speaking the non-Welsh manuscripts, are briefly described in volume I of the *Handlist,* pp.1-22, with the exception of a small number of manuscripts which did not come to the Library in 1909. All the Peniarth manuscripts which were of Hengwrt provenance were among those which came to the Library in 1909. Those manuscripts which did not come in 1909 were all 'Ancient Peniarth MSS'; of these, Peniarth 481-2, two exceptionally fine manuscripts, were acquired later, and a larger group in 1981. The latter group is described in a typescript catalogue

4

(1990). This group included a few previously unnumbered Peniarth manuscripts. The collection now extends to Peniarth MS 561.

It is convenient here to mention the other manuscript collections which were described in *RMWL*. The **Mostyn** manuscripts included in *RMWL* were, with the exception of MS 1 (now in the library of the University of Wales, Bangor), acquired by NLW in 1918, together with other Mostyn manuscripts of Welsh interest; they are now NLW MSS 3021-76. Another group of Mostyn manuscripts was bought at the 1974 sale; these are now NLW MSS 21238-54, described in a typescript catalogue. A few strays from the 1920 Mostyn sale which were acquired later are also incorporated in NLW MSS (on this series see below).

The **Llanstephan** manuscripts formed part of the collection of Sir John Williams, the principal benefactor of the Library, and came to the Library in 1909. MSS 1-154, originally the collection of Moses Williams (1685-1742), had been acquired by Sir John *en bloc* from the Shirburn Castle collection in 1899; MSS 155-200 are of diverse origins. For the remainder of Sir John Williams's collection see below under NLW MSS (p.6).

The **Panton** manuscripts were acquired in 1914 and are now NLW MSS 1970-2068.

MSS 1-50 of the **Cwrtmawr** collection, the collection made by Principal J.H. Davies, were catalogued in *RMWL* and were given to the Library in 1925. The remainder of the collection, MSS 51-1492, came to the Library as a bequest after the death of Principal Davies in 1926. The Cwrtmawr MSS have not been incorporated in NLW MSS. The whole collection is briefly listed in a typescript handlist. The most important part of the collection has now been described in detail; volumes I-III of the new typescript catalogue cover MSS 1-750, while other descriptions may be seen on request.

Of the other collections catalogued in *RMWL*, the manuscripts of **Shrewsbury School, Cardiff Free Library** (now Central Library, South Glamorgan Libraries), **Jesus College,** Oxford (deposited in the Bodleian Library) and the **British Museum** (now the British Library) remain effectively where they were; the **Havod** manuscripts are at Cardiff Central Library; the **Wrexham** manuscripts are now NLW MSS 872-4; of the **Llanwrin** manuscripts, MS 1 is now Cwrtmawr MS 530, MS 2 is NLW MS 15533, while the whereabouts of MSS 3 and 4 are unknown; the **Merthyr Tydvil MS** is NLW MS 970; **Aberdare MSS** 1-2 are NLW MSS 5474-5.

Many manuscript collections have been incorporated in NLW MSS, including several of those mentioned in the Library's charter, among them those of Sir Lewis Morris, Henry Owen, Sir Edward Anwyl, Sir Daniel Lleufer Thomas and Richard Williams, Celynog. Collections are listed on the contents pages of the *Handlist*. NLW MSS also include many very notable collections acquired by the Library in later years; among these are the collection made by Francis Bourdillon (NLW MSS 5001-148), the Llanover MSS (NLW MSS 13061-184) and, in part, the Gwysaney MSS (NLW MSS 17110-62). Besides collections which have been incorporated in NLW MSS there are other collections of manuscripts of comparable importance which are preserved in association with related archives. These are treated under the heading *Archives and Collections*, see below, p.11. Outstanding among these are the collections from Bodewryd, Brogyntyn, Chirk Castle, Powis Castle and Wynnstay.

NLW MSS
The manuscripts known as National Library of Wales MSS 1-446 are described in J.H. Davies, *Catalogue of Manuscripts, Volume I, Additional Manuscripts in the Collections of Sir John Williams, Bart., G.C.V.O.* (Aberystwyth, 1921). This volume is indexed; no subsequent volume appeared. The 'Additional' in the title shows the relationship to the Llanstephan MSS (see p.5). Recommended practice is to refer to these manuscripts simply as NLW MSS 1-446.

NLW MSS from 447 onwards are described in the *Handlist*. NLW MSS 447-500 are in fact further 'additional manuscripts' in the collection of Sir John Williams. NLW MSS 501 onwards follow a heading in the *Handlist* 'The General Collection'. 'General' does indeed describe the nature of NLW MSS. It is an open-ended series of manuscripts, numbering 23233 on 31 March 1994. To this series are added, singly or in groups, all manuscripts received by donation or purchase which are (1) physically compatible with NLW MSS, i.e. are manuscript books or rolls, or unbound material which is capable of being bound or filed, and (2) not an integral part of an archive or collection which is to be treated as a separate entity. It is among the NLW MSS that most literary, historical and antiquarian manuscripts will be found. NLW MSS also include much material of archival origin, notably correspondence, and even integral archives. Within the series there is no classification by language or subject.

Volumes I-IV of the *Handlist* were published as numbers 1-34 of a Supplement, Series II, to the *National Library of Wales Journal* between 1940 and 1986. The index to volumes I-II is at the end of volume II; volumes III and IV each have their own index.

Cataloguing of NLW MSS, other than current accessions, ceased in 1982 and was not resumed until 1992. Volume V will begin with NLW MS 13686. Volume VIII, the next to be published, will begin with MS 21701 and contain accessions for 1981-91. In future the *Handlist* will be published by volume rather than in parts, as a publication in its own right.

Generally speaking, NLW MSS appear in the *Handlist* in the order of their accession by the Library. There are, however, notable deviations from this rule. On the one hand there are single manuscripts or, more often, groups of manuscripts which were not incorporated in NLW MSS until many years after their arrival in the Library. On the other hand, manuscripts (mostly facsimiles) which were in the first place given NLW MSS numbers have sometimes been removed from the series and relocated; the gaps in the series which were thus created were filled by accessions of a later date. This needs mention by way of warning because in volumes I-IV of the *Handlist* the date of accession of individual manuscripts is not given. Thus, for example, volume IV of the *Handlist* contains for the most part manuscripts acquired in the years 1937-40. It also includes, however, the Llanover manuscripts which were deposited in the Library in 1916 and converted into a donation in 1939, and another group acquired in 1928-9, while gaps have been filled by some ninety manuscripts acquired, mostly singly, in the years 1960-77. It should be said that manuscripts are not removed from the series once they have been fixed by publication of the *Handlist*.

NLW MSS are shelved according to size. The six sizes (see the beginning of any volume of the *Handlist*) are denoted by the letters A-F following the MS number. These letters are not an essential part of a bibliographical reference but readers are requested to include them in the call-number. Since 1981 the letter G has been used for rolls and other awkward-shaped manuscripts which do not fit the normal shelf.

Descriptions of NLW MSS prepared for future volumes of the *Handlist* (currently only volumes VIII and IX) are available in files in the catalogue room. A complete but brief listing of NLW MSS 13686-21700, those to be described in volumes V-VII of the *Handlist*, is available in the catalogue room. Where manuscripts constitute a group there is in many cases a typescript schedule of the group in which the manuscripts are more fully described. For an explanation of the 'schedules' see below, pp.13-14. There are individual descriptions of the most important manuscripts in the appropriate *Annual Report*.

In conjunction with the preparation of descriptions of NLW MSS for volumes VIII and IX of the *Handlist* indexes have been compiled. Unlike the indexes to volumes I-IV of the *Handlist*, these fuller indexes are made from the manuscripts themselves and not from the descriptions. They are at present on cards.

Apart from the indexes produced by renewed work on the *Handlist*, NLW MSS 13686-21700 are covered by a general card index, far from comprehensive, kept in the catalogue room.

An automated 'Index to Welsh poetry in manuscript' (including some 40,000 poems) allows search by first line, name of poet or subject. On this index, see *NLWJ*, 27 (1991-2), pp.353-8. A user's guide is available.

NLW ex
This class consists of manuscripts excluded from NLW MSS, for which class they might otherwise be eligible, on the grounds of the insubstantial or secondary quality of their contents. Types of manuscript commonly placed in this class are volumes of newspaper cuttings, scrap-books, dissertations and research papers. The series begins with NLW ex 416. It is a continuation of a closed series known as 'Miscellaneous Volumes' (or 'Misc. Vols'). 'Misc. Vols' 1-415 are described in a manuscript register, not yet indexed. NLW ex, accessioned after June 1981, are described in files kept in the catalogue room and indexed in the *Index to Schedules* (see below, p.14).

NLW DEEDS
This is a series of deeds and documents of all kinds which have come to the Library singly or in groups too small to be treated as archives or collections. Less than 1% of the Department's holdings of deeds and documents is comprised in NLW Deeds; the remainder will be found among archives or collections. Nevertheless, NLW Deeds includes some valuable documents.

Several series which had existed in parallel with NLW Deeds were closed in 1981: NLW Wills, NLW Manorial, NLW Miscellaneous Records and a series known as 'Miscellaneous Documents' which had been arranged by county. The first two series have now been subsumed in NLW Deeds.

Post-June-1981 accessions to NLW Deeds (currently nos. 1242-1815) are described in a series of volumes in the catalogue room. They are indexed in the *Index to Schedules* (see below, p. 14). For pre-July-1981 accessions to NLW Deeds and the other parallel series, the primary finding aid is a manuscript register, not indexed. All pre-July-1981 accessions in the several series will eventually be described in a consolidated list, on the pattern of the schedules, and indexed accordingly.

NLW ROLLS

A series comprising material which is now divorced from archives and collections and which is in roll form. The series consists in the main of pedigree rolls, 15th-20th cent., including copies and facsimiles. The series also includes other documents whose format happens to be that of a large roll; addresses; oriental rolls; palm-leaf books; and a few non-manuscript items.

The series was numbered in 1992. Previously the rolls had been identified only by box numbers or had been unnumbered. The series numbers 305 items and is described in a typescript list, *NLW Rolls* (1993).

Since 1981 the older and more valuable rolls acquired have been included in NLW MSS, size G.

NLW FACSIMILES

This class includes photographs, photostats and photocopies. Much of the material consists of facsimiles of manuscripts and archives in other libraries and record offices. There is also, however, material of which the original is in private hands.

Facsimiles accessioned after June 1981 are listed in a file kept in the catalogue room. These are indexed in the *Index to Schedules*. Facsimiles accessioned before July 1981 are listed in a register and roughly indexed, often only under the name of the library or record office, in a separate index of facsimiles.

A point to be reflected on is that the boundary between manuscripts and facsimiles has become very indistinct since the arrival of cheap copying machines and printers. While authors' typescripts or carbons have long been accepted as manuscripts, today a photocopy or print may have the same potential status as an author's holograph.

MICROFILM AND MICROFICHE

The past two decades have seen a huge increase in the holdings. The nucleus of the collection is microfilm of manuscripts in Welsh and of Welsh interest in other major libraries: the British Library; Jesus College and the Bodleian Library, Oxford; and South Glamorgan Libraries (Cardiff Central Library).[1] The collection of the University of Wales, Bangor, is the one major collection notable by its absence. The Hereford Cathedral manuscripts are available on film (not only those of Welsh interest). A quantity of Welsh material from the Public Record Office is available, and some from other record offices and overseas libraries and archive repositories. All these films are listed in the typescript *Manuscripts of Welsh interest in places other than NLW on Microfilm*. Apart from British Library manuscripts (*NLW Film BL*) and the Cardiff manuscripts (*DC*), all this material is included in the series *NLW Film*.

Commercially produced microform which has been bought by the Library has so far been predominantly of archives rather than manuscript collections. It includes the Public Record Office Kew Lists (microfiche edition), kept on the open shelves, the State Papers Domestic, some Home Office papers, Parliamentary Papers and archives of British political parties (all these are in the series *MFC* or *MFL,* listed in the typescript *List of published microforms at the National Library of Wales*). The records of the ecclesiastical Court of the Arches are available (*NLW Fiche*). The Chadwyck-Healey *National Inventory of Documentary Sources in the United Kingdom and Ireland (NIDS)*, is available on fiche and also on CD-Rom.

Such other material in microform as will be mentioned here is all of particular interest to the genealogical searcher: census returns for Wales for the censuses of 1841-81 on microfilm, those for 1891 on fiche; indexes to the registers of births, marriages and deaths of the Office of Population, Censuses and Surveys for 1837-1983 (*OPCS*

---

1. A summary catalogue of the Cardiff (South Glamorgan Libraries) manuscripts (over 4000 in number) was prepared at NLW when the manuscripts came to Aberystwyth to be filmed. A copy of the catalogue is available in the reading room.

microfiches); the non-parochial (i.e. nonconformist) registers for Wales in the Public Record Office (*NPR* microfilms); abstracts and indexes of wills prepared by the Genealogical Society of Utah from the Welsh probate records in NLW (*AIW* microfiches); the *International Genealogical Index*, for Wales, England, Ireland, Scotland and the Channel Islands (Genealogical Society of Utah, 1988 edition) (*IGI* microfiches); publications on microfiche of the Welsh family history societies (included in *NLW Fiche*).

ARCHIVES AND COLLECTIONS
In terms of bulk, the material comprised under this heading probably accounts for over 95% of the holdings of the Department. Some important archives which belong under this head are described separately below: records of the court of Great Sessions in Wales, the Welsh probate records, local government records, records of the Church in Wales, nonconformist records. For the rest, the predominant type of archive among the older records is that of the landed family and its estates, and, among more recent archives, that of the institution or the individual.

Outstanding among the many archives of landed families, comprising in almost every instance estate records and family papers, often much more, are those of Badminton (Welsh estates), Brogyntyn, Bronwydd, Bute, Chirk Castle, Dolaucothi, Penrice and Margam, Powis Castle, Tredegar, and Wynnstay. A related category of archives is that which derives from solicitors' offices; those from the offices of Longueville & Co. of Oswestry, solicitors for many prominent north Wales families, Eaton Evans & Williams of Haverfordwest, and D.T.M. Jones of Carmarthen are notable examples.

While the muniments of all large landed estates are likely to include good series of rentals and accumulations of title deeds, not all Welsh estates will be represented by long series of manorial records. The manorial system never came to full development in the counties of the medieval Principality, in west Wales. The Marcher lordships on the other hand generated a wealth of manorial records. In the north, fine series of records survive in the Chirk Castle and Aston Hall archives; the Powis Castle archives have extensive records; the Badminton, Bute and Tredegar archives include the records of many lordships and manors of south east Wales, and the Penrice and Margam archives the records of many Glamorgan lordships and manors. An invaluable guide to Welsh manors and their ownership (and likely location of surviving records) is Appendix M of *Report of the Royal Commission on Land in Wales* (1896) pp.439-75. The compilation of a database of Welsh manorial records both in the Library and elsewhere is a current project.

Much of the early industrial history of Wales is to be found in the archives of landed families: the early iron and coal industries of north-east Wales in the Chirk Castle archives, for instance; those of south-east Wales in the Tredegar and Bute archives (primary sources for the nineteenth-century growth of the towns of Newport and Cardiff respectively); early industry in the Swansea area in the Badminton archives and the beginnings of its copper industry in the Vivian archives. The list of relevant estate archives could be extended to include industry in all parts of Wales. Overtly industrial archives are fewer in number; they include those described in Appendix I under the titles Beaumont, Crawshay, Evans & Bevan, Llandinam and Nevill. Maybery and Portmadoc are two solicitors' archives rich in industrial content.

Among the most bulky archives are those of institutions. Those in the Library include bodies of an official nature: the Association of Welsh Local Councils, the Council for the Principality, the Committee of Welsh District Councils, the Welsh Arts Council; cultural bodies such as the National Eisteddfod, the Welsh National Opera Company, the Honourable Society of Cymmrodorion, Urdd Gobaith Cymru; bodies of a professional or business nature: the South Wales and Monmouthshire Coalowners Association, the Royal Welsh Agricultural Society, the Welsh Plant Breeding Station (now incorporated in the Institute of Grassland and Environmental Research). Political archives are discussed below under the head of the Welsh Political Archive.

Personal archives probably represent the area of most rapid expansion in recent decades. For an earlier period these archives commonly survive embodied in family archives. Today they commonly subsist in their own right. There are a few outstanding examples from the last century: Edward Williams ('Iolo Morganwg'), G.T. Clark, Nassau Senior.

It is with the outstanding generation of Welsh politicians and public figures whose activity spanned the period of the establishment of the National Library that surviving personal archives begin to feature on a large scale. Among the important archives of that period are those of T.E. Ellis, D.R. Daniel, Lord Rendel, Sir O.M. Edwards, Samuel T. Evans, E.T. John, Thomas Charles Edwards and Sir John Herbert Lewis. A large part of the fragmented archive of David Lloyd George himself is in NLW, together with that of his secretary A.J. Sylvester. The extraordinarily full archive of Thomas Jones, C.H., has a strong Lloyd George ingredient, but has other wide interest besides. The extensive archives of politicians of later generations are mentioned below.

The written word being itself the end product, archives of writers have a value beyond that of other archives. The holdings of literary archives for both modern writers in Welsh and Welsh writers in English are very comprehensive. On the one hand there are the archives of T. Gwynn Jones, R. Williams Parry, T.H. Parry-Williams, W.J. Gruffydd, Kate Roberts, Saunders Lewis; on the other, archives or large collections of papers of Caradoc Evans, Jack Jones, Alun Lewis, John Cowper Powys, Brenda Chamberlain, Gwyn Thomas, Rhys Davies, David Jones, Vernon Watkins, Idris Davies, Gwyn Jones and Raymond Williams. In parallel with the archives of writers are those of publishers such as Thomas Gee and Hughes a'i Fab, and of literary journals such as *Y Llenor, The Anglo-Welsh Review, Planet* and *Poetry Wales*. A useful guide to some of the main modern Welsh literary archives in the Department is the typescript *Awduron Cymraeg yr Ugeinfed Ganrif* (1985). English-language literary archives are well covered in *Location Register to Twentieth Century English Manuscripts and Letters* (London, 1988).

Again, there are the archives of artists -- Gwen John, Augustus John, David Jones, Ceri Richards -- and of composers -- John Thomas ('Pencerdd Gwalia'), Joseph Parry, David Vaughan-Thomas, William Mathias. Papers of scholars abound, particularly of those concerned with Welsh literature and history: Sir John Rhŷs, Sir Henry Lewis, Sir Goronwy Edwards, David Williams and Sir Idris Foster may be named. Papers of scientists do not feature large but include those of O.T. Jones, the geologist, Ben Davies (with important papers relating to Sir Oliver Lodge), Griffith Evans, the bacteriologist, and H.J. Fleure, the anthropologist.

Archives and collections in the Department are listed or catalogued in 'schedules' which are normally typescript. For a large archive there may be a dozen or so volumes. The shelves of the catalogue room hold some 800 volumes, the slimmest of them comprising only a few pages. Schedules vary greatly in the level and depth of

13

description and in quality. Typically they correspond to what the archivist understands by a 'descriptive list'; a few verge on being calendars; many, especially among the more recent, could be described as summary lists; some, betraying earlier hopes, go under the title 'Preliminary Schedule' (usually a box-list or bundle-list). The word 'schedule' itself, a lawyer's word, was adopted in the Department in its early days and can designate any form of catalogue or list. Particulars of all schedules, catalogues and lists are given in Appendix I.

Few of the large archives or collections in the Department are not represented by a schedule of some sort, though the schedule may only be a 'preliminary' one, or may cover only part of the archive. Few schedules have indexes of their own, other than personal name indexes in some cases, but some two thirds of them have by now been covered by the *Index to Schedules* (see below). Apart from archives and collections represented by schedules which are not yet indexed, the main area at present difficult of quick access is that of the small archives and collections which often consist of only a few boxes. Many of these are covered by schedules, but many again are covered only by summary descriptions in the Annual Reports. There is a full personal name card index to the Annual Reports; this is now being largely superseded by automated free-text database of descriptions contained in the Annual Reports.

The uncharted area represented by the small archives and collections for which no schedules exist is one which virtually disappears for accessions after June 1981. Archives and collections which were received after that date and which are not covered by a schedule (or due to be covered by one) are covered in a series of annual volumes: *Minor Lists and Summaries.* Each of these volumes covers a twelve-month period corresponding to that of the *Annual Report* and contains summary lists or descriptions of perhaps fifty or so archives or collections, most of them small ones. These volumes are indexed in the *Index to Schedules.*

INDEX TO SCHEDULES

The *Index to Schedules* is a large card index, or, rather, a series of card indexes. Some two thirds of the schedules have been indexed. A file kept above the index cabinets indicates which schedules have been indexed, and by what abbreviations they are identified in the index. The scope of the index and the principles on which it is based are explained in a booklet *Index to Schedules: Introduction* (1978), and, more briefly, in a departmental pamphlet *Indexes*. References in the index are not normally to document numbers but rather to the pages in the schedules on which descriptions with further details will be found. Exceptions are documents of a standard type such as wills and marriage settlements; for these, document numbers are given directly, as they are also for documents in the series NLW ex, NLW Deeds, NLW Facsimiles and Minor Deposits. The main divisions of the *Index to Schedules* are as follows.

Topographical Index. An index covering the British Isles, based on the divisions of the pre-1974 counties and parishes. The Welsh counties come first, followed by the English counties, followed by Ireland, Scotland, the Channel Islands, the Isle of Man. Under each county there are divisions for the county itself, parishes, townships, manors, capital messuages (big houses). Countries outside Britain and Ireland are to be found in the subject index under 'Foreign'.

Estate Index. An index of landed estates by name.

Subject Index. Based on a system of subject classification with up to three levels of sub-division set out and more fully explained in *Index to Schedules: Introduction.* This index should be used in conjunction with its Word-key which will refer the searcher to the point or points in the classification where any given subject matter is to be found.

Select Personal Name Index. The principles of selection are explained in *Index to Schedules: Introduction.* In this, as in the other personal name indexes, names are indexed under standardized spellings. Names of the Welsh patronymic pattern and surnames are kept apart and indexed in two separate sections.

Index to Wills. An index to wills, letters of administration, etc., other than those in the records of the probate courts and registries (for these see below, p.22).

Index to Inquisitions post mortem.

Index to Marriage Settlements.

Index to Maps. Merely an index of maps which happen to remain in the Department. Most maps received as archives are transferred to the custody of the Department of Pictures and Maps.

Index to Private Bills and Acts of Parliament. Merely the holdings of the Department. The Library's main holdings are in the Department of Printed Books.

THE WELSH POLITICAL ARCHIVE

The Welsh Political Archive was established by the National Library in 1983 to co-ordinate the collection of all materials concerning politics in Wales, whether printed, manuscript or audio-visual. Its activities are not confined to a single department in the Library. The Archive has no curatorial role: materials collected are placed in the custody of the appropriate department. In this Guide we restrict ourselves to the holdings of the Department of Manuscripts and Records; the Library's information leaflet on the Archive gives a more general description.[1] The archives mentioned below are, or will be all, covered by schedules.

Party records held include national and some local records of all the major political parties active in Wales. The Labour Party (Wales) Archive comprises a complete set of minutes dating back to 1937 as well as files of correspondence and papers dating from the 1950s to the present day. Among the local Labour Party records held are those of Brecon and Radnor, Ebbw Vale and Caerphilly. The records of the Welsh Liberal Party date from its formation in the 1960s and those of the SDP in Wales from 1981. Locally, the most important Liberal Party records held are those of Ceredigion, Montgomery and Caernarfon. Several Conservative and Unionist Associations, notably those of Cardiff, Monmouth, Caernarfon and Conwy, have deposited their records. Some of these records go back to the early decades of the 20th century. The largest party archive is that of Plaid Cymru, which dates back to the party's foundation in 1925. To complement these Welsh records, there are available on microfilm copies of central party records of all the main British parties.

---

1. See also Gwyn Jenkins, 'The Welsh Political Archive', *The Journal of Contemporary British History,* 7 (1993) pp.174-180.

Mention has already been made of the papers of Lloyd George and his contemporaries. The papers of many more recent politicians are held, among them those of four of the first five holders of the post of Secretary of State for Wales : James Griffiths, Cledwyn Hughes (Lord Cledwyn of Penrhos), George Thomas (Viscount Tonypandy) and John Morris; of Clement Davies, Leader of the Liberal Party, Lord Elwyn-Jones, Lord Chancellor 1974-9, Gwynfor Evans, President of Plaid Cymru 1945-81, and Beata Brookes, Conservative MEP for North Wales 1979-89, and of many long-serving backbench MPs: Leo Abse, Emlyn Hooson (Lord Hooson), Ted Rowlands, Dafydd Wigley, to name a few.

There are also records of organisations such as the Welsh National Council of the United Nations Association, formerly the League of Nations Union, 1923-56, and the Association of Welsh Local Authorities, 1928-70s, and records and papers relating to campaigns and pressure groups, for example, minutes and papers of the Parliament for Wales Campaign, 1953-6, the records of Cymdeithas yr Iaith Gymraeg, and the papers of several recent radical and nationalist pressure groups.

Some of the more recent political archives are subject to embargo or conditional access.

The Welsh Political Archive publishes a *Newsletter* twice a year. It is distributed to libraries and record offices and any interested persons.

MINOR DEPOSITS
This is a numbered series currently reaching 1572. The deposits included in it are minor in the sense that they consist of single items, or small groups of documents or papers where the group has been treated as a single item. There is one medieval missal, a few literary manuscripts, a large number of registers and other records from chapels, and much else. Minor Deposits 1-1200 are described in a typescript *Schedule of Minor Deposits* (1975) which has its own index. Minor Deposits above 1200 are described in a file in the catalogue room and indexed in the *Index to Schedules*.

PUBLIC RECORDS
RECORDS OF THE COURT OF GREAT SESSIONS
The Court of Great Sessions was established by the Second Act of Union in 1543. This Act brought Wales fully under English law.

Twelve of the thirteen Welsh counties were divided into four circuits:

Chester	Flint, Denbigh and Montgomery[1]
North Wales	Anglesey, Caernarfon and Merioneth
Brecon	Brecon, Glamorgan and Radnor
Carmarthen	Cardigan, Carmarthen and Pembroke

The thirteenth county, Monmouthshire, was assigned to the Oxford assize circuit.

Great Sessions were held twice yearly in the twelve counties, each sessions in each county lasting six days. Sessions were held regularly, with very few lapses, until the abolition of the court in 1830. After 1830 the whole of Wales was divided into assize circuits. All assize records, including those for Monmouthshire from 1542, are in the Public Record Office.

The records of Great Sessions, such as had survived, were taken from the Welsh counties to the newly built Public Record Office in Chancery Lane in 1854. In 1909 many of the post-1660 minor classes were presented to the National Library. In 1962 the main body of records was transferred from London to Aberystwyth. For some counties, notably those of the Chester circuit, the records are exceptionally well preserved from the very beginning. Being somewhat daunting, however, the Great Sessions records are the least tapped of the major Welsh historical sources for their period.

The main activity of the court of Great Sessions was hearing civil actions. According to the 1543 Act it was to hear all pleas 'in as large and ample a manner' as the courts of Kings Bench and Common Pleas. It also functioned as a criminal court, corresponding to the Crown side of assizes in an English county. And, although the Act made no such provision, Great Sessions evidently exercised equitable jurisdiction from the outset. In other words, it had a Chancery side, though never a very active one. Most Welsh cases in equity went either directly to the court of Chancery in London, or, until 1641 and,

---

1. Flintshire had an anomalous position, one explained by its having been administered before 1543 as part of the Palatinate of Chester. Earlier practices survived beyond 1543. Throughout the period of the Court of Great Sessions the Flintshire records show some entanglement with those of Chester.

18

to a lesser extent, in the years 1660-89, to the court of the Council of Wales and the Marches at Ludlow.[1]

Following a precedent established in 1723, the removal of actions from Great Sessions to neighbouring English counties by writ of *certiorari* became increasingly common; and, following a precedent set in 1769, it became possible to begin actions in English courts. This effectively ended the court's independent jurisdiction. Appeal from Great Sessions was in pleas of realty and mixed pleas to the Kings Bench and in personal pleas to the court of the Council of Wales and the Marches and, after 1689, to the House of Lords.

The records

The records are best understood in the light of the distinction between common law and equity, and, on the common law side, between civil and Crown (or criminal) actions. The great bulk of the records relate to common law side, and these in turn to civil rather than Crown actions.

Court procedure varied to some extent from circuit to circuit as did the record-keeping and filing, and the names given to some files. There were also some changes in the course of time.

The primary records on the common law side are what may be called sessional records: each sessions in each county produced one roll (apart from the North Wales circuit which produced only one annual roll for each county) and four files. On the civil side there were the plea roll, the prothonotary's file, the file of feet of fines and the file of writs; on the Crown side, the gaol file. The plea roll is the formal record of civil actions. Before 1600 it may also include enrolled deeds and indictments; the latter to 1680 on the Brecon circuit. The prothonotary's files are files of papers in civil actions, seldom of primary importance before *c.* 1700. After that date they contain the only record of actions which did not reach issue and

1. The records of this important court, which had common law and equitable jurisdiction concurrent with that of Great Sessions, have almost entirely been lost: there survive a few stray registers and precedent books; a group of records in the Public Record Office, SP Dom. 46/3/1-20, mainly for the 1540s and 50s, including pleadings and correspondence (see PRO, List and Index Society, vol 222 (1986)); and among the papers of the second earl of Bridgewater in the Huntington Library, San Marino, California, a small group of records from the period of his presidency in the 1630s, including the process books. The process books are available on microfilm in NLW.

which were not, therefore, enrolled on the plea rolls. The feet of fines correspond to their English counterparts in the records of the court of Common Pleas. There is also a regular sessional file of writs, both original and judicial.

The gaol files, the one sessional record produced on the Crown side, constitute what is by far the most interesting class of records of Great Sessions. These files include calendars of prisoners, indictments, presentments, writs and recognizances; they also include, though not always, the examinations of witnesses. On the Chester circuit examinations were regularly filed, as also were informations and other papers sent down to Great Sessions by the Court in the Marches, and contribute to a source of extraordinary richness. Gaol files also commonly include coroners' inquisitions.

The survival of sessional records county by county is roughly indicated in the table below, in which the dates of the earliest surviving records are given. The earliest sessions in some counties antedate the Act.

	Plea rolls	Prothonotary's Papers	Fines	Writs	Gaol files
Flint	1541	1542	1542	1543	1542
Denb.	1541	1548	1557	1556	1545
Mont.	1541	1551	1559	1543	1554
Ang.	1576**	1703*	1685	1708*	1708*
Caern.	1550**	1649*	1603	1703	1621**
Mer.	1547**	1682*	1609	1682*	1702*
Brec.	1542*	1559	1559	1559	1559
Glam.	1541	1548*	1542	1542	1542*
Rad.	1542	1541	1554	1541*	1542*
Card.	1541*	1546*	1552*	1562*	1542*
Carm.	1541*	1543*	1560*	1618*	1542*
Pemb.	1542	1558*	1549*	1542*	1547*

* indicates that there are significant gaps
** indicates that the series is very incomplete

For most purposes searchers are advised to begin not with the sessional records but with one or more of the series of rolls and books compiled by court officials as summary records of the business of court. Several of these serve as indexes; they provide a quick way to trace parties or types of action. For civil actions the key class is the docket rolls (or docket books) and, for the Carmarthen circuit, the precipe books. These specify, sessions by sessions, names of parties to actions (including those which had not reached issue), the nature of the action, and the stage reached at the end of each session. Order books, rule books, minute books and imparlance books may help in tracing the progress of an action through the court and in discovering judgements but are of no value for the initial search.

There survive for four counties the calendar rolls, in effect sessional indexes to the gaol files, and, for Flintshire, a series of Crown Books. A feature of the Brecon circuit are the 'Black Books', likewise a summary of Crown actions sessions by sessions. These series are all valuable for a quick search of the Crown records. Order Books can be of help in discovering the outcome of criminal actions, by way of orders to execute sentences.

The survival of the main series of court 'index' rolls and books is shown in the table below.

	Docket rolls or books	Precipe books	Rule books &c	Calendar rolls	Crown books	Black books
Flint	1617-1697		1574-1830		1564-1756*	
Denb.	1617-1791		1738-1830			
Mont.	1546-1830		1738-1830			
Ang.	1660-1821*		1783-1830			
Caern.	1576-1819*		1783-1830			
Mer.	1582-1819*		1783-1830			
Brec.	1559-1830		1725-1830			1726-1830
Glam.	1545-1830		1725-1830	1553-1601		1726-1830
Rad.	1553-1830		1725-1830	1553-1659*		1726-1830
Card.	1667-1733**	1698-1830	1661-1807	1541-1602*		
Carm.	1559-1733**	1642-1830	1661-1807			
Pemb.	1544-1654**	1655-1830	1661-1807	1541-1674		

Equity records of Great Sessions only survive in significant numbers from 1689. They were kept by circuit, not by county. The substance of causes in equity is to be found in the 'pleadings' (bills, answers etc). Unfortunately the pleadings are arranged in an unhelpful way. Causes are best traced by the Bill Books. The progress of causes through the court can be followed with the help of the Order Books, whilst the judgements (decrees) of the court can be found in the Decree Books. The survival of these classes is shown

21

in the table below

	Pleadings	Bill Books	Order Books &c
Chester	1730-	1742-61	1731-
N. Wales	1693-	1706-	1717-
Brecon	1690-	1779-	1710-
Carmarthen	1689-	1731-	1745-1811

Most of the main classes of records of Great Sessions are listed in the Public Record Office, *Lists and Indexes*, volumes iv and xl. Copies of these, with corrections and typescript additions, constitute the present working list. A completely revised list, which includes also those classes previously unlisted, by Glyn Parry, *A Guide to the Records of Great Sessions in Wales,* is in the press. Meanwhile a departmental pamphlet *Records of the Court of Great Sessions* will be found useful. It includes a bibliography.

PROBATE RECORDS
Pre-1858 : Jurisdiction

The pre-1858 probate records deposited in the Library comprise those of the episcopal consistory courts of St Asaph, Bangor, St Davids, and Llandaff, the consistory court of the archdeaconry of Brecon, the peculiar of Hawarden, and the Welsh wills proved at the episcopal consistory court of Chester. There were no ecclesiastical courts in Wales below the diocesan level. In probate matters the consistory court of the archdeaconry of Brecon, one of the four archdeaconries of the diocese of St Davids, acted as the bishop's court in a local capacity and not the archdeacon's.

The probate records of the diocese, deanery, and peculiar courts of Hereford, together with those of eight of the Salop peculiar courts, all of which were housed for many years at the National Library, have been transferred to the Hereford Record Office and the Lichfield Joint Record Office respectively.

Information concerning the probate courts having jurisdiction in Wales, the counties and parishes they covered, and the dates of surviving records is given in a typescript schedule of probate records available in the Department of Manuscripts and Records and in a departmental leaflet *Probate Records in the National Library of Wales.* Details have also been published in A.J. Camp, *Wills and Their Whereabouts* (London, 1974), now outdated in some respects, and J.S.W. Gibson, *A Simplified Guide to Probate Jurisdictions,*

Where to Look for Wills (Federation of Family History Societies, 1989).

Below is set out the jurisdiction of the probate courts, by county:

St Asaph   Most of Denbigh, Flint and Montgomery; parts of Caernarfon, Merioneth (deaneries of Mawddwy, Edeirnion and Penllyn) and Salop.

Bangor   Anglesey; most of Caernarfon and Merioneth; parts of Denbigh (deanery of Dyffryn Clwyd) and Montgomery (deanery of Arwystli).

St Davids   Cardigan, Carmarthen and Pembroke; part of Glamorgan (deanery of Gower).

Llandaff   Most of Glamorgan and Monmouth.

Brecon   Brecon; most of Radnor; parts of Monmouth, Montgomery and Hereford.

Hawarden   Parish of Hawarden, co. Flint.

Chester   Parts of Flint and Denbigh (one parish, Holt).

Hereford (Records at Hereford Record Office)   Parts of Monmouth, Montgomery, and Radnor. This court also had jurisdiction in those parishes which were partly in Shropshire and partly in Montgomery, i.e. Alberbury, Mainstone, and Worthen.

Pre-1858 : the records

Original wills and administration bonds generally survive from about 1600, except for Bangor, where very few have survived prior to 1635. The earliest surviving volumes of register copy wills are for St Asaph (from 1565) and Brecon (from 1543), both pre-dating the surviving original records. During the Interregnum, ecclesiastical jurisdiction was abolished, with resulting gaps in the Bangor and St Asaph records between 1648 and 1660. In the dioceses of Llandaff and St Davids registration continued nevertheless, on a reduced scale, there being very few St Davids wills after 1653. The records of the Court of Civil Commission which functioned during the Commonwealth are at the Public Record Office.

Probate act books are available for all the courts except Bangor and Brecon (and except for the Welsh wills proved at Chester). The incomplete series for St Asaph goes back to 1584 and the series for Llandaff to 1692.

A project to index anew all the pre-1858 probate records, employing an automated database, is well advanced. Both an automated and a print-out index are available for the period 1750-1858 for the Bangor, St. Asaph and Llandaff records (the latter from 1753). Until completion of the project in 1995 copies of the manuscript indexes may still have to be used for the remaining post-1750 and for the pre-1750 records. For the earliest wills, however, two volumes of a definitive index have been published by the Library: *An Index of the Probate Records of the Bangor Consistory Court, Vol. I : Pre-1700* (1980) and *Archdeaconry of Brecon Probate Records, Vol. I : Pre-1660 (1989)*. Abstracts and indexes of most of the pre-1858 wills for the consistory courts of Bangor, St Asaph, Llandaff and St Davids, and the archdeaconry of Brecon are available on microfiche prepared by the Genealogical Society of Utah *(AIW microfiches)*.

The following is a summary of the holdings for each court, giving covering dates only. Gaps in the series have not been noted.

St Asaph   Original wills etc, 1583-1858. Register copy wills, 1565-1709. MS indexes, 1583-1858. Card index, 1729-1820. Revised index up to 1648 (in progress). Automated and print-out indexes, 1750-1858.

Bangor   Original wills etc, 1635-1858. (There are very few wills before 1635). Register copy wills and administrations, 1790, 1851-8. Published index to pre-1700 records. MS indexes, 1700-1858. Automated and print-out indexes, 1750-1858.

St Davids   Original wills etc, 1556-1858. Register copy wills, 1703-1858. MS indexes, 1600-1858 (archdeaconries of St Davids (Pembrokeshire), Cardigan and Carmarthen). [The archdeaconries are roughly equivalent to the historic counties, but the archdeaconry of Cardigan included a number of north Pembrokeshire and some Carmarthenshire parishes, and the archdeaconry of Carmarthen included 23 Glamorgan parishes, the deanery of Gower]. Card index for wills proved at Carmarthen 1817-36 which includes some Cardiganshire wills.

Llandaff	Original wills etc, 1568-1857. Register copy wills, 1695-1844. MS indexes, 1575-1857. Automated and print-out indexes, 1753-1857.
Brecon	Original wills etc, 1557-1857. Register copy wills, 1543-1858. Published index to pre-1660 records. MS indexes, 1660-1858.
Hawarden	Original wills etc, 1554-1858. Printed index, 1554-1800, in *Publications of the Flintshire Historical Society*, vol. 4. MS indexes, 1752-1858.
Chester	Original wills etc, 1521-1858. Typescript indexes (Welsh wills). Printed indexes, 1545-1837, in *Publications of the Lancashire and Cheshire Record Society* vols. 2, 4 etc.

Post-1858 : Jurisdiction

The post-1858 records are those of the district registries at St Asaph, Bangor, Carmarthen, Llandaff and Hereford. The one Welsh county not covered is Montgomeryshire. Territorial jurisdiction was abolished in 1926, and the registries at St Asaph and Hereford were closed in 1928. The jurisdiction of the district registries was as follows:

St Asaph	Denbigh, Flint and Merioneth.
Bangor	Anglesey and Caernarfon.
Carmarthen	Cardigan, Carmarthen, Pembroke, and part of Glamorgan (Gower).
Llandaff	Monmouth and Glamorgan (except Gower).
Hereford	Brecon, Radnor and Hereford.

Post-1858 : the records

The post-1858 records consist of series of large bound volumes of copy wills spanning the years 1858 to 1941, when all registries ceased to copy wills into registers. The records in NLW cover all the historic counties of Wales except for Montgomeryshire, and one English county, Herefordshire. Post-1858 Montgomeryshire wills were proved at the Shrewsbury District Registry whose register copy wills are at the Shropshire Record Office.

Contemporary manuscript indexes together with modern card indexes cover most of the records. Comprehensive coverage will be found in the printed **Calendar of Grants**, an annual index of all wills proved and administrations granted in England and Wales since 1858. A set of the **Calendar of Grants** for the period 1858-1972 is available on the open shelves in the main reading room.

The holdings for each registry are:

St Asaph   Register copy wills, 1858-1928. There are no separate MS indexes, but indexes can be found in the volumes for 1860-1 and 1865-1923.

Bangor   Register copy wills, 1858-1941. Card index, 1858-1941.

Carmarthen   Register copy wills, 1858-1941. MS indexes, 1858-1923. Card index, 1924-41.

Llandaff   Register copy wills, 1858-1940. MS indexes, 1858-1905.

Hereford   Register copy wills, 1858-1928. MS indexes, 1858-1928.

Other probate records

In addition to the pre-1858 probate records transferred to the district registries and thence to the National Library, some wills and inventories and other papers associated with probate can be found in the consistory court papers deposited with the diocesan records of the Church in Wales. These documents are listed in the typescript schedules of the Church in Wales records available in the Department. Thousands of wills will also be found in the Department's collections of family, estate and personal papers; some of these wills may not survive in the official probate records, or may never have been proved, or may have been proved outside Wales. A card index to these wills forms part of the *Index to Schedules*.

For abstracts of wills relating to south Wales, the searcher should find the papers of David Jones (NLW MSS 18470-87, mainly Glamorgan) and Francis Green (mainly Dyfed, bound photocopies kept in the catalogue room) of value.

COUNTY AND LOCAL GOVERNMENT RECORDS

This section is included as much to prevent misapprehension as to provide guidance to holdings of the Department. The National Library has in its time had custody of the Quarter Sessions records of seven Welsh counties, not to mention county and district council records of the pre-1974 authorities and other official county records. Most of these records have long since been transferred to county record offices. The last major transfer, to Powys County Record Office at Llandrindod Wells, of the Breconshire, Montgomeryshire and Radnorshire Quarter Sessions records, took place in 1990. What remains in the Library is a quantity of stray records, often embedded in the archives of landed families (one striking example being the early Denbighshire Quarter Sessions records among the Chirk Castle archives) and a number of small groups, including some of the few surviving Cardiganshire Quarter Sessions records and the records of a number of boroughs, notably Aberystwyth and Welshpool. A body of pre-1974 Montgomeryshire Rural and Urban District Council records also remains on deposit in the Library.

The Quarter Sessions Order Books for Breconshire, Montgomeryshire and Radnorshire are available in the Department on microfilm. A convenient guide to surviving Quarter Sessions records is J. Gibson, *Quarter Sessions Records for Family Historians,* 3rd edition, (Birmingham, 1992).

RECORDS OF THE CHURCH IN WALES
Diocesan and capitular records

The Church in Wales came formally into being in 1920 when the disestablishment of the Church of England within Wales (including Monmouthshire) took effect. Until 1920 the four ancient Welsh dioceses -- Bangor, Llandaff, St Asaph and St Davids -- were part of the province of Canterbury. Two new dioceses, that of Monmouth

27

and that of Swansea and Brecon, were created soon after disestablishment. By a decision of the Governing Body of the Church in Wales in 1944 all the early diocesan and capitular records were transferred to the National Library. A good survey of these records will be found in J. Conway Davies, 'The records of the Church in Wales', *NLWJ*, 4 (1945), pp. 1-34. The records are listed in twenty nine typescript volumes: Bangor (4), Llandaff (10), St Asaph (3) and St Davids (12).

The ecclesiastical archives of Wales have suffered great losses. Few records apart from bishops' registers survive from before 1660. The main classes and dates of surviving records, where they begin earlier than 1800, are set out below by diocese. Particulars of bishops' registers to 1646 can be found in David M. Smith, *Guide to Bishops' Registers of England and Wales* (London, 1981); particulars of bishops' transcripts of parish registers can be found in C. J. Williams and J. Watts-Williams, *Cofrestri Plwyf Cymru / Parish Registers of Wales* (Aberystwyth, 1986). The diocesan sets of the tithe maps and apportionments are held by the Department of Pictures and Maps; gaps in the holdings have been made good by copies from the Tithe Commissioners' set. All surviving pre-1837 marriage bonds and allegations are accessible through an automated index.

Further deposits of records have been made from time to time, mainly by the dioceses of Llandaff, St Davids and St Asaph and modern records of the diocese of Swansea and Brecon have also been deposited. Brief details may be found in the Library's Annual Reports. Records are closed for a minimum of 25 years from the date of creation.

BANGOR
Episcopal records
Bishops' registers: 1408-17, 1512-25, 1534-8, 1542-1637, 1682-1794, 1800-14, 1821-64. The registers from 1512 to 1899 have been 'digested' by A.I. Pryce in *The Diocese of Bangor in the Sixteenth Century* (Bangor, 1923) and *The Diocese of Bangor During Three Centuries* (Cardiff, 1929).
Subscription books: from 1720
Ordination papers: from 1728, a few 1690-1702
Appointments and resignations: a few from 1661, more numerous in 18th cent., largely post-1800

Bishops'transcripts: particulars in C.Williams and J. Watts-Williams, *Parish Registers of Wales* (Aberystwyth, 1986)

Marriage bonds and allegations: from 1760, a few 1691, 1693, 1696 and 1757-8

Faculties: all post-1800, mostly 20th cent.

Petitions for the registration of dissenters' meeting houses: all post-1800 but with a return of licences granted from 1774 onward

Terriers: series for many parishes beginning in 1776, for a few as early as 1630

Visitation articles ('queries and answers'): 1567-1632 (cathedral), 1690 (dean of Bangor and archdeacon of Merioneth only), 1749, from 1771

Other visitation records: from 1675

Consistory court act books: 1730-69, from 1790

Correction mandates: 1752, from 1773

Consistory court papers: 1683, from 1734

Consistory court probate papers: from 1745, a few wills from 1587

Miscellanea (vols and papers): from 15th cent. Includes a vol. containing particulars of benefices, 1778

Deeds and estate records: from 15th cent. (see also the Welsh Church Commission archive)

Correspondence: from 1739

Chapter records

Act books: from 1680 (first vol. incomplete)

Accounts: from 1690

Other records: from late 17th cent., mostly post-1800

ST ASAPH

Episcopal records

Bishops' registers and other records of episcopal acts: 1506-71 (register for 1536-58), 1631-45 (acts), 1660-8 (acts), 1681-1755 (institutions, with various other acts including ordinations 1683-8 and 1721-53), 1748-1945 (two series of registers from 1889, one only to 1935)

Subscription books: 1682-92, from 1704

Ordination papers: from 1746, a few from 1714. Other clergy papers almost all post-1800 (a few 18th cent. resignations)

Bishops' transcripts: particulars in C.J. Williams and John Watts-Williams, *Parish Registers of Wales* (Aberystwyth, 1986)

Terriers: series for some parishes beginning in 1630

Registers of faculties (also include licensing of meeting houses, surgeons, etc.): from 1713

Marriage bonds and allegations: from 1690, a few from 1616

Visitations articles ('queries and answers'): 1738-53, 1791-1812, from 1871

Visitation books: from 1682

Reports on rural deaneries: from 1709

Consistory court act books: from 1580, a number of gaps in the series

Correspondence: from 1684

Miscellanea: from 1600, a few items from the late 14th/early 15th cent. Include a few deeds and other estate records, transcripts of earlier records including parts of the lost 14th century diocesan record known as *Llyfr Coch Asaph*, detailed parochial returns 1681-7, particulars of benefices compiled at various times from the early 18th cent. onward and early 18th cent. transcripts of 16th cent. and undated particulars.

Chapter records
Act books: from 1667

Other records: from 1670

ST DAVIDS
Episcopal records
Bishops' registers: 1397-1414, 1415 (facsimile), 1482-1518, 1554-66, 1636-8, 1661-1907. The register for 1397-1414 and 1482-1518 was published in the Cymmrodorion Record Series, no. 7 (3 vols, 1917-20)

Subscription books: 1660-84, from 1744

Ordination papers: from 1660, large gaps in the series before 1835

Other clergy papers (appointments, etc.): from 1660, mostly post-1800. Also some appointments to schools, from 1660

Bishops' transcripts: particulars in C. J. Williams and J. Watts-Williams, *Parish Registers of Wales* (Aberystwyth, 1986). Only a very few transcripts survive for parishes in the archdeaconries of Cardigan and St Davids between 1712 and 1794

Marriage bonds and allegations: a few from 1601, increasingly numerous from 1717

Consecration papers: 1717 (Llandyfrïog), 1787 (Aberystwyth), others post-1800

Faculty papers: a few from 1740, mostly late 19th and 20th cent.

Sequestration papers: a few from 1753, mostly post-1800
Queen Anne's Bounty papers: from 1707
Petitions for the registration of dissenters' meeting houses: from 1715
Papers relating to episcopal revenues: from 1661 (with transcripts of earlier records)
Brecon Collegiate Church papers: from 1664 (with transcripts of earlier records)
Miscellaneous books: from second half of 16th cent., including particulars of benefices, 18th and 19th cent.
Miscellaneous deeds: 1687, 1711, from 1743
Consistory court act books: from 1661 (archdeaconry of Brecon); 1590-3, 1660-8, from 1679 (archdeaconry of Carmarthen); 1668-71, 1698-9 (archdeaconry of Cardigan); from 1670, large gap in series between 1712 and 1763 (archdeaconry of St Davids)
Consistory court papers: from 1662 (no papers for the archdeaconries of Cardigan and St Davids for the greater part of the 18th cent.)
Consistory court probate papers: from 1661, a few from 1600 (very few papers for the archdeaconries of Cardigan and St Davids between 1710 and 1780)
Visitation articles ('queries and answers'): 1755-62, from 1799 (archdeaconry of Brecon); 1755, from 1799 (other archdeaconries)
Visitation books: from 1688 (clergy), from 1663 (wardens)
Churchwardens' returns and presentments: from 1672 (only for the archdeaconry of Carmarthen do many returns survive post-1700. The archdeaconry of Brecon presentments, 1699-1789, mostly only survive in abstract form)
Correspondence: from 1669
Miscellaneous papers: from 1570, including some terriers from 1674 (copy), 1681 (for other terriers see the typescript 'Schedule of the Maybery Collection', vol. III, see below, p.128)

Chapter records
Act books: from 1561
Account books: from 1384 (the earlier entries only extant in an early 17th cent. transcript).
Other chapter records beginning in the 17th and 18th centuries include registers of leases (not a continuous series), chapter acts, proxies, accounts (some relating to the fabric), leases, letters, papers relating to repairs to the cathedral and visitation records. There are

also 17th and 18th cent. copies of the statutes and the manuscript of Edward Yardley's *Menevia Sacra*, compiled around the middle of the 18th cent. but not published until 1927, by the Cambrian Archaeological Association.

LLANDAFF
Episcopal records
Bishops' registers (entitled act books) and other records of episcopal acts: 1660-78 (acts), 1679-1724 (institutions and ordinations), 1729-37 (institutions and ordinations, the latter to 1735), 1782-90 (institutions by commission), 1817-19 (draft register entries), 1819-51 (facsimile register), 1852-1927 (registers), 1870-1937 and 1967-84 (draft registers), 1919-21 and 1937-66 (registers). The acts for 1660-78 and the institutions and ordinations for 1679-1724 have been published in *Llandaff Records*, vols II-IV, ed. J.A. Bradney (Cardiff, 1908-9, and London, 1912)

Subscription books: from 1660

Precedent and form books: from 1670

Ordination papers: from 1745, a few from 1721, one 1465 and one 1668 (most after 1800)

Appointments to curacies: a few from 1742, mostly post-1800

Appointments to benefices: from 1660, one 1643

Resignations: from 1661

Appointments of surrogates, etc.: from 1726

Bishops' transcripts: particulars in C. J. Williams and J. Watts-Williams, *Parish Registers of Wales* (Aberystwyth, 1986)

Marriage bonds and allegations: from 1665, for every year from 1734 to 1941 except 1741

Terriers: 1771 for some parishes, a few from 1631 (copy), 1636

Faculty papers: some from 1738, largely 20th cent.

Sequestration papers: from 1670, mostly post-1800, also sequestration books, 1767-1858 (some gaps)

Queen Anne's Bounty papers: from 1707

Petitions for the registration of dissenters' meeting houses: from 1754, mostly 19th cent.

Particulars of benefices: from *c.* 1771

Visitation articles ('queries and answers'): from 1763

Visitation books: from 1703

Miscellaneous deeds: from 1659, largely post-1800

Letter books and miscellaneous correspondence: from 1720 (letter

book for 1746-50, others post-1800)
Account books: from 1711 (mostly registrar's accounts)
Miscellanea (vols and papers): from 17th cent.
Consistory court act books: 1693-6, from 1722
Consistory court papers: from 1710, a few from 1674
Consistory court probate papers: some from 1602 (largely inventories),
    more from 1662, increasingly numerous in 18th cent.

Chapter records
Act books: 1573-1817 (early entries transcribed from a dilapidated
    volume which survives in part)
Registers of leases and patents: from 1661
Account books: from 1694 (proctor general), from 1775 (inspector of
    the fabric)
Miscellaneous papers: a considerable body, mostly post-1800
Some 19th and 20th century chapter records have been deposited at
the Glamorgan Record Office, Cardiff. They have been listed as
'Llandaff Cathedral Archives'

PARISH RECORDS
A few parish records reached the Library before 1950, generally in
order to allow the Library to make photostat copies. By an
agreement with the Representative Body of the Church in Wales in
1950 the Library was able to begin actively to collect parish registers
and other parochial records. In 1976, following agreements between
the Representative Body and the Welsh county councils (apart from
Powys, still at that date without a record office), the Welsh county
record offices were also designated repositories for ecclesiastical
parish records. By the early 1980s registers of all but a few of the
ancient parishes had been deposited either in the National Library
or in a county record office. Particulars of surviving Welsh parish
registers and their locations, together with particulars of surviving
bishops' transcripts, facsimiles, microfilms and other copies of
registers, will be found in C. J. Williams and J. Watts-Williams,
Cofrestri Plwyf Cymru / Parish Registers of Wales (Aberystwyth,
1986). Over half the surviving Welsh registers only begin after
1700.
    Ecclesiastical parish records other than registers, sometimes
including pre-1895 civil records, have generally been deposited in
the same repository as the registers, i.e. either in the National

Library or a county record office. Civil parish records, for whose custody there are statutory provisions, are normally to be found in county record offices; among the exceptions are stray records which have found their way into family and personal archives now in the National Library. Details of all officially deposited parochial records other than registers will be found in a series of loose-leaf files in the catalogue room. Details of stray parochial records to be found in other archives will be found via the *Index to Schedules* and other indexes.

For conservation reasons, readers are normally required to consult parish registers in a microfilm copy (listed in the series *CPD*) rather than the original register. Parish registers held in Clwyd County Record Office are also available in NLW on microfilm (in the series *NLW Film*).

CENTRAL RECORDS OF THE CHURCH IN WALES

Following the 1914 Welsh Church Act central institutions had to be created for the disestablished Church in Wales that came into existence in 1920. The Representative Body holds in trust the property of the Church in Wales (including the churches) and administers its finances. The Governing Body, an assembly of bishops, clergy and laity, acts as the legislative body of the church. Records of these and other central bodies have been deposited and briefly listed. None of the records are available for consultation at present without written permission from the depositing body.

RECORDS OF THE WELSH CHURCH COMMISSION

The Church of England was disestablished and disendowed in Wales by the Welsh Church Act, 1914. Under Section 29 of the Act, the registrars of the Welsh dioceses, the Ecclesiastical Commissioners for England and the Governors of Queen Anne's Bounty were to hand over to the Welsh Church Commissioners all documents relating to lands vested in the Welsh Commissioners by the Act. Such documents were to be deposited by the Commissioners in the National Library of Wales when no longer required for the execution of the Commission's duties. In accordance with this directive, seven separate deposits of material found their way into the Library between 1933 and 1947. The first five of these consisted exclusively of material acquired by the Commissioners from other bodies, notably the Ecclesiastical Commissioners, and are made up of estate management files, deeds and documents and a small group of early manuscripts relating to church lands in Wales. The first five groups are described in a series of five schedules. See E.D. Jones, 'Welsh Church Commission Records', *NLWJ*, 2 (1941-2), pp.82-3, for brief details of the early records.

No provision was made in the 1914 Act for the deposit of records created by the Commissioners. In 1943 the University of Wales Estates Committee deposited in the Library a large body of material concerning episcopal and capitular estates and manors in Wales. In 1945 the Master of the Rolls directed that tithe apportionments and maps should also be deposited in the National Library. When the dissolution of the Welsh Church Commission was under consideration in 1945 and 1946, it was agreed that the National Library would be the most suitable repository for its records. In 1946 and 1947, a large body of records generated by the Commission was deposited. This was made up of three classes of material : parish files relating to the administration of lands while in the hands of the Commissioners; conveyances and transfer orders concerning property in 462 parishes, in all the counties of Wales; and a series of files on specific matters such as lay patronage, University of Wales estates, border parishes, receivership, inland revenue. Also deposited were files relating to the collection of tithe rent charges, files which came from the offices of the agents employed by the Commissioners such as John Francis, Carmarthen, G.W. David, Cardiff, and Boscawen and Richmond, Wrexham.

Work is in progress on a comprehensive list of Welsh Church Commission records, one which will take the place of the present schedules and the working lists of the 1946 and 1947 deposits.

NONCONFORMIST RECORDS

Common to all nonconformist archives is one main field: the records of the individual church (congregation) or meeting house or chapel. In some denominations the individual church is totally autonomous; there is no higher authority and consequently no hierarchy of archives. Such was the case until recent times with the Baptists and Congregationalists. Methodism, on the other hand, was associated from the beginning with a regional structure and this is reflected in the records. One denomination only, the Presbyterian Church of Wales (the Welsh Calvinistic Methodists) has as a matter of policy, like the Church in Wales, centralized its archives in the National

Library. For the remainder, the pattern of survival and custody of archives has been haphazard, to a greater or lesser degree.

Taking as a basis the list of nonconformist churches in the 1851 Religious Census, the Department has established an automated database recording the location of all known archives (including registers), whether in the National Library, the Public Record Office or local record offices. A by-product of the database is *Cofrestri Anghydffurfiol Cymru / Nonconformist Registers of Wales*, ed. Dafydd Ifans (Aberystwyth, 1994), a guide to surviving Welsh nonconformist registers. There follow here a few general observations on the archives of the main Welsh denominations.

BAPTIST

Before the 19th century Baptist records exist on one level only, that of the autonomous church and its meeting house or chapel. Many churches have deposited records in the Library (the earliest register is of Llanwenarth, beginning in 1655), as also in local record offices. More recent records, of the 19th and 20th centuries, include those of quarterly meetings, associations, unions and colleges; also, of course, those of ministers and historians of the denomination.

Some Baptist archives are listed in individual schedules. The typescript *List of Records of Baptist Churches* (1974) offers a useful summary list. The subject section of the *Index to Schedules* contains sections on all denominational records, including stray material among other archives. All accessions from July 1981 are detailed in files in the catalogue room.

CONGREGATIONALIST (INDEPENDENT)

There are a few records from the 17th century, rather more from the 18th century and many from the 19th and 20th. The pattern is similar to that for the Baptists. Apart from the records of single churches and personal archives there are, from the 19th and 20th centuries, records of quarterly meetings and associations and colleges.

Many Congregationalist archives are listed in individual schedules. There is a typescript *List of Records of Congregationalist Churches* (1962). The *Index to Schedules* contains a relevant section. Post-June 1981 accessions are described in a file in the catalogue room.

CALVINISTIC METHODIST ARCHIVES

The records of the Welsh Calvinistic Methodists, now the Presbyterian Church of Wales, are notably well preserved from the beginnings of the Methodist movement in Wales. This is for two reasons perhaps: there existed from the start a degree of central control; and there seems to have developed early an archival awareness. When an agreement for the deposit of the records was made between the Presbyterian Church of Wales and the National Library in 1934 the 'C.M. Archives' already had a recognised existence with a designated Curator. Accessions to the archive still come to NLW through the Curator. Regular lists of accessions to the archive have appeared in the *Journal of the Calvinistic Methodist Historical Society* since 1922. A good account of the archive by K. Monica Davies and Gildas Tibbott will be found in *NLWJ*, 5 (1947), pp.13-49. Although the policy of the denomination has been to centralize records in the National Library, some records have also been deposited in local record offices.

The records deposited in 1934 included two major groups, the 'Trevecka Group' and the 'Bala College Group'. The former, which represents the largely autonomous 18th-century development of Methodism in Wales, beginning in the 1730s, is centred on the archives of the founding father of Welsh Methodism, Howell Harris, and of the religious community which he established, the 'Trevecka Family'. Besides the 290 volumes of Howell Harris's diaries (for 1735-73), listed in a schedule [*c.* 1941], it comprises some 3000 letters, accounts of Societies (individual groups of adherents) and records of Associations. An inventory of the correspondence is provided in M.H. Jones, *The Trevecka Letters* (Caernarfon, 1932). There is a typescript index to this volume (1970). An additional group of Trevecka papers is listed in a typescript schedule [1938].

The 'Bala College Group' represents the development of Methodism during the 19th century, its spread in North Wales, the separation from the Established Church in 1811 and the formation of the Confession of Faith in 1823. This group is listed in a schedule [1936] with small supplementary schedules (1938 and 1964). Other small supplementary groups are 'Bala College Safe' [1934] and Trevecka College (1964).

A further five volumes (1941-74) list in a single unclassified series the 'General Collection' which embraces all accessions made to the 'C.M. Archives' during the period 1934-74, some 29000 items. This series includes the records of Associations, District Meetings, colleges, individual churches and personal archives, both those of ministers and laymen. These five volumes are provided with an index (1992). The accessions for 1974-83 are listed in a second series, differing from the first in that it is classified (vol. VI, 1988). In content, the accessions of these years are distinguished from those of the earlier period by the high proportion of records of individual churches, many of them deposited because of the closure of the church. A third series, following a classification similar to that of the second, lists accessions from July 1983 (vols VII and VIII, 1991 and 1992).

The records of the North Cardiganshire Presbytery, detailed in a schedule [c. 1940], have been withdrawn.

Particular mention should be made of the archives of the Foreign Mission, which cover the missionary work of the Church in North East India from its beginning in the 1840s.

Some material, notably the Howell Harris diaries and the Foreign Mission archives, may only be consulted by special permission.

WESLEYAN METHODISTS

From early in the 19th century Welsh Wesleyan Methodism has been organized in districts and, within districts, circuits. District records survive from 1816. Surviving records are divided between the National Library and local record offices. A major archive of Welsh Wesleyan Methodism was assembled by Mr R.J. Thomas at Amgueddfa'r Hen Gapel, Tre'r-ddôl, and subsequently deposited in the National Library. This archive includes district and circuit records as well as those of churches and individuals; it is listed in a schedule, *Welsh Methodist (Wesleyan) Archives* (1978) and indexed in an accompanying volume. *List of Records of (Wesleyan) Methodist Interest* (1978) provides a guide to Wesleyan records other than those in the Amgueddfa'r Hen Gapel archive. A few records of English language circuits in Wales are included in the Amgueddfa'r Hen Gapel archive; others have been deposited subsequently, notably the records for the Aberystwyth and Welshpool circuits. All Wesleyan Methodist accessions from 1978 are detailed in a file in the catalogue room.

OTHER DENOMINATIONS

There are no major holdings of records for other denominations. No major deposit of Roman Catholic records has yet been made.

Unitarian records, mostly unofficial deposits or donations, are detailed in a list, *Manuscripts of Unitarian interest* (1980), while in relation to the Society of Friends (Quakers), for which no official deposits are held, it is worth drawing attention to the papers of J.R. Hughes which include a wealth of transcripts and other material on Quaker history in Wales. Otherwise, searchers should turn to the indexes.

UNIVERSITY DISSERTATIONS

The National Library is the place of deposit for the University Registry copies of dissertations for higher degrees of the University of Wales (theses). They are in the custody of the Department. The earliest deposited dissertations are from 1900. Up to 1984, dissertations are listed by author in a series of typescript volumes. There is a corresponding subject card-index. Since 1985 dissertations have been included in the Library's automated printed-book database. Annual print-outs are made, arranged by author.

READER SERVICES

Information on the National Library's service for readers is given in a series of leaflets, notably those titled *General Information* and *Rules for Readers*. The following details provide only basic information for readers using the holdings of the Department of Manuscripts and Records.

General

The Library's reading rooms are open from 9.30 a.m. to 6.00 p.m. on weekdays and 9.30 a.m. to 5.00 p.m. on Saturdays. The Library is closed on bank holidays and during the first full week in October. Both long and short-term readers' tickets may be issued to applicants over eighteen years of age. These are obtainable at the General Office. The Library's photocopying service includes xerox copying, microprinting (for copies from a bound manuscript volume), and provision of black-and-white and colour photographic prints, slides and transparencies. Application forms for obtaining photocopies of documents, together with a leaflet listing charges, are available at the enquiries desk or by post.

The Catalogue Room

Enquiries and orders for documents may be made in the Department's catalogue room. An explanatory leaflet, *How to order documents,* is available there. Located in the catalogue room are the Department's schedules, lists and indexes together with reference books (see plan). Ultra-violet lamp facilities are located in a recess in the catalogue room. Also located in this recess are a computer terminal providing access to the Index to Welsh Poetry in Manuscript (see p.8) and a personal computer on which searches may be made of the indexes to probate records (see p.24), the marriage bonds index (see p.28) and a free-text database of the Minor Lists and Summaries series and of the appendixes to the Library's Annual Reports.

The Reading Room
The reading room seats 30 readers. All manuscripts and documents must be read in this room but University of Wales theses may be read in the reading room of the Department of Printed Books. Reference books are available on open shelves together with catalogues and lists of archives and manuscripts in other libraries and record offices (see plan). The use of ink is prohibited in the reading room. The use of lap-top computers is permitted provided that they do not cause disturbance to other readers. Readers with special needs (e.g. typing, recording) may make use of a specially designated room, the Erina Morris Room, adjacent to the microform reading room.

Microform Reading Room
The Department's microfilm and microfiche holdings (see above, pp.10-11) may be read in the microform reading room which is located at present at the east end of the main reading room of the Department of Printed Books It houses both microfilm and microfiche readers, and a member of staff is on duty at the counter to assist readers.

Postal enquiries
In response to postal enquiries, the Department will provide information as to sources held by the Department, except where lengthy searches of catalogues and indexes are necessary, and verification of a single entry from documents or records where precise references and details are provided by the enquirer. For more detailed searches, including genealogical searches, a fee-paid research service is available.

Exhibition

A selection of important and representative manuscripts may be viewed in the Library's permanent exhibition, *Trysorfa Cenedl / A Nation's Heritage,* in the Gregynog Gallery. Examples of the Department's recent accessions are displayed in a case outside the entrance to the Catalogue Room.

CATALOGUE ROOM AND READING ROOM

Plan

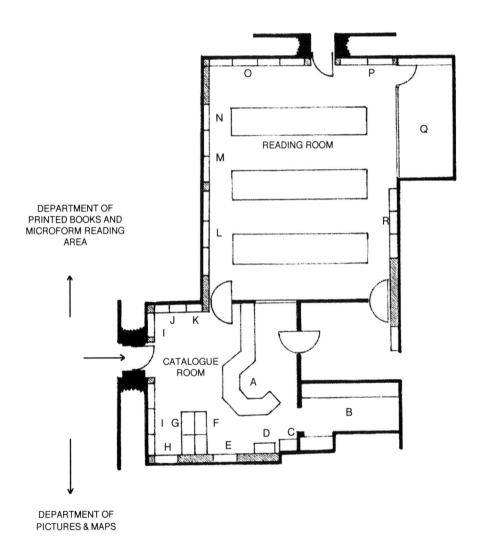

O

P

N

Q

READING ROOM

M

DEPARTMENT OF
PRINTED BOOKS AND
MICROFORM READING
AREA

L

R

J K

I

CATALOGUE
ROOM

A

I G

F

B

H

E

D C

DEPARTMENT OF
PICTURES & MAPS

CATALOGUE ROOM AND READING ROOM

Key to plan

A   Enquiry desk

B   Computer terminals; ultra-violet lamp; microfilm reader (for use only when microfilm has to be compared with original manuscripts)

C   Card index to NLW MSS 13686-

D   Card index to NLW *Annual Report*

E   NLW *Annual Report*; manuscript catalogues; lists of parish registers and bishop's transcripts, microfilms, Minor Deposits, NLW ex, NLW Deeds, NLW Facsimiles; nonconformist files (recent accessions)

F   Card indexes to some probate records and to theses (both becoming superseded)

G   Card index to schedules

H   Lists of University of Wales theses (dissertations)

I   Schedules (archives and collections)

J   Church in Wales lists; lists of parochial records, including those in other record offices; nonconformist lists; Minor Lists and Summaries; special and subject lists; probate indexes

K   Some key reference books; guides and annual reports of Welsh record offices

L   Lists from other Welsh record repositories

M   Manuscript catalogues of British and Irish libraries

N   Guides to English local record offices; manuscript catalogues of European and American libraries; subject guides

O   Public Record Office and Royal Commission on Historical Manuscripts publications

P   Dictionaries; general reference books on archival science, local history, genealogy, palaeography, seals, watermarks etc

Q   Supervisor of the reading room

R   Editions of Welsh literary texts; reference books on Welsh history, Welsh county histories, pedigree books, Welsh americana; *National Library of Wales Journal*

APPENDIX I

ARCHIVES AND COLLECTIONS

This appendix is intended to be a guide to the archives and collections in the Department. Specifically, it aims at providing a complete list of catalogues, schedules and lists available on the shelves of the catalogue room of the Department at the end of March 1994. Its completeness is a bibliographical one, not as a list of archives and collections held in the Department, though the main uncatalogued archives and collections are also included. Most of the catalogues, schedules and lists are typescript, a few are printed (these will be recognised by indication of place of publication, as well as date); most were produced within the Library, a few of them arrived with the archives. They are, for the great part, as noted above, also available at the National Register of Archives and, apart from those produced since 1985, on microfiche and CD-Rom in the Chadwyck-Healey *National Inventory of Documentary Sources* and, selectively, in local Welsh record offices and university libraries.

The volumes which are listed below describe themselves variously on their title pages as 'catalogue', 'schedule' (commonly), 'preliminary schedule', 'list', 'handlist'; while the material is denoted variously as 'collection', 'muniments', 'archives', 'records', 'manuscripts and papers', 'deeds and documents', 'documents and correspondence', or by other permutations of these words. The choice of words on title pages is often arbitrary. Rather than reproduce an array of titles such as 'A schedule of correspondence, deeds, documents and maps deposited by XYZ', full and exact titles have largely been eschewed. Exact forms of titles are given in the bibliographical details when short and helpful, and otherwise the bare word 'schedule', to cover all manner of catalogues and lists. A key word or words from the title (though sometimes not even part of the title) is given in bold as a heading: this serves to identify the archive or collection and is, typically, the name of an organisation, of a house (the seat of an estate) or of a person. It is in alphabetical order of these names, which appear on the spines or covers of the volumes, that the volumes are shelved in the catalogue room. Abbreviations of these names are used for indexing in the index to schedules. It has to be said that some of the names themselves are somewhat arbitrary (representing perhaps the accidental source of a collection); for all their occasional arbitrariness, they have, nevertheless, established themselves as working titles.

Following the short title comes, in the first paragraph, a very brief description of the archive or collection, and in a following paragraph come particulars of schedules and published descriptions. The date of the schedule is given, or, if it is undated, an ascertainable or a suggested date

44

is given in square brackets. This is followed by the number of pages in the schedule. High numbers of pages can be equivocal: they may be an indication either of the large extent of an archive or of a high level of cataloguing. Reference is then given to such summary descriptions of archives and collections as are available in print, in the Library's *Annual Report (AR)* and, more fully, in some cases, elsewhere, notably in the *National Library of Wales Journal (NLWJ)*; also to other relevant publications. The symbol @ following references to the *Annual Report* denotes additional accessions which are not detailed in the *Annual Report*. No companion to this appendix will be of greater value than the *Dictionary of Welsh Biography*.

The archives and collections described in schedules were sometimes at a later date incorporated, in whole or in part, in NLW MSS. Where this is the case, NLW MSS numbers are given. Even when an archive or collection has been wholly incorporated in NLW MSS and covered by the *Handlist of Manuscripts* the schedule may remain on the catalogue room shelf if its descriptions (as sometimes, for example, of correspondence) offer greater detail than the *Handlist*.

Many archives and collections once held in the Department have been transferred to other record offices, sometimes after having been catalogued. Particulars of transferred archives and collections are retained in this list for the convenience of those who may be under the misapprehension that the archive or collection is still in the Library, and for the added reason that references to transferred material are still embedded in departmental indexes.

Where an archive or collection is known to be divided between the Library and another library or record office, or when other closely related material is held elsewhere, reference is made to other locations. It is to be feared that some such cross-references will have been overlooked.

Entries have been made for archives or collections in the Department for which no schedule is yet available in so far as they are both distinctive (identifiable by a simple title, whether of a person or family or organisation or estate) and important. The words 'working list' in such entries indicate that a list (or schedule) is available for a substantial part or even the whole of the archive or collection, but not yet in form to be placed in the catalogue room. In effect, 'working list' means that some sort of finding aid is available upon request. There remain a good number of small unlisted archives and collections not included in this appendix for which the only published reference will be in the Annual Reports.

Readers will notice inconsistencies in the spelling of place-names, those of houses, in particular. The Guide reproduces forms adopted in schedules (conspicuously so in titles), which in turn often represent traditional anglicised forms of Welsh names. Following current departmental practice, pre-1974 county names are used throughout for purposes of identifying places. The words 'Also **Maps**' at the end of the bibliographical data indicate that maps integral to the archive or collection have been transferred to the Department of Pictures and Maps. Many of the early schedules of estate records neither list estate maps nor indicate that a transfer has taken place. 'Also **Maps** (schedule)' indicates that a separate schedule of transferred maps is available. Where no schedule of maps is available readers should use the indexes of the Department of Pictures and Maps, bearing in mind that the parish index is comprehensive while the estate index is not.[1]

The words 'conditional access' indicate that access to the archive or collection, or part of it, is in some way restricted and serve in general as a warning that written permission may be required. Potential users of such archives or collections are advised to enquire about the conditions before visiting the Library.

1. *Estate Maps of Wales, 1600-1836* (Aberystwyth, 1982) provides a useful introduction.

ABERFAN
Papers relating to the Public Inquiry into the Aberfan tip disaster of 1966.

Schedule (1984), 13pp.*AR 1983-84*, p.44.

ABERGAVENNY
Rentals, 1586-1627, and court books, 1767-1867, of the lordship of Abergavenny; and deeds, 1395-1915, relating to the lordship of Abergavenny in co. Monmouth and to other estates of the Nevill family, marquesses of Abergavenny, in co. Hereford. Other records in Gwent R O *s.n.* Gabb, Price & Fisher.

Schedule (1933), 302pp. *AR 1932-33*, pp.25, 34.

ABERGLASNEY
Records of the family of Philipps of Aberglasney, co. Carmarthen, 17th-19th cent. *Transferred to Dyfed R O (Carmarthen).*

AR 1940-41, p.27.

ABERPERGWM
Family and estate records, 17th-early 20th cent., of Williams of Aberpergwm, relating mainly to cos Glamorgan, Monmouth, Brecon and Carmarthen; records of industrial interest, mainly relating to collieries; correspondence of the Williams family and the associated families of Smith of Castellau and Lloyd of Castellau and Aberpergwm, co. Glamorgan, and Bush of Durcot, co. Oxford. Other records in West Glamorgan R O.

Schedules (1964), 143pp. (correspondence); (1968), 116pp. (deeds and documents); (1993), i + 26pp. *AR 1939-40*, p.35; *1949-50*, p.39; *1964-65*, pp. 60-1; *1965-66*, p.62; *1990-91*, p.64. See also *AR 1978-79*, p.52.

ABERTHIN
Documents relating mainly to Aberthin, parish of Llanblethian, co. Glamorgan, 1631-1913.

Schedule (1947), 37pp. *AR 1947-48*, p.36.

ABERTRINANT
Deeds, 1716-1807, relating to the Abertrinant estate, mainly in the parish of Llanfihangel-y-Creuddyn, co. Cardigan. *Withdrawn*. See also **Griffith E. Owen**.

Schedule (1939), 31pp.

ABERYSTWYTH BOROUGH
Borough records, 17th-20th cent., including court leet records, 1693-1882; harbour records, 1780-1906. See also **Glan-paith**.

Schedule [?1950s + suppl. 1970], 8pp. *AR 1939-40*, p.32. @.

ABERYSTWYTH CORN AND GENERAL MARKET CO.
Records of the company covering the whole period of its existence, 1870-1922.

Schedule (1978), ii + 89pp. *AR 1952-53*, p.28.

ABERYSTWYTH, ST MICHAEL'S CHURCH
Records, 1762-1933, relating to St Michael's Church, St Mary's Welsh Church and the 'Ysgoldy', Aberystwyth, and the National Schools of Aberystwyth and Penparcau, co. Cardigan. Later deposits listed as parochial records.

Schedule (1933), 36pp. *AR 1933-34*, pp.45-6.

47

ABERYSTWYTH SHIPPING

Crew lists and agreements for the port of Aberystwyth, 1863-1913. These represent records dispersed by the PRO in 1971 after retention of a sample; records for other Welsh ports are in county record offices.

List with index of ships (1985), 70pp. *AR 1971-72*, p.80.

ABERYSTWYTH, UCW, SRC & SOCIETIES

Records of the Students' Representative Council and various societies of the University College of Wales, 1892-1948.

UCW, Aberystwyth, SRC and Societies Records (1990), 3pp. *AR 1927-28*, p.48; *1930-31*, p.49; *1954-55*, p.56.

DANNIE ABSE

Papers of Dannie Abse (1923-   ), poet. *NLW MSS 21973-4, 21997-8, 22425-9.*

Dannie Abse Papers (1990), 11pp.; (1992), vol. II, i + 9pp. *AR 1987-88*, p.61; 1992-93, p.59.

LEO ABSE

Papers of Leo Abse (1917-   ), Labour MP for Pontypool, 1958-87. *Conditional access.*

AR 1990-91, p.59.

YR ACADEMI GYMREIG

Archives of Yr Academi Gymreig (including the English Language Section) from its foundation in 1958. *Conditional access.*

Archifau'r Academi Gymreig (1993), ii + 10pp. *AR 1972-73*, p.66; *1974-75*, p.62; *1984-85*, p.41; *1990-91*, p.64.

ACREFAIR

Papers of John Williams of Dowlais and Acrefair (d. 1898) and his family. They relate largely to the New British Iron Co., Acrefair, co. Flint, of which he was manager, and to Calvinistic Methodism.

Schedule (1989), 602pp. in two vols. *AR 1947-48*, p.32.

ALAW DDU

Papers of William Thomas Rees ('Alaw Ddu', 1838-1904), composer.

Rhestr o Bapurau Alaw Ddu (1981), i + 31pp.

W. E. R. ALLEN
Deeds (donated by W.E.R. Allen) relating to co. Pembroke, 1753-1850.

Schedules (Miscellaneous II, n d.), 4pp.; (1937), 4pp. *AR 1929-30*, p.19; *1937-38*, p.28.

ALLT-LWYD
Deeds and documents, 1617-1869, of the Hughes family of Allt-lwyd, parish of Llansanffraid, relating to cos Cardigan, Carmarthen and Pembroke. See also **Roberts & Evans** and **Llidiardau**.

Schedule (1974), 28pp.

AMGUEDDFA'R HEN GAPEL, TRE'R-DDÔL see above, p.38

AMPHLETT LEWIS & EVANS
Records from the office of Amphlett Lewis & Evans, Newcastle Emlyn (earlier D. Roy Evans), solicitors. Include deeds relating to estates in the surrounding areas of cos Cardigan and Carmarthen, 1708-1943, mainly the Llysnewydd and Pigeonsford estates; various Petty Sessions records, 1861-1936. See also **D. Roy Evans**.

AR 1967-68, pp. 50-51. Also **Maps**.

G.T.D. ANGEL
Deeds and documents (deposited by G.T.D. Angel), 1860-94, relating to the parishes of Llanllawddog and Abergorlech, co. Carmarthen. (*Minor Deposit 36B*).

Schedule (1958), 6pp. *AR 1957-58*, p.35.

ANGLO-WELSH REVIEW
Archives of the journal *Anglo-Welsh Review*, 1957-88.

Anglo-Welsh Review Archives (1993), 22pp. Frequent accessions since 1965, references to *AR* not detailed here.

ANTHROPOS
Papers of Robert David Rowlands ('Anthropos', ?1853-1944), author.

AR 1953-54, p.36; @.

BODFAN ANWYL
Papers of John Bodvan Anwyl ('Bodfan', 1875-1949), minister and lexicographer, with a few relating to his brother Sir Edward Anwyl (1866-

1914). See also **Minor Lists 1987** and **1991** for Anwyl family papers.

Schedule (1981), iv + 246pp. *AR 1976-77*, p.36; @.

AP NATHAN
Papers of James Ednyfed Rees ('Ap Nathan', 1876-1960) together with those of his father, Jonathan Rees ('Nathan Wyn', 1841-1905) and uncle, Evan Rees ('Dyfed', 1850-1923), Archdruid, and those of David Watkin Jones ('Dafydd Morganwg', 1832-1905) and Tom Jones, Trealaw (1871-1938).

Schedule (1984), 32pp. *AR 1984-85*, p.44.

ARUNDEL
Ministers' accounts and rentals for Marcher lordships of the earls of Arundel, including Wrockwardine, 1307-1466, Gower, 14-15th cent., Gwynllŵg, 1500-16, Oswestry, 15th-16th cent. *Returned to Arundel.*

Schedule (1943), 32pp.

ASHBURNHAM
Records of the Welsh estates of the earls of Ashburnham, 1392-1923. The estates descended from the Vaughan family of Bredwardine, co. Hereford. The chief estates were Porthamal, co. Brecon, and that in the parishes of Llanddeusant, Myddfai and Pembrey, co. Carmarthen. The main Ashburnham archive is in East Sussex R O. See also **BRA 1933**.

Schedules (1954), 62pp.; (1984), 42pp. Also **Maps**. *AR 1954-55*, pp. 47-8; *1964-65*, p.55; *1981-82*, p.80.

ASSOCIATION OF WELSH LOCAL AUTHORITIES
Records of the Association, 1928-76, including minutes, 1952-73, of annual and council meetings, and papers concerning finance, administration, and the withdrawal of railway services in Wales during the 1960s.

Schedule (1981), ii + 17pp. *AR 1981-82*, p.80.

ASTON HALL
Family and estate records, 12th-20th cent., of Lloyd of Aston Hall, near Oswestry, co. Salop, and Foxhall, co. Denbigh, and Harvey of Rolls Park, co. Essex; include records of the manors of Aston, from 1354, Sandford, from 1337, Middleton, from 1407 and Whittington, from 1362, with a few earlier strays; correspondence from 1642. See also **Longueville**.

Aston Hall Deeds and Documents (1955, 1964), 1072pp. in three vols; *Aston Hall Correspondence* (1964), 1734pp. in four vols. *AR 1948-49*, pp. 48-9.

BACHYMBYD

Estate and family records of Salusbury of Rhug, co. Merioneth, and Bachymbyd and Pool Park, co. Denbigh, later the barons Bagot, 1243-1801. Some records relating to English estates have been deposited by NLW in Staffordshire R O with the main Bagot archive. Include ministers' accounts relating to the Devereux estates, 1404-9 and 1525-52.

Schedule (1955), 333pp.; (1992), i + 4pp. (rentals). Also **Maps** *s.n.* Bagot. *AR 1942-43*, pp. 29-30, *1943-44*, p.29; *1974-75*, p.63. See also *AR 1941-42*, p.18 (*s.n.* Foyer). The early correspondence is calendared in W. J. Smith, *Calendar of Salusbury Correspondence 1553-circa 1700* (Cardiff, 1954). Most of the later records remain uncatalogued (1994).

BADMINTON

Records of the Welsh estates of the dukes of Beaufort, earlier of the earls of Worcester and William Herbert, earl of Pembroke (d. 1469). These include records for the Breconshire lordships of Crickhowell, from 1382, and Tretower, from 1532; ministers' accounts for Monmouthshire lordships from 1387 and manorial records for the lordship of Chepstow, from 1568, Monmouth, from 1416, Porthgaseg, from 1262, Raglan, from 1364, Treleck, from 1508, and for the lordship of Usk, from 1517; records of the Seignory of Gower and Kilvey from 1366 and for the borough and manor of Swansea, 1657-1835. Deeds from the 13th cent. and industrial records from the 16th cent. Plans in West Glamorgan R O.

Schedules: *Manorial Records : Vol I Brecknockshire* (1941), 287pp.; *Vols II and III Monmouthshire* (1946), 238 and 275pp.; *Vols IV and V Glamorgan* (1946), 169 and 154pp.; *Vol. VI Miscellaneous Counties* (1946), 285pp.; *Deeds and Documents* (1946), 540pp. in two vols; *Manuscripts and Records* (1965) 398pp. Also **Maps**. *AR 1940-1*, p.26; *1941-42*, p.25; *1960-61*, p.51; *1962-63*, pp. 45-52; *1964-65*, p.54; *1987-88*, p.62; *1989-90*, p.64. *NLWJ*, 5 (1947-8), pp. 55-6. Working list available for the 1987-88 and 1989-90 deposits.

BAKER-GABB see GABB

SIR JOHN BALLINGER

Papers of Sir John Ballinger (1860-1933), relating to library administration and literary, historical and archaeological research (*NLW MSS 9929-54*).

Schedule (1933), 7pp. *AR 1933-34*, p.27.

LUCIE BARBIER

Papers of Lucie Barbier (1875-1963), singer and pianist, including correspondence with French and English composers relating to La Société des Concerts Français, a society with which she was closely involved, 1907-1916 (*NLW MSS 22692-8*).

Lucie Barbier Papers (1993), 34pp. *AR 1988-89*, p.66.

BARMOUTH HARBOUR TRUST
Records covering the whole period during which the Trust was in operation, 1797-1929. Other records in Gwynedd R O (Dolgellau).

Barmouth Harbour Trust Records (1978), ii + 54pp. *AR 1944-45*, p.30; *1960-61*, p.51.

P.M. BARNARD
Deeds (purchased from P.M. Barnard), relating mainly to co. Monmouth, 1481-1780, a number of them concerning the Kemeys family of Bertholey, parish of Llantrissent.

Schedule (1979), iii + 18pp.

BATHAFARN AND LLANBEDR
Records of the estates of the Thelwall family of Bathafarn Park and Llanbedr Hall, co. Denbigh, lying mainly in that county, 1483-1864.

Schedule (1973), v + 167pp. *AR 1939-40*, p.31.

BEAUMONT
Records (donated by S.L. Beaumont) of the Trimsaran Coal, Iron and Steel Co. Ltd, the Ynisarwed Resolven Colliery Co. Ltd., and the Yniscedwyn Iron, Steel and Coal Co. Ltd, 1837-76.

Schedule (1948), 25pp.

BEDFORDSHIRE COUNTY COUNCIL
Deeds (donated by Bedfordshire County Council), 1600-53.

Schedule (1936), 2pp.

BEHRENS
Deeds and documents (donated by Mrs Helen E. Behrens), 1720-1938, of the Davies family of Llwyn, co. Cardigan, and Ffrwdfâl and Rhosybedw, co. Carmarthen, relating to cos Cardigan, Carmarthen and Pembroke (see also NLW MSS 11760-88).

Schedule (1962), 77pp. *AR 1937-38*, p.29.

SIR IDRIS BELL
Papers of Sir Harold Idris Bell (1879-1967), papyrologist and translator of

Welsh literature.

AR 1943-44, p.17; *1967-68*, pp. 21-2; *1968-69*, p.21.

T. G. BELLIS

Deeds (deposited by T.G. Bellis), relating to the parishes of Pennant and Llanrhaeadr-ym-Mochnant, 1618-1861. *Withdrawn.*

Schedule (1967), 5pp. *AR 1967-68*, p.49.

BELMONT ABBEY

Antiquarian collections (deposited by Belmont Abbey) of Robert Biddulph Phillipps (1798-1864). *Returned to Belmont Abbey. Some copied in NLW Facs 746.*

Schedule (1954), 21pp.

NICHOLAS BENNETT

Papers of Nicholas Bennett (1949-), Conservative MP for Pembroke, 1987-92. Conditional access.

AR 1992-93, pp.53-4.

AUGUSTA BERRY

Deeds (donated by Mrs J. Augusta Berry), 1753-1865, relating to properties in cos Glamorgan, Pembroke and Carmarthen.

Schedule (1938), 8pp. *AR 1938-39*, p.28.

BERTH-LWYD

Records of the Berth-lwyd and Dôl-llys estates, co. Montgomery, 1789-1888.

AR 1961-62, p.49.

KEITH BEST

Papers of Keith Best, MP for Ynys Môn 1979-87. *Conditional access.*

Keith Best Papers (1987), 12pp. *AR 1986-87*, p.58.

BETTISFIELD

Estate records and correspondence, 13th-19th cent., of the Hanmer family of Bettisfield, co. Flint. Includes manuscripts of Sir Thomas Hanmer (d. 1678), the horticulturalist.

Schedule (1947), 354pp. Also **Maps**. *AR 1938-39*, p.46; *1962-63*, p.54. *NLWJ*, 5 (1947-8), p.57.

PERCIVAL BEVAN

Stray records (donated by Percival Bevan) relating to the Wynnstay estates in co. Montgomery, including court rolls, 19th cent., and copies of Strata Marcella charters. See **Wynnstay**.

AR 1963-64, p.23.

ALISON BIELSKI

Papers of Alison Bielski (1925-   ), poet.

Alison Bielski Papers (1990), 12pp. *AR 1974-75*, pp. 63-4; *1980-81*, p.73; *1983-84*, p.53; *1988-89*, p.60.

BIRDSALL BOOKBINDING COLLECTIONS

A collection of materials relating to the bookbinding firm of Birdsall & Co., Northampton, closed 1961, and to bookbinding in general.

Birdsall Bookbinding Collection (1993), 5pp. *AR 1981-82*, p.36; *1991-92*, p.60.

BIRMINGHAM CORPORATION

Records from the Elan Estate Office, Rhaeadr, some relating to waterworks, mainly however the papers of Stephen William Williams (1837-99), surveyor and antiquary, including papers relating to his work as county surveyor of Radnorshire; deeds and other papers, mostly relating to co. Radnor, 1543-1933. See also **Penralley**.

AR 1961-62, p.45. Also **Maps**.

BODEWRYD

Estate records and papers of the Wynne family of Bodewryd, co. Anglesey, 13th-19th cent., with records also of the Bodowyr estate (Bodedern), co. Anglesey, and Plas Einion estate, co. Denbigh. Include important Welsh literary manuscripts, the antiquarian collections of Edward Wynne, chancellor of Hereford (d. 1755), relating to Wales and the diocese of Hereford, and part of the collection of Humphrey Humphreys, bishop of Bangor and later of Hereford (1648-1712). See also **Sotheby**.

Bodewryd Manuscripts and Documents [1933], 83pp.; *Correspondence and documents* [1951], 95pp. *AR 1932-33*, pp.43-4; *1943-44*, p.31.

BODFACH

Deeds and documents, 1737-1846, relating to the estate of the families of Bell Lloyd and Price Lloyd of Bodfach mainly in co. Montgomery.

Bodfach Deeds and Documents (1961), 45pp. *AR 1960-61*, pp.61-2.

BODFEAN

Deeds and papers relating to the Bodfean estate and the Wynn family, co. Caernarfon, 1474-1911. *Transferred to Gwynedd R O (Caernarfon).*

Schedule (1953), 21pp. *AR 1953-54*, p.51.

BODRHYDDAN

Court books, 1794-1841, and other records of the manor of Rhuddlan; records of the estates of Bodrhyddan, Aberkinsey and Bryniorkin in cos Flint and Denbigh, 1606-1794; correspondence, 18th-19th cent., including a group relating to plantations in Nevis and St Kitts in the West Indies. A larger group of Bodrhyddan archives is in UW, Bangor.

Bodrhyddan Documents [1936], 17pp.; *Bodrhyddan Correspondence* [*c*. 1940], two vols of transcripts, 385 and 140pp. Also **Maps**. *AR 1935-36*, p.48; *1938-39*, p.44.

BODVEL

Records of the Bodvel estate, co. Caernarfon, 1593-1754. *Transferred to Gwynedd R O (Caernarfon).*

Schedules (1936), 2pp.; (1947), 15pp. *AR 1935-36*, p.55; *1946-47*, p.46.

BODYNFOEL

Deeds, 1627-1823, relating to Bodynfoel, parish of Llanfechain, co. Montgomery.

Schedule (1933), 6pp. *AR 1932-33*, p.42.

BONSALL

Manuscripts, deeds and documents, 1674-1919, of the Bonsall family of Fronfraith, Llanbadarn Fawr, co. Cardigan, relating mainly to the Fronfraith estate in co. Cardigan and to the Galltyllan estate in co. Montgomery (some now *NLW MSS 3113-9*). See also **Minor Lists 1992** and **Roberts & Evans**.

Schedule (1932), 15pp. Also **Maps**. *AR 1932-33*, p.26.

BONTDOLGADFAN

Papers of William Williams ('Gwilym Cyfeiliog', 1801-76), of Bontdolgadfan, Llanbryn-mair, and members of his family (*NLW MSS 16728-89*).

Schedule (1947), 55pp. *AR 1942-43*, pp.26-7. See also *AR 1962-63*, p.35 (NLW MSS 18435-7); *1971-72*, pp.49-50; *1976-77*, p.39.

BORTH CONGREGATIONAL CHURCH
Records, 1869-1967, relating to the Congregational churches at Borth, Bow Street and Clarach, co. Cardigan (*Minor Deposit 361-4*).

Schedule (1967), 5pp. *AR 1953-54*, p.44. @.

BORTH-Y-GEST
Literary and historical manuscripts, mainly 18th-19th cent., collected by R. E. Jones, Borth-y-gest, mainly of north Wales interest, and slate quarrying records from the Ffestiniog area, co. Merioneth, 1863-1919. (The greater part now *NLW MSS 18262-418*.)

AR 1959-60, pp.42-3; *1960-61*, p.45; *1961-62*, pp.37-8.

BORTH-Y-GEST, EGLWYS BETHEL
Papers, 1871-1967, mainly relating to Bethel Welsh Congregational church, Borth-y-gest, co. Caernarfon.

Schedule (Welsh) (1971), 8pp. *AR 1970-71*, p.35.

DAVID BOWEN ('MYFYR HEFIN')
Papers of David Bowen ('Myfyr Hefin', 1874-1955), Baptist minister and author. Include papers of Ben Bowen (1878-1903), poet, his brother.

AR 1960-61, pp.22-3.

BRADNEY
Transcripts and extracts from parish registers, wills and other documents, and genealogical notes, made by or for Sir Joseph Bradney (1859-1933) in the course of his researches into the history of Monmouthshire (*NLW MSS 7561-7767*).

Schedule [*c*. 1933], 34pp. *AR 1933-34*, p.27. *NLWJ*, 5 (1947-8), 229-31.

BRADNEY DEEDS
Deeds donated by Sir Joseph Bradney or purchased through him, mostly relating to co. Monmouth, mostly 16th-19th cent. The 1921 group also includes deeds relating to co. Cardigan, including the Alltyrodyn and Castell Howell estates, and to co. Glamorgan, 16th-19th cent.

Bradney Deeds (1923 Group) [*c*. 1923], 25pp. *AR 1920-21*, p.12; *1923 (Oct.)*, p.9; *1931-32*, p.34. Only the 1923 group is catalogued (1994).

BRAWDY
Deeds and documents (purchased from Mrs E. Jones, connected with the Jones family of Brawdy) mostly of Pembrokeshire interest, 1490-1866.

The associated manuscripts are NLW MSS 11790-813 and 12166-74.

AR 1938-39, p.41.

BRECON BOROUGH CHARTER
Charter of incorporation of the borough of Brecon, 1556.

English translation (1963), 55pp. *AR 1962-63*, p.52.

BRECON AND RADNOR DIVISIONAL LABOUR PARTY
Records of the Brecon and Radnor Divisional Labour Party, 1924-85. *Conditional access.*

Schedule (1986), 11pp. *AR 1985-86*, p.61.

BRECONSHIRE QUARTER SESSIONS
Quarter Sessions records for co. Brecon, from 1670. *Transferred to Powys R O.* Microfilm is available in NLW of the Quarter Sessions Order Books, enclosure awards and deposited plans.

Preliminary schedule (1971), 37pp. *AR 1971-72*, p.82.

BREESE
Correspondence and papers, 19th-20th cent., from the library of Major Charles E. Breese (*NLW MSS 9471-89*).

Schedule (1933), 24pp. *AR 1932-33*, pp.26.

BRIGSTOCKE
Deeds relating to co. Carmarthen, 1813-*c*.1870; genealogical notes and transcripts relating to Brigstocke and other west Wales families. See also **W. Evans George** and **Griffith E. Owen**. Other Brigstocke records in Dyfed R O (Carmarthen).

Schedules [*c*. 1947], 3pp.; [*c*. 1957], 6pp. *AR 1946-47*, p.18; *1956-57* p.23. See also **Miscellaneous II** and *AR 1930-31*, p.29.

BBC (WALES)
Scripts, in Welsh and English, of the Welsh region of the BBC, from 1932.

BBC (Wales) Archives : Scripts, vol.i (1986, suppl. 1989), 45pp.; vol. ii (1986), 278pp.; vol. iii (1986), 198pp. Frequent reports in *AR* from 1960, not detailed here.

BRITISH RECORD SOCIETY
Deeds (received through the British Record Society) relating to most

Welsh counties, 1465-1883.

Schedule [*c.* 1932], 64pp. *AR 1931-32*, p.51.

BRITISH RECORDS ASSOCIATION

Records received through the British Records Association from various sources, mostly London solicitors' offices. Most Welsh counties are represented. Schedules are designated by years, as below. Summaries of contents are given only when there is a substantial body of records relating to a particular family, estate or activity.

1933, 42pp. Also **Maps**. *AR 1933-34*, p.37.
Deeds and manorial records, 17th-19th cent., relating to the Welsh estates of the earls of Ashburnham. See **Ashburnham**.

1934-35, 21pp. *AR 1934-35*, p.43.

1934-36, 24pp. *AR 1934-35*, p.43; *1935-36*, p.47.

1937, 10pp. *AR 1937-38*, p.29.

1940, 59pp. *AR 1939-40*, p.25.

1955, 167pp.

1956, 52pp.
Deeds and documents, 1707-1842, relating mainly to the estates of the Griffith family of Cefnamwlch, co. Caernarfon. See **Voelas and Cefnamwlch**.

1958, 72pp. *AR 1958-59*, pp.50-1.
Records relating to the development of Milford Haven, co. Pembroke, largely of the Milford Haven Dock and Railway Co., 1790-1921.

1963, 24pp. *AR 1963-64*, pp.23, 36, 48, 54.
Documents, 1867-85, relating to the Holyhead Shipbuilding and Trading Company Ltd.; deeds and documents, 1557-1904, relating to the Glandyfi estate and other properties in co. Cardigan, and in co. Montgomery; and deeds and documents, 1769-1855, relating to the families of Tickell of Whitechapel, co. Middlesex, and Cheltenham, co. Gloucester, and Jones of Gwynfryn, co. Cardigan.

1966, 41pp. *AR 1966-67*, pp.53, 54, 55, 56, 61.
Estate and family records, 1708-1894, of Mostyn of Plas Kynaston, co. Denbigh, and Owen of Woodhouse, co. Salop; and of Thelwall of Efenechtyd and Llanbedr Dyffryn Clwyd and Wynne of Prion, co. Denbigh.

1968, 27pp. *AR 1968-69*, pp.21, 25, 27, 35, 47, 50, 52, 53.

1975, 27pp. *AR 1975-76*, pp.47, 76, 81.
Deeds and documents, 1757-1858, relating to the Slwch, co. Brecon, and Bow, co. Middlesex, estates of the barons Tredegar. See **Tredegar**.

1977, iii + 45pp. *AR 1976-77*, pp.42-3, 47.
Deeds and documents, 1771-1918, mostly relating to a portion of the Glanusk estate in cos Brecon and Radnor of the Bailey family of Nant-y-glo. The main Glanusk archive is in Powys R O.

Other distinctive groups received through the BRA and remaining uncatalogued (1994) relate to: Hanmer of Bettisfield, co. Flint, 1733-1891 (*AR 1948-49*, pp.24-5); Corbet of Ynysmaengwyn, co. Merioneth, 1838-1912 (*AR 1948-49*, p.24); Breconshire, notably the Great Forest of Brecon, 1692-1878 (*AR 1950-51*, p.20); and Lewis, Morgan and Davies of Aberclydach and Cwrtygollen, co. Brecon, 1585-19th cent. (*AR 1970-71*, p.68).

BRITON FERRY
Deeds and documents, relating to the Briton Ferry estate in co. Glamorgan, of the Mansel family and the earls of Jersey, 1627-1879. Other records in West Glamorgan R O.

Schedule (1952), 113pp. *AR 1951-52*, p.34.

BROGYNTYN
Valuable medieval manuscripts and later Welsh and English literary manuscripts (the 'Brogyntyn', formerly 'Porkington', MSS); estate records and family correspondence of Owen of Brogyntyn, Wynne of Clenennau, Glyn and Ystumcegid, Maurice of Clenennau, Owen of Penrhos, Mostyn of Nant, Anwyl of Parc, Vaughan of Corsygedol, Longueville, Godolphin and Owen of Glasynys and Ormsby-Gore, barons Harlech, 14th-20th cent. The estates lay mainly in cos Caernarfon, Flint, Merioneth, Montgomery and Salop.

Schedules (1937), 42pp. (the first series of 'Brogyntyn MSS'); (1938), 289pp.; (1938), 142pp.; (1958, Longueville group), 87pp. Also **Maps**. *AR 1933-34*, pp.39-40 (catalogued in the 1937 and 1938 schedules); *1937-38*, pp.59-66 (lists the second series of 'Brogyntyn MSS'); *1938-39*, p.47; *1939-40*, p.33; *1947-48*, p.37; *1948-49*, pp.25-26; *1949-50*, p.28; *1953-54*, p.27; *1955-56*, pp.31-38; 1958-59, p.56 (Longueville group); *1992-93*, pp.57-8. The manuscripts are described (under shelf-numbers no longer current) in Royal Commission on Historical Manuscripts, *Second Report* (1871), pp.84-88, and idem, *Fourth Report* (1874), pp.379-97. The early correspondence is calendared in T. Jones Pierce, *Clenennau Letters and Papers*, Part I (Aberystwyth, 1947). Part II of this calendar was never published, being found seriously unreliable, but may be consulted in partly corrected page proofs in the catalogue room. No schedule is yet available for many of the estate records or for the later family papers. Cataloguing of these is in progress, as is a definitive catalogue of the Brogyntyn MSS.

BRONWYDD

Manuscripts and records relating to the family of Lloyd of Bronwydd, co. Cardigan, and their ancestors, the Owens of Henllys, co. Pembroke, including literary, genealogical and historical manuscripts of George Owen of Henllys (*c.* 1552-1613); manorial records relating to the hundred and barony of Cemais in Pembrokeshire; and deeds, mostly 16th-18th cent. See also **Minor Lists 1992.**

Schedules (1933), 101pp.; (1952), 779pp. in two vols. *AR 1932-33*, pp.39-41. *NLWJ*, 3 (1943-4), pp.33-5; 7 (1951-2), pp 67-9.

BRONWYLFA

Deeds and documents, 1660-1922, from Bronwylfa, Llandderfel, relating to the Fronheulog estate and to other properties, mainly in co. Merioneth.

Schedule [*c.* 1933], 71pp.

BRONYGRAIG

Documents (donated by Mrs L. Lloyd of Bron-y-graig), 1776-1881, mainly relating to the family of Lloyd of Brunant, co. Carmarthen.

Schedule [1934], 12pp. *AR 1933-34*, p.33.

BROOM HALL

Manuscripts from Broom Hall, co. Caernarfon, and records of the Jones and Evans families and the Broom Hall estate in co. Caernarfon, mainly 18th-20th cent.; and deeds, 1724-1854, relating to the Bodfel estate in cos Anglesey and Caernarfon. Other records in UW, Bangor.

Schedule (1953), iv + 361pp. Also **Maps.** *AR 1946-47*, pp. 23-4; *1949-50*, pp.40-41.

L. J. BROWN

Diaries and other papers of Leonard Joseph Brown (d. 1951), mountaineer, notably in Wales.

AR 1951-52, p.22.

BRUCE

Deeds (deposited by G.L. Bruce), of lands in co. Glamorgan, 1728-1856. *Transferred to Glamorgan R O (Cardiff).*

Schedule (1933), 8pp. *AR 1932-33*, p.36.

MRS C. H. BRYAN

Deeds (donated by Mrs C.H. Bryan) relating to the Llanfyllin area of co. Montgomery and to co. Salop, 1591-1901, (*NLW Deeds 643-661*).

Schedule [c. 1955], 5pp. *AR 1954-55*, p 23.

BRYFDIR

Manuscripts of the literary works of Humphrey Jones ('Bryfdir', 1867-1947). Other papers in Gwynedd R O (Dolgellau).

Gweithiau Barddonol 'Bryfdir' (1972), i + 22pp. *AR 1972-73*, p.41.

BRYNBELLA 'PIOZZIANA'

Deeds, 1564-1857, relating to the Bachegraig estate, co. Flint; diaries of Gabriel and Hester Lynch Piozzi and documents relating to the Piozzi family (some now *NLW MSS 11096-104*).

Schedule [?c. 1945], 12pp. Also **Maps**. *AR 1943-44*, p.28.

BUNSEN AND WADDINGTON

Papers of the Waddington, Bunsen and Chisholm families, consisting mainly of some 1,200 letters, 1817-63, to Mrs Georgina Waddington of Llanover, Thomas Waddington of St Rémy and his wife Janet (née Chisholm), and to various members of the Chisholm family. See also **Llanover Papers**.

Bunsen and Waddington Letters, vol. i (1981), vii + 199pp. Volume ii has yet to appear (1994). *AR 1973-74*, p.52. Some of the letters are published in A.J.C. Hare, *Life and Letters of Baroness Bunsen* (London, 1879).

BURCHINSHAW

Deeds and documents relating to the family of Burchinshaw of Llansannan, co. Denbigh, 1557-1863.

Schedule [1971], 10pp. *AR 1969-70*, p.27.

BURDON

Deeds and documents (purchased from H. Burdon), 1719-1855.

Schedule (1975), 8pp.

BUTE

Records of the Welsh estates of the marquesses of Bute, comprising much of what in 16th-17th cent. were estates of the earls of Pembroke, later of Lord Windsor. Include manorial records, from 14th cent., for many manors in cos Glamorgan and Monmouth; surveys, rentals, deeds, from

16th cent.; industrial records, from 16th cent.; some Cardiff borough records, from 16th cent., and extensive records for the 19th-cent. growth of the city; correspondence relating to industrial disputes and the Merthyr Riots, 1830s-40s. Further Bute records are in Glamorgan R O.

Preliminary schedule [1955], i + 211pp. This will be superseded by a completely revised schedule, almost completed (1994). Also **Maps**. *AR 1950-51*, pp.33-7; *NLWJ*, 7 (1951-2), pp.246-58; John Davies, *Cardiff and the Marquesses of Bute* (Cardiff, 1981).

BWLCHGWYN
Records of Bwlchgwyn Silica Co. and Bwlchgwyn Roadstone Co., Bwlchgwyn, co. Denbigh, 1830-1960.

AR 1976-77, p.36.

BWLCH-HAFOD-Y-GOF
Deeds, 1629-1833, relating to the families of Lucas and Matthews of Bwlch-hafod-y-gof, Llangurig, co. Montgomery.

Schedule (1973), 9pp. *AR 1972-73*, p.34.

BWRDD FFILMIAU CYMRAEG
Archives of Bwrdd Ffilmiau Cymraeg (the Welsh Film Board) from formation in 1972 to dissolution in 1986.

Archifau'r Bwrdd Ffilmiau Cymraeg (1992), i + 12pp. *AR 1988-89*, p.62.

CAERHUN
Records of the Caerhun estate in cos Anglesey and Caernarfon, the Downing estate in cos Denbigh and Flint, and the Llechweddygarth estate in co. Montgomery, and the families of Davies and Davies Griffith of Caerhun and Lloyd and Thomas of Downing, 1446-1935.

Caerhun Deeds and Documents (1970), 190pp. Also **Maps**. *AR 1943-44*, p.30.

CAERNARVON COURT ROLLS
Court rolls of the borough courts of Caernarfon, 1361-1402. See also **Arthur Ivor Pryce**. The main body of borough records is in Gwynedd R O (Caernarfon).

Caernarvon Court Rolls, 1361-1402, ed. G. P.Jones & Hugh Owen (Caernarvonshire Historical Society, Record Series, I, 1951).

CAERYNWCH
Deeds, 16th-19th cent., relating to property in cos Merioneth, Denbigh

and Flint, and letters and documents, mostly connected with the Edwards family of Cerrigllwydion and Dolserau and the Richards family of Caerynwch. Other records in Gwynedd R O (Dolgellau).

Schedule (1946), 83pp. Also **Maps**. *AR 1938-39*, p.49

CAMBRIAN ARCHAEOLOGICAL ASSOCIATION
Records of the Association from 1846.

Schedules (1977 + suppl.), i + 26pp.; (1988), 5pp.; (1992), i + 3pp. *AR 1966-67*, p.60; *1983-84*, p.53; *1984-85*, p.41; @.

CAMBRIAN IRON WORKS
Records of the Cambrian Iron Works, Wrexham, 1874-1927.

AR 1963-64, pp.36-7.

CAMBRIAN NEWS SALVAGE
Material preserved from salvage collected in campaigns organized by *The Cambrian News* during the Second World War: includes many tradesmen's and business records, largely of Cardiganshire interest, 1818-1941.

Schedule (1976), iv + 13pp. *AR 1943-44*, p.26. @.

IAN AND THALIA CAMPBELL
Papers and ephemera collected by Ian and Thalia Campbell relating to the Peace Movement, notably Greenham Common, and the Labour Party, mostly 1970s and 80s.

Schedule (1993), i + 8pp. *AR 1989-90*, p.64.

CARDIGAN BOROUGH
Cardigan Borough Order Books, 1653-1907.

AR 1958-59, p.51.

CARDIGANSHIRE BOARDS OF GUARDIANS
Records of the Boards of Guardians of Cardiganshire, from 1837. *Transferred to Dyfed R O (Aberystwyth).*

Schedule [*c.* 1986], 38pp.

CARDIGANSHIRE COUNTY ROADS BOARD
Records of the Aberystwyth section, 1770-1845, and Cardigan section, 1803-44, of the Cardiganshire Turnpike Trust, and of the Cardiganshire

County Roads Board, 1844-70. See also **Roberts & Evans**. Other records in Dyfed R O (Aberystwyth).

Schedule (1980), ii + 3pp. *AR 1938-39*, p.45; *1949-50*, p.40.

CARDIGANSHIRE EDUCATION AUTHORITY
Records of the Education Committee of Cardiganshire County Council, including School Board records and school log books. *Transferred to Dyfed R O (Aberystwyth)*.

Schedule (1951 + suppl.), 88pp.

CARDIGANSHIRE LIBERAL ASSOCIATION
Records of the Association, 1921-74.

Cardiganshire Liberal Association Records (1987), ii + 15pp. *AR 1986-87*. p.65.

CARDIGANSHIRE QUARTER SESSIONS
A group of the otherwise poorly surviving records of the Quarter Sessions of Cardiganshire, comprising Order Books from 1739, sessions files from 1949, appeals from 1926, committee papers from 1952 and a few stray pre-1900 documents. See also **Cardiganshire County Roads Board** and **Roberts & Evans**.

Schedule (1974), 9pp. Also **Maps**. *AR 1934-35*, p.43; *1959-60*, p.50; *1967-68*, p.49; *1973-74*, p.70.

CAREY EVANS see EVANS

CARMARTHENSHIRE ANTIQUARIAN SOCIETY
Deeds and documents (deposited by the Carmarthenshire Antiquarian Society), mostly relating to co. Carmarthen, including material on enclosure, canals and tramroads, 1609-1873. Further records in Dyfed R O (Carmarthen).

Schedule [c. 1933 + suppl.], 21pp. *AR 1932-33*, p.36; *1936-37*, p.30.

CARNEDDOG
Papers of Richard Griffith ('Carneddog', 1861-1947), poet and local historian. See also NLW MSS 7234-53.

AR 1946-47, p.25; *1956-57*, p.29. Working list available.

CARREG-LWYD
Estate and family records of Griffith of Carreg-lwyd and Holland of Berw, co. Anglesey, and Trygarn of Trygarn, co. Caernarfon, 14th-19th cent.; valuable papers relating to affairs of state, early 17th cent. (John Griffith

was secretary to Henry Howard, 1st earl of Northampton), and to local affairs, 17th-18th cent.

Schedule [pre - 1928], 478pp. *AR 1924 (Oct.)*, pp.9-10; *1925 (May)*, pp.18-20. The schedule is a notoriously unsatisfactory one. Many of the more important documents are described in Royal Commission on Historical Manuscripts, *Fifth Report* (1876), pp.405-23, more fully and satisfactorily than in the schedule. See also *AR 1964-65*, p.58.

CARTER
Documents, 1586-1909, relating to the Morgan family of Chepstow, co. Monmouth, and the Carter family of Chepstow, afterwards of Clifton.

Schedule (1958), 54pp. *AR 1957-58*, p.38; *1958-59*, p.54.

F. C. CARTER
A collection of Welsh deeds and documents of diverse origins (purchased from F.C. Carter), 14th cent.-1820.

Schedule (1979), pp.v + 67.

CASTELL GORFOD
Manuscripts and documents from the collection made by the antiquary, Joseph Joseph of Brecon, and enlarged by James Buckley of Castellgorfod, co. Brecon. The collection includes a transcript of the Golden Grove Book of pedigrees.

Schedule [pre-1934], 20pp. *AR 1920 (Oct.)*, pp.4-5.

CASTLE HILL
Estate records, 13th-20th, but mainly 18th and 19th cent., relating to cos Cardigan, Stafford and Salop, and to the Williams family of Pantyseiri and Castle Hill, co. Cardigan, and the Loxdale family of Castle Hill. Include records of the Company of Shearmen and Clothworkers of Shrewsbury, 15th-18th cent.

Schedule (1953), 10 + 342pp. *NLWJ*, 8 (1953-4), pp.109-112. See also *AR 1942-43*, p.23; *1959-60*, pp.62-3; *1960-61*, p.58; *1970-71*, p.71; *1971-72*, p.78; @.

CEFNBRYNTALCH
Records of the Bryntalch (otherwise Cefnbryntalch) estate, co. Montgomery, 1535-1910; some local political correspondence, mid 19th cent.

Schedule (1962), 129pp. *AR 1937-38*, pp.67-8.

CELLAN
Deeds relating to the parish of Cellan, co. Cardigan, 1694-1831.

Cellan Deeds (1981), 6pp. *AR 1978-79*, p.43.

CELYNOG
Deeds, 1514-1813, evidently collected by the antiquary, Richard Williams of Celynog (1835-1906), relating to cos Flint, Merioneth and Montgomery. See also NLW MSS 527-92.

Schedule (1975), i + 26pp.

CENTRAL WELSH BOARD
Records of the Central Welsh Board, 1896-1949, and other papers relating to education in Wales.

AR 1978-79, p.56.

CERNIOGE
Records relating to the Cernioge estate in co. Denbigh, to the Gethin family of Cernioge and the Kenrick family of Nantclwyd, including some lands of Aberconway abbey, 1502-1856.

Schedule (1962), 74pp. *AR 1954-55*, p.26; *1955-56*, p.44; *1956-57*, pp.28, 35; *1958-59*, p.43. See also *AR 1964-65*, p.43.

THE CHAIN
Papers of the Baker-Gabb and Paterson family of The Chain, Abergavenny, 19th-20th cent., supplementing **Baker-Gabb**.

Schedule (1993), i + 17pp. *AR 1983-84*, pp.55-6.

BRENDA CHAMBERLAIN
Papers of Brenda Chamberlain (1912-71), artist and writer. *(NLW MSS 21484-525, 22493-4)*.

Brenda Chamberlain Manuscripts (1973), 12pp. *AR 1972-73*, pp.44 and 53.

EDGAR CHAPPELL
Papers of Edgar Leyshon Chappell (1879-1949), local politician in Cardiff, worker for social reform and local historian. Other papers in Cardiff Central Library (South Glamorgan Libraries).

Uncatalogued (1994).

CHARLES AND DAVIES
Letters and papers, 1791-1889, relating mainly to the Charles family of Carmarthen and the Davies family of Aberystwyth and Cwrtmawr. See also NLW MSS 10549-50 and 12894.

Schedule (1959), ii + 29pp. *AR 1958-59*, pp.52-3.

D.M.C. CHARLES
Records (deposited by D.M.C. Charles) deriving from the office of Barker, Morris & Owen of Carmarthen, solicitors. Include records of many Carmarthenshire estates, 17th-20th cent. and papers relating to the work of the registrar of the diocese of St Davids, 19th cent.; office records, 1864-1949. See also **Griffith E. Owen**. Other records in Dyfed R O (Carmarthen).

AR 1970-71, pp.58-9.

CHARTISM IN MONTGOMERYSHIRE
Correspondence of the earl of Powis and other papers relating to Chartism in Llanidloes, Newtown and elsewhere in Montgomeryshire, 1831-42. See also **Powis**.

Calendar (1935), 52pp.

CHARTISM IN SHROPSHIRE
Correspondence of the earl of Powis and other papers relating to Chartism in Shropshire, 1842. *Withdrawn*. See also **Powis**.

Calendar (1941), 21pp. (1949), 23pp.

CHIRK CASTLE
Estate and family records of the Chirk Castle estate, mainly in co. Denbigh, from 1595 the estate of the Myddelton family. Includes records of the lordship of Chirk and Chirkland, from 1322; deeds, from 13th cent.; records of coal, iron and lead industry, from 17th cent.; the records of Denbighshire Quarter Sessions, including order books and sessions files, 1641-99; parliamentary election papers for the county and borough of Denbigh, 1681-1852; records of Sir Thomas Myddelton (1550-1631) as a London merchant; correspondence, from *c.* 1600; literary manuscripts. See also **Longueville, Plas Power** and **Ruthin**.

Schedules: vol. I [1957], 211pp. (MSS, Quarter Sessions, election papers, manorial records); vols II-IV (1939), 667pp. in three vols (correspondence); vols V-VII [1956-7], 1270pp. in three vols (deeds and documents). *AR 1931-32*, pp.53-5; *1950-51*, pp.37-8. *NLWJ*, 1 (1939-40), pp.83-8; 8 (1953-4), pp.335-48.

CILGWYN

Records of the Cilgwyn estate in cos Cardigan, Carmarthen and Pembroke, and in Paddington, co. Middlesex, and the families of Lloyd, Hall and Fitzwilliams, 1509-1936; records of the borough of Adpar, *c*. 1670-1832; records of the New Quay Harbour Co. and Llandyssul Market Co., 1834-1900.

Schedules (1934), 76pp.; (1956), 7pp.; (1989), ix + 26pp. Also **Maps**. *AR 1933-34*, p.38; *1964-65*, p.57; *1985-86*, p.61. *NLWJ*, 3 (1943-4), p.35

CIL-RHIW

Deeds (donated by B.W. Allen of Cil-rhiw) relating to the parishes of Crinow and Llanbedr Felffre, co. Pembroke, 1595-1777.

Schedule (1949), 9pp.

CILYBEBYLL

Records of the estate of the families of Herbert, Turberville and Lloyd of Cilybebyll, co. Glamorgan, 1465-1854. See also **Ethel Lloyd**. Other records in West Glamorgan R O.

Schedule (1942), 63pp.; (1957), 146pp. See also *AR 1962-63*, p.59.

CILYMAENLLWYD

Estate records, 1541-*c*. 1864, and correspondence, 18th cent., (deposited by Lady Howard Stepney of Cilymaenllwyd) relating mainly to the family of Stepney of Prendergast and Llanelli and estates in cos Carmarthen and Pembroke.

Schedule (1949), 66pp. *AR 1948-49*, pp.58-9.

G. T. CLARK

Papers of George Thomas Clark (1809-98), engineer, associated in particular with the Dowlais iron works, and antiquary, including Clark family papers and documents collected by him (donated by Wyndham D. Clark). Much of the antiquarian material is now *NLW MSS 5171-234* and some family records and diaries are now *NLW MSS 14991-15061*. A group of G. T. Clark deeds is listed in **Miscellaneous I**.

AR 1922 (May), pp.5-6; *1922 (Oct)*, p.6; *1948-49*, pp.20-1; *1955-56*, pp.25-6; *1957-58*, p.20; *1958-59*, pp.24-5. A working list of the correspondence is available.

LORD CLEDWYN

Papers of Cledwyn Hughes, later Lord Cledwyn of Penrhos (1916-   ), MP for Anglesey, 1951-79, Secretary of State for Wales, 1966-8, Chairman of the Parliamentary Labour Party, 1974-9. *Conditional Access.*

Lord Cledwyn Papers (1994), iii + 18pp. *AR 1990-91*, p.59.

CLEMENSTONE

Records of the Clemenstone estate, co. Glamorgan, 1579-1903; papers of Daniel Durel, headmaster of Cowbridge Grammar School, 1719-66; deeds relating to Hertfordshire, 1273-1727. *Transferred to Glamorgan R O (Cardiff).*

Schedule (1929), 41 or 50pp. (two typings). *AR 1929-30*, p.39.

CLENENNAU see BROGYNTYN

CLIVE

Papers of Robert, Lord Clive (1725-1774) and Edward Clive, earl of Powis (1754-1837). See also **Powis**. A related group of papers ('First Series') is in the India Office Library.

Clive MSS and Papers (Second Series) (1954), 178pp. See *NLWJ*, 24 (1985-6), pp.244-7.

CLYNFIEW

Estate records and family papers, 16th-19th cent., relating to Lewis of Llwyngrawys, co. Cardigan, and Clynfiew, co. Pembroke, Williams of Tre-fach, co. Pembroke, and Bowen of Pantyderi, co. Pembroke, and Cardigan.

Preliminary schedule (1973), 27pp. *AR 1972-73*, pp.70-71.

CLYTHA

Estate records associated with Clytha House, parish of Llan-arth, mid 17th-mid 19th century, mostly relating to co. Monmouth, including copies of deeds relating to the Hanbury Williams family of Coldbrook. Other records in Gwent R O.

Schedule (1980), ii + 62pp. *AR 1925-26*, p.23.

COALOWNERS' ASSOCIATION

Records of the Monmouthshire and South Wales Coalowners' Association from 1864 until its dissolution in 1955.

Schedule (1954), 115pp. In process of re-cataloguing. *AR 1947-48*, p.39; *1953-54*, pp.45-48; *1954-55*, pp.50-51; *1955-56*, p.50.

COED COCH

Estate and family records of Wynne of Coed Coch and the estates of Trovarth and Coed Coch, co. Denbigh, 1246-1894, and Teirdan, also co. Denbigh, 18th-19th cent.; correspondence, 18th-19th cent. See also NLW MSS 4571-7 and 6616-9.

Schedules, vols I and II (1978), IIIA (1980), IIIB and IV (1981), continuous pagination, iv + 1678pp. *AR 1929-30*, p.18.

COEDYMAEN

Group I: papers of Sir William Williams ('Speaker Williams', 1634-1700). See also **Trevor Owen** and **Wynnstay**.

Schedule (1983), 34pp., superseding an earlier schedule (1924), 19pp. AR 1925 (May), pp.21-3.

Group II: papers of Charles Watkin Williams-Wynn (1775-1850), politician, including extensive correspondence with Lord Grenville and others of his family.

Schedule (1959), 5pp. A more detailed working list available. *AR 1958-59*, p.54. See also *NLWJ*, 1 (1939-40), pp.159-60.

SPENCE-COLBY

Deeds, 1507-1810, relating mainly to estates in co. Pembroke later owned by the Colby family of Ffynone; Pembrokeshire militia papers, 1780-1800. See also **Owen & Colby**.

Schedule [after 1927], 40pp. *AR 1926-27*, p.54. *NLWJ*, 9, (1955-6), pp.106-8.

COLEMAN

Deeds collected by James Coleman, relating to most Welsh counties, 16th-19th cent.

Calendar of Deeds and Documents. Vol. 1: The Coleman Deeds (Aberystwyth, 1921), 466pp. *AR 1909-10*, pp.36-7.

COMMITTEE OF WELSH DISTRICT COUNCILS

Records of the committee established in 1983 as a successor to the Council for the Principality (q.v.), 1983-6. *Conditional access.*

Schedule (1990 + suppl.), 27pp. *AR 1989-90*, p.65; *1991-92*, p.61.

CORBETT DEEDS

Deeds relating to estates of the Corbett family in cos Montgomery and Stafford, 1549-1762.

AR 1949-50, p.36.

CORBETT-WINDER see **WINDER**

CORSTON
Records of the Leach family of Corston, co. Pembroke, 1652-1900, including correspondence and family papers, 18th-19th cent., and deeds, mostly relating to south Pembrokeshire, some relating to coal mines, 1652-1890 (part now *NLW MSS 11162-228)*. Other records in Dyfed R O (Haverfordwest).

AR 1936-37, p.31.

CORWEN ELECTRIC LIGHT CO.
Records of Corwen Electric Light Co., 1922-51.

AR 1960-61, pp.33, 35; *1968-69*, p.29.

COTTESMORE
Estate and family records of Massy of Cottesmore, co. Pembroke; estates in co. Pembroke, 18th-19th cent., in co. Limerick, Ireland, 17th-19th cent.

Schedule (1937), 20pp.

COUNCIL FOR THE PRESERVATION OF RURAL WALES
Records of the Council from its establishment in 1928. *Conditional access.*

Schedule (1966 + suppl.), 16pp. *AR 1966-67*, p.53.

COUNCIL FOR THE PRINCIPALITY
Records of the Council for the Principality established in 1974 to co-ordinate the work of district councils, 1974-83. *Conditional access.*

Schedule (1986), 20pp. *AR 1985-86*, p.60.

COURTFIELD
Estate records of the Vaughan family of Courtfield, Welsh Bicknor, co. Hereford, and associated families of Vaughan of Ruardean, co. Gloucester, Besington of Crowarne, co. Hereford, and Weld of Lulworth, co. Dorset, 13th-20th cent.; lands in cos Monmouth, Radnor, Hereford and elsewhere. The Vaughans were notable adherents to Roman Catholicism. See also **Sir L. Twiston Davies**.

Schedule (1905), 93pp. The schedule, compiled by J. Hobson Matthews, does not cover all the records in NLW. A revised schedule is in progress (1994). *AR 1948-49*, pp.59-61. *NLWJ*, 7 (1951-2), pp.258-68.

COURT HENRY
Records of the Court Henry estate, co. Carmarthen, 1770-1905.

Schedule (1939), 26pp.

COWETHAS FLAMANK
Archives of Cowethas Flamank, a Cornish current affairs and research group, from 1969.

List (1987), 7pp. *AR 1986-87*, p.58.

CRAFNANT AND GERDDI BLUOG
Deeds and documents, 1572-1868, relating to the Crafnant and Gerddi Bluog estates and to properties mainly in co. Merioneth.

Schedule (1948), pp.i + 14; (1951), 6pp. *AR 1947-48*, p.41. @.

CRAWSHAY-WILLIAMS see WILLIAMS

CRIDDLE
Deeds (purchased from M.E. Criddle), 1608-1794.

Criddle Deeds (1975), i + 11pp.

CROESOR SLATE QUARRIES
Records of Croesor Slate Quarries, Croesor, co. Merioneth, 1878-1920. Other records in Gwynedd R O (Dolgellau).

Schedule (1994), i + 2pp.

CROSSE OF SHAW HILL
Records of the family of Thelwall of Nantclwyd, Bathafarn Park and Plas Coch, co. Denbigh, and of the associated families of Parry of Nantclwyd and Ruthin, Gethin of Cernioge and Kenrick of Woore, co. Salop, London and Chester, including letters and papers of Civil War interest. The main portion consists of deeds, 1550-1675, relating to Parry and Thelwall properties in co. Denbigh. See also **Bathafarn and Llanbedr**. The main Crosse archive is in Lancashire RO.

Schedule (1947), 276pp. *AR 1946-47*, pp.36-38.

CROSSWOOD
Estate and family records of Vaughan of Crosswood (Trawsgoed), co. Cardigan, later the earls of Lisburne, 1527-1939. See also **Roberts & Evans**.

Calendar of Deeds and Documents. Vol. II: The Crosswood Deeds (Aberystwyth, 1927), 478 pp. A second group is catalogued in a typescript schedule [1920s], 122pp. Also **Maps**. *AR 1923 (May)*, p.7; *1946-47*, p.41 (the second group); *1949-50*, pp.41-2; *1958-59*, p.56; *1963-64*, p.53. *NLWJ*, 2 (1941-2), pp.21-3

CROYDON
Deeds (originally deposited by H. Johnes Lloyd of Croydon, Herts) relating to the Dolaucothi estate, co. Carmarthen, 1610-1899. See also **Dolaucothi**.

Schedule (1927), 69pp. *AR 1926-27*, p.53.

CWMCYNFELYN
Records of the Williams family of Cwmcynfelyn, Llangorwen, co. Cardigan, 1814-98, and deeds, 1577-1887. See also **Roberts & Evans**.

AR 1944-45, p.27. Working list available.

CWM DU
Deeds, 1609-1924, relating to property in the parishes of Llanfihangel Cwm Du, Cathedin, Talgarth, Llangynidr and Trallong, co. Brecon.

Schedule (1976), i + 24pp. *AR 1976-77*, p.41.

CWMGWILI
Estate records, 1576-1936, relating to the family of Philipps of Cwmgwili, co. Carmarthen, and the family of Jenkins of Cilbronnau, Llangoedmor, co. Cardigan. See also **Griffith E. Owen**. Other records in Dyfed R O (Carmarthen).

Schedule (1955), 14 + 202 pp. *AR 1947-48*, pp.40-1. *NLWJ*, 9 (1955-6), pp.102-5.

CWRTMAWR
An important collection of Welsh manuscripts made by John Humphreys Davies of Cwrtmawr (1871-1926), Principal of the University College of Wales, Aberystwyth, 1919-26, together with a collection of documents made by him and his own personal papers. Manuscripts collected by him include the earlier collection of John Jones ('Myrddin Fardd', 1836-1921), that of the Richards family of Darowen, and the papers of the scholar Daniel Silvan Evans (1818-1903). Among the documents are early archives of the Nanteos estate, co. Cardigan, 16th-18th cent.

RMWL, ii, pp.871-937 (MSS 1-50 only); *Handlist of Cwrt Mawr Manuscripts* (1939), 103pp. (lists all 1492 MSS in brief); *A catalogue of the Cwrtmawr Manuscripts* (1980-94), xvi + 657pp. in three vols (to date describing MSS 1-750);

Cwrt Mawr Deeds (1956), 541pp. *AR 1925 (Oct.)*, p.6; *1925-26*, pp.2-3; *1926-27*, pp.21-2. The personal papers of J. H. Davies and Daniel Silvan Evans remain uncatalogued (1994).

CYFARTHFA
Records, including letter-books and accounts, relating to the industrial concerns of the Crawshay family of Cyfarthfa, co. Glamorgan, especially to the iron works at Cyfarthfa, Hirwaun and Forest, from 1813, with a few earlier documents.

Schedule [1958], 988pp. in two vols. *AR 1935-36*, p.48; *1939-40*, p.33; *1952-53*, pp.22-3; *1972-73*, p.67. *NLWJ*, 1 (1939-40), p.146. Partly uncatalogued (1994).

CYFRONNYDD
Deeds, 1568-1939, relating to the Cyfronnydd estate in cos Denbigh, Merioneth and Montgomery, and records relating to Aberllefenni Slate Quarry, 1850-1946.

Schedule (1959), 4pp. *AR 1958-59*, pp.36-7.

CYMERAU
Family and estate papers of Pugh of Cymerau and Aber-mad, co. Cardigan, 1612-1978.

Schedule (1972), 62pp. *AR 1938-39*, p.49; *1977-78*, p.74; *1979-80*, p.80; *1982-83*, pp.52-3. The later groups are uncatalogued (1994).

CYMMRODORION
Records of the Honourable Society of Cymmrodorion, 1873-1970.

AR 1937-38, p.56; *1951-52*, p.33; *1960-61*, p.53; *1975-76*, p.77; *1977-78*, p.68; *1978-79*, p.76; *1980-81*, p.76.

CYMREIGYDDION Y FENNI
Literary works submitted to the eisteddfodau of Cymdeithas Cymreigyddion y Fenni, with adjudications, 1834-53 (now *NLW MSS 13959-62*, see also NLW MSS 13958, 13963-70 and 13182-5).

Schedule (1935), 29pp.

CYNLLAITH OWEN
Court records of the manor of Cynllaith Owen, co. Denbigh, 1736-1835.

Schedule (1932), i + 3pp. *AR 1932-33*, p.44.

CYNWYL GAEO
Records relating to the family of Johnes and Hills-Johnes of Dolaucothi, Cynwyl Gaeo, co. Carmarthen, 1566-1940. See also **Dolaucothi**.

AR 1949-50, pp.50-1; *1973-74*, p.50.

CYSULOG
Deeds and documents (deposited by J. Roberts Jones of Cysulog) relating to Cefn Trefor Isaf and other properties in the parish of Llanfihangel-y-traethau, co. Merioneth, 1648-1878.

Schedule (1938), 10pp. *AR 1938-39*, p.47.

D. R. DANIEL
Papers of David Robert Daniel (1859-1931), political commentator, including diaries and correspondence of Thomas Edward Ellis, material relating to Lloyd George, and papers, 1878-1914, relating to the North Wales Quarrymen's Union and the Penrhyn Quarry strikes.

Schedule [1959], 55pp.

DAN-YR-ALLT
Deeds relating to the Lloyd family of Dan-yr-allt, Llangadog, co. Carmarthen, 1537-1674. Other records in Dyfed R O (Carmarthen).

AR 1982-83, p.50. Working list available.

DAVID & DAVID
Valuations of properties in south Wales and adjoining counties of England by Messrs David & David, land agents and surveyors, of Cardiff, 1846-1933.

David & David Valuations (1994), i + 36pp.

DAVIES, GREGYNOG
Deeds (deposited by the Misses Davies, Gregynog) relating to properties in co. Montgomery, 1597-1832. See also **Gregynog**.

Schedule (1947), 8pp. *AR 1946-47*, p.38.

DAVIES, PORTMADOC
Records of Messrs Davies Brothers, Porthmadog, slate quarry owners, including records of many quarries in cos Caernarfon, Merioneth and Pembroke, 1859-1956, papers relating to the slate industry, and papers

relating to local railways, 1867-1921. Other records in Gwynedd R O (Caernarfon).

AR 1949-50, p.23; *1956-57*, pp.25-7.

ANEIRIN TALFAN DAVIES
Papers of Aneirin Talfan Davies (1909-80), writer and broadcaster. *Conditional access.*

Casgliad Aneirin Talfan Davies : rhestr ragarweiniol (1980), 10pp. *AR 1980-81*, pp.74-5.

BENJAMIN DAVIES
Papers of Benjamin Davies (1863-1957), scientist, communist and spiritualist; they cover his long collaboration with Sir Oliver Lodge, from whom there are some 900 letters, 1885-1941.

Benjamin Davies Papers (1982), iii + 19pp. *AR 1981-82*, p.63.

CLEMENT DAVIES
Papers of Clement Davies (1884-1962), MP and leader of the Liberal Party. *Conditional access.*

Clement Davies Papers (1981), xiv + 984pp. in four volumes. *AR 1977-78*, p.67; @.

D. R. DAVIES
Over 150 scrapbooks compiled by D.R. Davies of Aberdare containing press cuttings, etc., 1900-1978, relating largely to Welsh drama, theatrical activities and popular entertainment in Wales and amongst Welsh communities in English cities, and Welsh actors on stage and screen.

Schedule (1978 + suppl.), [vi] + 43pp. *AR 1973-74*, p.55; *1974-75*, p.48; *1978-79*, p.63; *1988-89*, p.64.

D. TEIFIGAR DAVIES
Papers of D. Teifigar Davies (d. 1961), embracing a group of papers of Richard Bennett (1860-1937), all relating mainly to the history of Calvinistic Methodism in upper Montgomeryshire.

Schedule (1963), 8pp. *AR 1962-63*, pp.23-4.

E. FRANCIS DAVIES
Estate records (deposited and bequeathed by E. Francis Davies) of Bodwenni, Llandderfel, co. Merioneth, and Serior, Llandrillo-yn-Edeirnion,

and the associated families of Roberts, Williams and Evans, and deeds relating to property elsewhere in north Wales, 13th-20th cent.; a few literary manuscripts, 16th-18th cent.

Schedules (1937-8), 56pp.; (1944), 7pp. *AR 1937-38*, pp.56-7; *1944-45*, p.29. See also *AR 1962-63*, p.22.

ELWYN AND MARGARET DAVIES
Papers of Elwyn Davies (1906-86), administrator, and Margaret Davies, his wife, geographer.

Schedule (1994), i + 36pp. *AR 1982-83*, p.35; *1986-87*, p.59. See also *AR 1980-81*, p.43. Also **Maps**.

GEORGE M. Ll. DAVIES
Papers of George Maitland Lloyd Davies (1880-1949), pacifist.

Schedule (1964), 90pp. See also *AR 1960-61*, p.25.

GLYN DAVIES
Deeds (donated by Glyn Davies) relating to co. Montgomery, and to local government and turnpike trusts, 1676-1874.

Schedule (1950), 8pp. *AR 1949-50*, p.23.

GWILYM DAVIES
Papers of Gwilym Davies (1879-1955), minister and worker for peace, relating to broadcasting, and to religious, cultural, Welsh and international affairs.

Schedule (1955 + suppl.), ii + 87pp. *AR 1954-55*, p.23; *1955-56*, p.26; *1958-59*, p.28. See also *AR 1966-67*, p.25.

HUBERT DAVIES
Music manuscripts of Hubert Davies (1893-1965), composer.

Music MSS of Hubert Davies (1970), 10pp. *AR 1969-70*, p.53.

MRS IFOR DAVIES
Deeds (donated by Mrs Ifor Davies) relating to co. Cardigan, 1720-1900.

Schedule (1967), 8pp. *AR 1966-67*, pp.24-5

J. CONWAY DAVIES
Papers of James Conway Davies (1891-1971), archivist and palaeographer.

Schedule (1992), ii + 50pp. *AR 1971-72*, p.35.

J. GLYN DAVIES

Papers of John Glyn Davies (1870-1953), poet and Celtic scholar; manuscripts collected by him; papers of his family, including the 'Tanycastell Collection' which contains papers of John Jones, Tal-y-sarn (1796-1857), and letters from Australia and New Zealand. Letters to J. Glyn Davies include some 400 from Robert Scourfield Mills (*alias* Arthur Owen Vaughan *alias* Owen Rhoscomyl, 1863-1919), author and adventurer, 1903-19.

Schedules: vol. I, *Manuscripts and Papers* ([1949] and suppl. 1984), 114pp.; vols II-V, *Correspondence* [1952-6], 388, 346, 281 and 259pp. *AR 1937-38*, pp.30 and 57; *1939-40*, p.33; *1940-41*, pp.19 and 26; *1942-43*, p.17; *1946-47*, pp.21 and 38-9; *1954-55*, p.41; *1963-64*, p.49; *1970-71*, pp.59-60; *1983-84*, p.45; *1992-93*, p.54.

SIR L. TWISTON DAVIES

The main part of this collection (donated by Sir L. Twiston Davies, 1894-1953) consists of the archive of the firm of Powles and Tyler, solicitors, of Monmouth, predominantly 1780-1880; prominent among the families served are Hardwick, Jones of Llanarth Court and Vaughan of Courtfield; there are many papers arising from the firm's activity as Conservative agents, in parliamentary elections, 1818-85. Besides the Powles and Tyler archive there is a small collection of manuscripts, some of them oriental, and documents. See also **M. P.Watkins**.

Schedule (1981), xiii + 1169pp. in four vols. *AR 1933-34*, p.28; *1934-35*, p.31; *1941-42*, p.16; *1942-43*, p.17; *1943-44*, p.17; *1944-45*, p.17; *1945-46*, p.21.

LL. AP IVAN DAVIES

A small collection of Welsh literary manuscripts and manuscripts and papers relating mostly to the area of Llanuwchllyn and Llandrillo-yn-Edeirnion, co. Merioneth, 17th-19th cent. (*NLW MSS 19660-74* and *21192-3*). (Donated by Dr Ll. ap Ivan Davies).

Schedule (1946 + suppls.), 15pp. *AR 1944-45*, p.30; *1958-59*, p.51; *1963-64*, p.49; *1965-66*, p.25; *1973-74*, p.36.

MOSES DAVIES

Business records of Moses Davies of Llanfyllin, auctioneer and estate agent, 1859-1916.

AR 1951-52, p.26.

O. GILBERT DAVIES

Deeds and documents (deposited by O. Gilbert Davies) relating to various

Welsh and Border counties, 1638-1897.

Schedule (1936), 25pp. Also **Maps**. *AR 1936-37*, p.30.

OWEN DAVIES

Manuscripts and papers from the library of Owen Davies (1840-1929), Baptist minister, Caernarfon, consisting largely of material relating to Welsh Baptists (*NLW MSS 19552-606*).

Schedule (1966), 11pp. *AR 1965-66*, pp.29-31.

PADARN DAVIES

Papers of John Davies (John Padarn Gildas Davies), Roman Catholic priest, ordained 1852, sometime priest at Brecon (*NLW MSS 19910-22*).

Schedule (1968), 3pp.

PERCIVAL V. DAVIES

Deeds and documents (donated by Percival V. Davies) mostly relating to small estates in the St David's area of co. Pembroke, 1694-1896.

Schedule (1962 + suppl.), 59pp. *AR 1961-62*, p.24; *1964-65*, p.27.

RHYS DAVIES

Manuscripts of Rhys Davies (1903-78), including autograph and typescript drafts of his novels and stories (*NLW MSS 21528-46*). The residue of his papers, including papers relating to Anna Kavan (Helen Ferguson, 1901-68), is comprised in the 1990-91 acquisition. See also NLW MSS 23106-9.

Rhys Davies Manuscripts (1974), 5pp. See also *AR 1990-91*, p.63; *1992-93*, p.58.

T. WITTON DAVIES

Papers of Thomas Witton Davies (1851-1923), Baptist minister and Semitic scholar.

AR 1923 (Oct.), p.5.

W. EMLYN DAVIES

Papers of William Emlyn Davies (1899-1973), a Swansea schoolteacher, including a large collection of 'calligrams' and calligraphy done by him, and correspondence with writers and artists.

W. Emlyn Davies: Papers & Calligrams (1987), 21pp. *AR 1987-88*, p.57.

DENTON CLARK & CO

Records from the office of Denton Clark & Co, Llanidloes, surveyors and land agents, relating to mid-Wales, notably to the Doldowlod estate, Nantmel, co. Radnor, 1871-1955.

AR 1970-71, p.61. Also **Maps**.

DERRY ORMOND
Records of the Derry Ormond estate, near Lampeter, co. Cardigan, 1621-1927, mainly dating from the late 18th cent. after its acquisition by the family of Jones, later Inglis-Jones.

Schedule (1976), xxi + 173pp. *AR 1960-61*, p.55. *NLWJ*, 22 (1981-2), pp.214-22.

DERWYDD
Records of the estates, mainly in co. Carmarthen, of the families of Vaughan of Golden Grove and Llanelli, Bevan of Laugharne (including Madam Bridget Bevan, 1698-1779), Stepney of Llanelli and Stepney-Gulston of Derwydd, 1525-1904. Other records in Dyfed R O (Carmarthen).

Schedule (1955), 201pp. *AR 1941-42*, p.27. *NLWJ*, 9 (1955-6), pp.262-3.

LEWIS WESTON DILLWYN
Thirty-six diaries of Lewis Weston Dillwyn (1778-1855) of Penlle'rgaer, Glamorgan, naturalist, 1817-52. *Temporarily withdrawn (1994)*.

Calendar (1931), three vols, 186, 185 and 196pp. Extracts printed in South Wales and Monmouth Record Society, *Publications*, No. 5 (1963).

WILLIAM DILLWYN
Thirteen volumes of diaries and journals of tours, 1774-90, by William Dillwyn of Walthamstow (?1743-1824), father of Lewis Weston Dillwyn.

Calendar [c. 1931], two vols, 110 and 115pp.

DINAS MAWDDWY
Court records of the borough of Dinas Mawddwy and the manor of Mawddwy, co. Merioneth, 1771-1915. *Transferred to Gwynedd R O (Dolgellau)*.

Schedule (1940), 39pp.

DINAS POWIS
Records of the family of Lee of Dinas Powis, co. Glamorgan, including rentals and surveys of the manor of Dinas Powis and the Dinas Powis estate and deeds relating to properties in cos Glamorgan, Monmouth and Brecon, 1455-1914.

Schedule (1933), 46pp.; (1971), 8pp. *AR 1933-34*, p.41; *1970-71*, p.70.

PAUL DIVERRES
Papers of Paul Diverres (1880-1946), Celtic scholar; an earlier antiquarian collection of H. Diverres relating to the history of Brittany; manuscripts in Breton, 18th-19th cent.

Schedule (1960), 50pp. Also **Maps**. *AR 1946-47*, p.22.

DIXON
Deeds (deposited by Mrs Alice M. Dixon) relating to co. Monmouth, 1447-1829; pocket-books and notebooks relating to the parish of Mynyddislwyn, 1782-1848.

Schedule (1949), i + 34pp. *AR 1949-50*, p.39.

DOBELL
A collection (acquired from Dobell, the bookseller) evidently made in the 19th cent. by a Shropshire antiquary, comprising deeds and an earlier, mid-18th cent., antiquarian collection relating mainly to Shrewsbury and north Wales.

Schedule (1975), i + 30pp.

DOLAUCOTHI
Estate and family records, 16th-20th cent., of Johnes and Hills-Johnes of Dolaucothi, co. Carmarthen, the estate mostly in that county; the correspondence is extensive, over 15,000 letters, 1688-20th cent; include military papers of Sir James Hills-Johnes. See also **Croydon, Cynwyl Gaeo** and **Herbert Lloyd-Johnes**.

Schedules: (1927), 16pp. (a summary list); *Dolaucothi Correspondence* (1980-81), 2995pp. in eleven vols (vol. xi an index); *Dolaucothi Correspondence*, vol. xii (1990), 222pp. Vols i-xi contain correspondence from late 18th cent. to early 20th cent., vol. xii from 1688 to mid 19th cent. Vol. xii replaces 'schedule II' in the 1927 list. The estate records and other papers are in process of cataloguing (1994). Also **Maps**. *AR 1926-27*, pp.14, 35; *1931-32*, p.36; *1932-33*, p.41; *1947-48*, p.27; *1948-49*, p.29; *1976-77*, p.69; *1983-84*, p.43; @.

DOLFRIOG
Records (received from Dolfriog, Beddgelert) of the estates and families of Williams of Hafodgaregog, Nanmor, and of Hughes and Priestley of Trefan, Llanystumdwy, the estates mainly in cos Caernarfon and Merioneth, 1448-1841; correspondence of Maurice Williams of Hafodgaregog, 1620-66.

Schedule [*c.* 1960], 258pp. *AR 1954-55*, pp.55-6.

DOLOBRAN
Deeds relating to the Lloyd family and to the Dolobran estate in the parishes of Meifod and Llanfihangel-yng-Ngwynfa, co. Montgomery, 1731-1878.

Schedule [pre-1934], 34pp. *AR 1930-31*, p.48.

DOL'RHYD
A small group of estate and family records (from Dol'rhyd, Dolgellau) of Nanney of Nannau, Vaughan of Hengwrt, Rhug and Nannau, and Owen of Garthangharad, Dolgellau, the estates mainly in co. Merioneth, 1539-1909. Other records in UW, Bangor, *s.n.* Nannau.

Schedule (1949), 11pp.

DESMOND DONNELLY
Papers of Desmond Louis Donnelly (1920-74), MP for Pembrokeshire, 1950-70. *Conditional access.*

AR 1977-78, pp.68-9.

DOVEY WOODLANDS LTD
Records of Dovey Woodlands Ltd, a co-operative forestry organization active in mid-Wales, 1948-68.

AR 1969-70, p.57.

DOWNING
Deeds relating to the estates, in cos Denbigh and Flint, of the Pennant families of Bychton and Downing, 1352-1802. Much of the Pennant archive, including many of the papers of Thomas Pennant (1726-98), has been dispersed at auction. Three groups of Pennant papers are NLW MSS 2521-98, 12706-20 and 15421-36. A substantial residue of the archive is in Warwick R O. Other records in Clwyd R O (Hawarden).

Schedule (1978), vii + 58pp. *AR 1922 (Oct.)*, p.9.

DRUID INN
Papers (acquired from the Druid Inn, Goginan, co. Cardigan) relating to the activities of the family of Francis as mining agents, mainly in the lead mines of North Cardiganshire and Flintshire, 1825-58.

Schedule (1976), 30pp. *AR 1955-56*, p.38; *1957-58*, p.26. See also *AR 1956-57*, p.28.

DUCHY OF CORNWALL

Records of the administration of the Duchy of Cornwall estates in Wales. The early records give an impression of random survival; they complement similar records of Crown estates in the Public Record Office. The records include ministers' accounts, 1461-1552; chamberlains' accounts, north Wales, 1481-82, 1519, and south Wales, 1519-20; receivers' accounts, 1544-1620; petitions, 1620-1723; certificates of survey, 1618-95; surveys of castles, 1618-25; other records, 1391-1872.

Duchy of Cornwall Welsh Records (1986), vii + 74pp. *AR 1984-85*, p.42. See also *AR 1968-69*, p.22.

DUNRAVEN

Records of the Dunraven estate, principally in Glamorgan, of the families of Wyndham and Wyndham-Quin of Dunraven Castle, co. Glamorgan, earls of Dunraven, and of Clearwell, co. Gloucester, and of the associated families of Edwin and Thomas of Llanfihangel-juxta-Cowbridge, Baynham and Throckmorton of Clearwell and Ashby of Isleworth, co. Middlesex, 14th-20th cent.; manorial records from 16th cent. Records of the Irish estates and family papers are in PRO Northern Ireland.

Preliminary schedules (1940), 32pp.; (1952-53), 50pp.; *Dunraven Estate Rentals* (1991), 8pp. (an expansion of part of the 1952-53 schedule). Also **Maps**. *AR 1940-41*, p.27; *1942-43*, p.32; *1952-53*, pp.41-5. *NLWJ*, 2 (1941-2), pp.81-2.

DYNEVOR

Estate records of the family of Rice of Newton and Dinefwr, later barons Dynevor, 1514-20th cent., the estates lying in cos Carmarthen, Glamorgan and Pembroke; records of the Neath Abbey estate include records of the manor of Cadoxton-juxta-Neath, from 1602, and coal-mining records, 18th-19th cent. Further records in Dyfed R O (Carmarthen) and West Glamorgan R O.

Schedules: *Group A* (1936), 33 + 4pp.; *Group B* (1936), 174 + 2pp., in two vols; *Preliminary Report and Schedule* [c. 1957], 18pp. (material not in groups A and B). *AR 1956-57*, p.41; *1958-59*, pp.51-52.

EATON EVANS & MORRIS

Deeds and documents deposited by Messrs Eaton Evans & Morris of Haverfordwest relating to cos Pembroke, Carmarthen and Gloucester, 1621-1891. See also **Haverfordwest** and **Eaton Evans & Williams**, parts of the same archive.

Schedule (1960), 7pp. *AR 1959-60*, p.50.

EATON EVANS & WILLIAMS

Deeds and documents deposited by Messrs Eaton Evans and Williams of Haverfordwest, 1296-1928, relating mainly to co. Pembroke; including records of the estates of the families of Phillips of Trelewelyn, Harry of Cwmwdig, Elliot of Earwere, Wogan of Wiston, Barlow of Slebech, Symmons of Llanstinan, Warren of Trewern, Laugharne of St. Brides, Harries of Tregwynt, Tancred of Dudwell, and Bowen of Upton; records of the manors of Manorbier, Penely, and Prendergast, 1618-1850. See also **Haverfordwest (Eaton Evans & Williams)**, to which archives these are a supplement, and **Eaton Evans & Morris**. Other records in Dyfed R O (Haverfordwest).

Schedule (1957), 928pp. in two vols. *AR 1937-38*, p.58.

WALTER EDDY

Papers of Walter Eddy of Fron, Llangollen, mining surveyor, 1835-92. The papers relate mainly to lead mines and collieries in north Wales.

AR 1966-67, p.28.

LADY EDWARDS

Deeds and papers, 1812-93 (donated by Lady Edwards), some relating to Hugh Hughes (1790-1863) of Aberystwyth, artist, and to his wife, Sarah, daughter of the Rev. David Charles, Carmarthen.

Schedule (1962), 4pp. *AR 1961-62*, p.25.

SIR GORONWY EDWARDS

Papers of Sir John Goronwy Edwards (1891-1976), historian.

Sir Goronwy Edwards Papers (1984), iii + 27pp. *AR 1980-81*, p.44; *1982-83*, p.43.

HUW T. EDWARDS

Papers of Huw Thomas Edwards (1892-1970), trade union leader and public figure. *Conditional access.*

AR 1973-74, pp.72-3. Working list available.

JACK EDWARDS

Letters home from Jack Edwards, later a bookseller in Aberystwyth, most of them written from Cincinnati, Ohio, 1880-7. (*NLW MS 20995*). See also NLW MSS 14741-96.

Calendar (1973), 41pp. *AR 1941-42*, p.21.

SIR O.M. EDWARDS

Manuscripts and printed books from the library of Sir Owen Morgan Edwards (1858-1920), the bulk of the manuscript material belonging to the 19th cent. and much of it consisting of original copy of matter published or sent for publication in *Cymru* and *Cyfres y Fil*. (*NLW MSS 8330-444*). The main body of Sir O.M. Edwards's papers is summarily described in the *Brasrestr* and is in process of being catalogued.

Schedule [*c.* 1931], 13 + 55pp. *AR 1930-31*, pp.30-1. *Brasrestr o bapurau Syr Owen M. Edwards* (n.d.), 9pp. Working list of part available. *AR 1980-81*, p.44.

SIR O.M. AND SIR IFAN AB OWEN EDWARDS

Association copies of printed books from the libraries of Sir Owen M. Edwards (1858-1920) and his son, Sir Ifan ab Owen Edwards (1895-1970).

Schedule (1974), 8pp.

THOMAS CHARLES EDWARDS

Papers of Thomas Charles Edwards (1837-1900), principal of the University College of Wales, Aberystwyth.

AR 1939-40, p.33; *1943-4*, p.29. Working list available. A selection published in *Thomas Charles Edwards Letters*, ed. T. I. Ellis (Aberystwyth, 1952-3).

EDWINSFORD

Records of the estate of the family of Williams, later Williams-Drummond, of Rhydodyn otherwise Edwinsford, co. Carmarthen, including deeds, 1472-1811, records of the manor of Talley, 1617-1744, correspondence, 1580-1863. Other records in Dyfed R O (Carmarthen) *s.n.* Trant.

Schedule (1971), 1056pp. in two vols. *AR 1946-47*, pp.44-6.

EIFION WYN

Papers of Eliseus Williams ('Eifion Wyn', 1867-1926), poet.

Schedule (1993) 62pp. *AR 1988-89*, p.66.

EISTEDDFOD GENEDLAETHOL CYMRU

Archives from the central office, established in 1978, of Eisteddfod Genedlaethol Cymru, with some earlier records. See also **National Eisteddfod of Wales**.

Schedule (Welsh, 1988) [i] + 48 pp.; vol. II (1994), [i] + 8pp. Several deposits since 1987, references to *AR* not detailed here.

ELIS-THOMAS see **THOMAS**

DOUGLAS J. ELLIOTT
Deeds and documents (donated by Douglas J. Elliott), 1767-1875, of the family of Jones of Glanyrafon-ddu, parish of Talley, co. Carmarthen, relating to properties in cos Carmarthen and Brecon.

Schedules (1960), 3pp.; (1962), 5pp. *AR 1959-60*, p.25; *1961-62*, p.25.

SIR CLOUGH WILLIAMS-ELLIS
Papers of Sir Clough Williams-Ellis (1883-1978), architect and conservationist. The papers mostly date from after 1951 in which year his early papers were largely destroyed by fire. His plans and drawings are at the Royal Institute of British Architects Library. *Conditional access.*

AR 1978-79, pp.84-5.

ROBERT ELLIS, 'CYNDDELW'
Manuscripts and papers of Robert Ellis ('Cynddelw', 1812-1875), Baptist minister, poet, and antiquary. (*NLW MSS 10216-74*).

Schedule [*c.* 1935], 45pp. *AR 1935-36*, pp.44 and 61.

T. E. ELLIS
Papers of Thomas Edward Ellis (1859-99), MP for Merioneth, 1886-99, and chief Liberal whip, 1894-5.

Schedules (1961), 268pp.; (1983), 107pp. *AR 1927-28*, p.28; *1960-61*, p.54; *1964-65*, pp.27 and 57; *1965-66*, pp.26-7; *1968-69*, pp.48-9.

T. I. ELLIS
Deeds and documents (deposited by T.I. Ellis), mainly 18th-19th cent., relating to the estate of the Davies family of Castle Green, Cardigan, and of Carnachenwen, near Fishguard, and to other properties in cos Cardigan and Pembroke.

Schedules (1940), 37pp.; (1956), 19pp. *AR 1955-56*, p.49.

ELLIS-GRIFFITH see **GRIFFITH**

ELWES
Deeds and documents (deposited by Harold T. Elwes), 14th-19th cent., relating to estates mainly in north Wales, particularly those of the families

of Lloyd of Halghton, Phillips of Gwernheulod, and Overton of Overton in co. Flint, and Wynn of Penhesgin, co. Anglesey.

Schedule (1976), 420pp. *AR 1954-55*, pp.48-49; *1958-59*, pp.53-4; *1964-65*, p.57; and *1967-68*, p.50.

ERIVIAT
Records of the estates of the family of Foulkes of Eriviat, Henllan, co. Denbigh, in cos Denbigh, Flint, Merioneth and Caernarfon, mainly 16th-18th cent.

Schedule (1953), 90pp. *AR 1952-53*, p.45.

ESGAIR AND PANTPERTHOG
Records of the Esgair and Pantperthog estates, co. Merioneth, and the Ruck family, and lands in cos Montgomery, Cardigan and Kent, 1509-1898; papers of Paul Panton the younger of Plas Gwyn, Anglesey, 1659-1822; and Welsh manuscripts of more than one Oliver Morris of Esgair Leferin, 17th-18th cent. See also **Panton** and **Plas Gwyn**.

Schedule (1950), 132pp. *AR 1949-50*, pp.47-8.

EVANS & BEVAN
Records of the Evans and Bevan group of anthracite collieries in the Vale of Neath, 1867-1912.

Schedule (1936), 9pp. *AR 1935-36*, p.49.

EVANS & GRIFFIN
Part of the archive of the Jones family of Gwynfryn (donated by Mrs Evans and Mrs Griffin), mainly comprising papers relating to the Llangynfelyn area, co. Cardigan, 19th cent. See also **Gwynfryn**.

Schedule (1950), 3pp.

A. W. WADE-EVANS
Papers of Arthur Wade Wade-Evans (1875-1964), historian and nationalist. See also **Titus & Elizabeth Evans** and **Minor Lists, 1988** *s.n.* Mali Evans.

AR 1964-65, p.36.

ALCWYN C. EVANS
Manuscripts of Alcwyn C. Evans (1828-1902), antiquary, relating mainly to the history and genealogy of the town and county of Carmarthen,

including volumes of pedigrees of the gentry of south Wales (*NLW MSS 12356-88*).

Schedule (1939), 15pp. *AR 1938-39*, p.34. *NLWJ*, 1 (1939-40), pp.97-8.

ANEURIN O. EVANS

Deeds (donated by Messrs Aneurin O. Evans & Co.) relating to the town of Denbigh and the parishes of Henllan and Eglwys-bach, co. Denbigh, 1709-1912.

Schedule (1965), 4pp. *AR 1964-65*, p.28.

BENNETT EVANS

Deeds and documents (deposited by Miss A.E. Bennett Evans) relating to the estate of the Brock family in co. Carmarthen, 1843-75, and others, 1774-1900.

Schedule (1977), 16pp. *AR 1976-77*, p.67.

C. J. O. EVANS

Deeds (deposited by C.J.O. Evans) relating to west Glamorgan, 1591-1857.

Schedule [*c.* 1935], 10pp. *AR 1935-36*, p.49.

D. D. EVANS

Deeds and papers (deposited by D.D. Evans) of the Jones family of Llanio Fawr, co. Cardigan, 1692-1833.

Schedule [*c.* 1934], 8pp. *AR 1934-35*, p.44.

D. ROY EVANS

Deeds and papers (deposited by D. Roy Evans) including manuscripts of the work of Mrs A.A. Puddicombe ('Allen Raine'); deeds relating to Laugharne, 1609-1756, and to cos Cardigan, Carmarthen and Pembroke, 1695-1877. See also **Amphlett Lewis & Evans**. Related records in Dyfed R O (Carmarthen) *s.n.* Beckingsdale.

Schedule [*c.* 1934], pp.44 + 12 + 3. *AR 1927-28*, p.28; *1931-32*, pp.51-2.

EIRLYS WATCYN EVANS

Deeds (donated by Mrs Eirlys Watcyn Evans) relating to the parish of Llywel, co. Brecon, 1753-1825.

Schedule (1972), 4pp. *AR 1971-72*, p.42.

GEORGE EYRE EVANS

Papers of George Eyre Evans (1857-1939), antiquary and historian of Welsh Unitarianism; papers of his father, the Rev. David Lewis Evans (1813-1902); papers of the Powell family of Colyton, Devon; deeds, 1565-1900. (Some now *NLW MSS 7963* and *13271-685*). See also NLW 14631-9.

Schedules [*c.* 1933], 22pp.; [*c.* 1940], 88pp.; (1971), 47pp. *AR 1933-34*, p.29; *1939-40*, p.24.

DR GRIFFITH EVANS

Papers of Griffith Evans (1835-1935), bacteriologist and pioneer of protozoon pathology.

Schedule (1979), iii + 97pp. *AR 1941-42*, p.17; *1946-47*, p.23; *1947-48*, p.23; *1958-59*, p.24; *1959-60*, p.23; *1960-61*, p.22; *1963-64*, p.27; *1965-66*, p.61; *1968-69*, p.24.

GWYNFOR EVANS

Papers of Gwynfor Evans (1912-   ), MP for Carmarthenshire, 1966-70 and 1974-79, President of Plaid Cymru, 1945-81. *Conditional access.*

AR 1972-73, p.68; *1978-79*, p.77; *1979-80*, p.74; *1982-83*, p.49; *1988-89*, p.61.

HENRY EVANS

Records from the office of Henry Evans, Machynlleth, solicitor, including local government and Petty Sessions records for the Machynlleth area, 19th-20th cent.

AR 1980-81, p.76; *1981-82*, p.82. Working list available.

HUGH EVANS

Correspondence of Isaac Foulkes and Hugh Evans of the Brython Press (Gwasg y Brython), Liverpool, 1895-1933; papers relating to the Llangwm area of co. Denbigh, 1809-95. See also NLW MSS 14406-23 and Gwasg y Brython Archives (**Minor Lists 1992**).

Schedule (1952), 30pp.

IVOR EVANS

Records from the office of Ivor Evans, Aberystwyth, solicitor, including records for several north Cardiganshire estates, 19th-20th cent., and some official county records for Cardiganshire, see **Cardiganshire County Roads Board** and **Cardiganshire Quarter Sessions**. See also **Roberts & Evans**.

AR 1938-39, p.45; *1949-50*, p.40; *1974-75*, p.65. Also **Maps**, *s.n.* Cardiganshire County Council.

J. GWENOGVRYN EVANS
Manuscripts and papers of John Gwenogvryn Evans (1852-1930), editor and cataloguer of Welsh manuscripts. See also **Timothy Lewis** and **Minor Lists 1985**.

Schedule [c. 1930], 32pp. *AR 1929-30*, p.39. See also *AR 1972-73*, p.69.

J. T. EVANS
Deeds (donated by the Rev. J.T. Evans) relating to cos Pembroke and Gloucester, 1584-1832. See also **Titus & Elizabeth Evans**.

Schedule [c. 1932], 2 + 1 + 2pp. *AR 1930-31*, p.32; *1931-32*, p.35.

M. BROADHEAD EVANS
Deeds and documents (deposited by Miss M. Broadhead Evans), mostly relating to Anglesey, 1678-1913, including some relating to the Rev. John Elias, Llanfechell (1774-1841), and his descendents.

Schedule [c. 1937], 38pp. *AR 1937-38*, p.58.

LADY OLWEN CAREY EVANS
Papers of Lady Olwen Carey Evans (1892-1990), daughter of David Lloyd George, with some medical papers of her husband, Sir Thomas Carey Evans (1884-1947); include a small group of Lloyd George's own papers.

Schedule (1991), 19pp. *AR 1990-91*, p.63.

R. H. EVANS
Deeds and documents, 1686-1911, relating mainly to cos Caernarfon, Denbigh and Merioneth; papers relating to local government in co. Caernarfon, in particular, in the Pwllheli district, 19th cent.

Schedule (1975), 120pp. Also **Maps**. *AR 1937-38*, pp.58-9.

RON EVANS
Papers of Ron Evans as Labour Party agent in the constituency of Ebbw Vale to Aneurin Bevan and Michael Foot, 1951-87.

Schedule (1988), 11pp. *AR 1987-88*, p.57.

S. J. EVANS
Papers of Samuel J. Evans (1870-1938), headmaster of Llangefni County School, including material on education and the history and antiquities of Anglesey.

Schedule (1978), v + 53pp. *AR 1960-61*, p.47.

SAMUEL T. EVANS
Papers of Samuel Thomas Evans (1859-1918), MP for Mid-Glamorgan, 1890-1910, Solicitor-General, 1908-10, and President of the Divorce, Probate and Admiralty Court, 1910-18. See also NLW MSS 2231-42.

Schedule (1974), 40pp. *AR 1973-74*, pp.52-3

TITUS AND ELIZABETH EVANS
Papers of John Thomas Evans (1869-1941, son of Titus and Elizabeth Evans), rector of Stow-on-the-Wold, author of catalogues of church plate. The papers are mainly those of J. T. Evans himself, largely antiquarian in interest, relating to cos Pembroke, Gloucester and Oxford, and of his brothers, notably Arthur Wade-Evans. See also **A. W. Wade-Evans**.

AR 1942-43, p.19. Working list available.

SIR VINCENT EVANS
Papers of Sir Evan Vincent Evans (1851-1934), public figure associated with the National Eisteddfod and the Honourable Society of Cymmrodorion.

AR 1943-44, p.18; *1984-85*, p.33.

W. A. EVANS
Deeds and documents (purchased from W.A. Evans) relating to cos Denbigh, Flint and Anglesey, 1310-1795.

Schedules (1958), 3pp.; (1962), 7pp.; (1963), 11pp.; (1964), 12pp. *AR 1957-58*, p.28; *1962-63*, p.41; *1963-64*, p.42.

W. EVANS GEORGE & SONS
Records from the office of W. Evans George & Sons, solicitors, of Newcastle Emlyn, co. Cardigan; predominantly relating to the Brigstocke family of Kidwelly and Llechdynny, co. Carmarthen, and Blaenpant, co. Cardigan, 1496-1910. See also **Brigstocke**. Other records in Dyfed R O (Carmarthen).

Schedule (1987), [xi] + 448, in two vols. Also **Maps** *s.n.* Blaenpant. *AR 1965-66*, p.53; *1967-68*, p.50; *1968-69*, pp.49-50.

WILLIAM EVANS, 'WIL IFAN'
Letters to William Evans, 'Wil Ifan' (1883-1968), poet. See also **Minor Lists 1983** and **Brinley Richards**.

Schedule (1965), 82pp. See also *AR 1949-50*, p.26; *1960-61*, p.28; *1965-66*, p.28; *1966-67*, p.27.

EWENNY
Records of the Ewenny Abbey estate, co. Glamorgan, including records of the manor of Ewenny, 17th-19th cent. *Transferred to Glamorgan R O. (Cardiff).*

Schedule [pre-1934], 122pp. *AR 1932-33*, p.44.

FALCONDALE
Records of the Falcondale and Peterwell estates of the Harford family, co. Cardigan, 18th-19th cent., and of the borough of Lampeter, 1741-1848. See also **Peterwell**.

Schedule [*c.* 1928], 35pp. *AR 1927-28*, p.46.

FFOSRHYDGALED
Records of the Ffosrhydgaled estate, mostly in the parish of Llanychaearn, co. Cardigan, and Aberystwyth, 1733-1920, with some shipping records. See NLW MSS 13870-9 for associated manuscripts, see also **Roberts & Evans**.

Schedule [*c.* 1934], 21pp. *AR 1934-35*, p.43. See also *AR 1940-41*, p.19.

JOHN FISHER
Papers of John Fisher (1862-1930), Chancellor of St Asaph and antiquary, including some papers of David Richard Thomas (1833-1916), fellow antiquary.

Schedule [?1950s], 10pp.

KYRLE FLETCHER
Several groups of deeds purchased from Kyrle Fletcher, including:

Deeds relating to cos Monmouth, Brecon and Glamorgan, 1586-1848.

Schedule [*c.* 1925], 9pp.

Deeds, 1520-1777, relating to cos Brecon and Glamorgan, notably to the Woods family of Brecon.

AR 1936-37, p.32.

Deeds, 1647-1876, relating to the Llandeilo area, co. Carmarthen.

AR 1937-38, p.53.

Records of the family of Jones of Llanarth, co. Monmouth, 17th-18th cent., with others relating to cos Monmouth and Glamorgan, 17th-19th cent. Other Jones of Llanarth records in Gwent R O.

Preliminary schedule [c. 1968], 11pp. *AR 1967-68*, pp.37-8.

H. J. FLEURE

Papers of Herbert John Fleure (1877-1969), anthropologist. See also **Minor Lists 1982**.

Schedule (1976), 6pp. *AR 1976-77*, pp.67-8.

BENJAMIN FLOWER

Correspondence of Benjamin Flower (1755-1829), journalist and printer, 1794-1808. (*NLW MS 13587*).

Schedule (1980), iii + 23pp. *AR 1939-40*, p.24.

FOLEY

Records of the estate of the family of Foley of Ridgeway, co. Pembroke, mainly in that county, 1366-1869.

Schedule (1964), 81pp. *AR 1963-64*, pp.54-5.

FONMON CASTLE

Family and estate records of Jones of Fonmon Castle, cos Glamorgan and Monmouth, 13th-19th cent. *Transferred to Glamorgan R O (Cardiff)*.

Schedule (1934), 81pp., 174pp., 190pp., in three vols. *AR 1932-33*, pp.35-6.

SIR IDRIS FOSTER

Papers of Sir Idris Foster (1912-84), Celtic scholar.

Schedule (1985), 7pp. *AR 1978-79*, pp. 77-9; *1984-85*, p.34.

MANSEL FRANKLEN

Manuscripts and papers of John Montgomery Traherne (1788-1860), antiquary, mostly relating to the history of Glamorgan, including papers of William Davies, Cringell (1756-1823); deeds, 1399-1817. (Mainly now *NLW MSS 6511-615*). (Donated by Lady Mansel Franklen).

Schedule [pre-1934], 219pp. *AR 1928-29*, pp.19-21.

MAXWELL FRASER

Papers of Maxwell Fraser (1902-80), author, and of Edgar Phillips ('Trefin', 1889-1962), poet, her husband. See also **Brinley Richards**.

Papurau Trefin, Archdderwydd Cymru (1994), i + 26pp. *AR 1980-81*, p.41; *1981-82*, p.45. Working list of Maxwell Fraser Papers available.

BAKER-GABB
Records, 14th-20th cent., of the Baker, Gabb, and Baker-Gabb families, comprising deeds and documents relating to lands mostly in cos Monmouth and Hereford; correspondence; and family papers. See also **The Chain**.

Schedule (1948), 301pp. Also **Maps**. *AR 1942-43*, pp.30-1.

GARN
Estate and family records of Griffiths of Garn, co. Denbigh, 1572-1943.

AR 1955-56, pp.29-31; *1958-59*, p.44. See T. A. Glenn, *The Family of Griffiths of Garn and Plasnewydd in the County of Denbigh* (London, 1934).

GEE PRINTING CO.
Archives of the printing and publishing firm of Thomas Gee, later Messrs Gee & Son, Denbigh, 1836-1937. See also NLW MSS 12138-61 and 22083-7 and **Kate Roberts.**

Schedule (1977), ii + 39pp. Supersedes two earlier schedules ('Morris T. Williams', both 1936). *AR 1935-36*, p.49; *1937-38*, p.59; *1938-39*, p.46.

GELLI
Deeds relating to Y Gelli estate, Llanfair Caereinion, co. Montgomery, 1610-1890

Schedule (1982), ii + 38pp. *AR 1939-40*, p.31.

LLOYD GEORGE
Papers of Dame Margaret Lloyd George, including over 2,000 letters from David Lloyd George, 1886-1936; a small part of Lloyd George's own archive; papers of Lady Megan Lloyd George. (*NLW MSS 20403-93*).

Schedule (1970), 20pp. *AR 1969-70*, p.40. K. O. Morgan, *Lloyd George Family Letters, 1885-1936* (Cardiff/Oxford, 1973).

Part of the archive of David Lloyd George, 1st Earl Lloyd-George of Dwyfor, acquired from the 3rd Earl Lloyd-George. (*NLW MSS 21514-37*). See also NLW MSS 21787-92. The main Lloyd George archive is in the House of Lords R O.

Schedule (1992), 49pp. *AR 1986-87*, p.64.

WILLIAM GEORGE
Papers of William George (1865-1967), brother of Lloyd George. They include diaries of Lloyd George, 1878-88, and some of Lloyd George's own papers; some 4,000 letters from Lloyd George to William George, mostly

1890-1916; diaries of Richard Lloyd ('Uncle Lloyd'), 1881-1913, and of William George, 1883-1915.

AR 1989-90, p.63. Working list of part of papers available.

WILLIAM GEORGE MUSIC MSS

Music manuscripts of William George, Ystalyfera (d. 1920), composer.

Schedules (1975), 17pp.; (1986), [ii] + 8pp. *AR 1971-72*, p.52; *AR 1985-86*, p.60.

JOHN GIBSON

Letters from John Gibson (1790-1866), sculptor, to Mrs Henry Sandbach of Liverpool and Hafodunos, Abergele, and Henry Sandbach, 1839-65. (*NLW MSS 20566-7*).

Schedule (1971), 36pp.

LEWIS GILBERTSON

Papers (donated by the Rev. Canon Lewis Gibertson) relating to ecclesiastical matters in the diocese of St Davids and the Gilbertson family of Dolycletwr, co. Cardigan, 1764-1813. (*NLW MSS 6203-4*). See also **Roberts & Evans.**

Schedule [? 1960s], 9pp. *AR 1927-28*, p.28.

GLANDENYS

Deeds relating to the Lampeter and Llandovery areas of cos Cardigan and Carmarthen, 1650-1890, including the Glandenys estate.

AR 1971-72, p.58.

GLANDOVAN

Estate and family records of Gower of Glandovan and Castle Malgwyn, parish of Cilgerran, co. Pembroke, mainly late 18th-19th cent., including industrial records.

AR 1957-58, pp.35-37; *1964-65*, pp.55-7.

GLAN-PAITH

Records accumulated by John Parry, Glan-paith, during his practice as a solicitor in Aberystwyth in the early 19th cent.; comprise deeds, largely relating to the Penglais estate in the Aberystwyth area, 1555-1918, and Aberystwyth borough records, 1759-1813. See also **Roberts & Evans.**

Schedule (1935), 76pp. *AR 1934-35*, p.47. See also *AR 1938-39*, p.49. *NLWJ*, 3 (1943-4), p.35.

GLANSEVERN

Records of the family of Owen, later Humphreys-Owen, of Glansevern, co. Montgomery, and Johnes of Garthmyl. Include papers of Arthur Charles Humphreys-Owen (1836-1905), including correspondence with Lord Rendel, 1877-1905 (schedule, vol. I); family correspondence, 17th-19th cent. (vols II-IV); estate and other records, 15th - 20th cent., including naval records of Captain William Owen, 1750-78, also deeds relating to Sheldon, co. Warwick, 13th-15th cent. (vols. V-VII).

Schedules (1966-74), 222pp., 196pp., 167pp., 214pp., 370pp., 368pp. and 161pp., in seven vols. Also **Maps**. *AR 1935-36*, pp.51-3; *1937-38*, p.70; *1938-39*, p.48; *1939-40*, pp.34-5; *1962-63*, pp.54-5; *1970-71*, pp.68-9. See also *AR 1962-63*, pp. 58-9; *1975-76*, p.78.

GLANSEVIN

Estate records, 16th-20th cent., of the family of Lloyd of Glansevin and Mandinam, Llangadog, and of the associated families of Harries of Llandovery and Price of Ystrad-ffin, co. Carmarthen, Lloyd of Wern Newydd and Edwards of Derry-odyn, co. Cardigan, and Price-Jones of Glanhafren, co. Montgomery. Other records in Dyfed R O (Carmarthen) *s.n.* Glasbrook.

Schedule (1971), 302pp. *AR 1948-49*, pp.49-51.

GLANYRAFON

Deeds relating mainly to the Glanyrafon and Bronheulog estates in Llansilin and Llangedwyn, co. Denbigh, 1576-1897.

AR 1939-40, p.33.

GLYNEIDDAN

Deeds and documents relating to Glyneiddan, Nantgaredig, co. Carmarthen, and elsewhere in the county, 18th-20th cent., and papers of Henry Jones-Davies (1870-1955) relating to local government and agriculture in the area.

Schedule [*c.* 1961], 21+7+4pp. *AR 1960-61*, pp.57-8.

GLYNLLIFON

Estate records of the Wynn family, later barons Newborough, of Glynllifon and Bodfean, co. Caernarfon, 15th-19th cent. *Transferred to Gwynedd R O (Caernarfon) and incorporated in the larger Glynllifon archive.*

Schedule (1938), 437pp. in two vols. *AR 1934-45*, pp.49-50.

Deeds and documents relating to the Glynllifon estate, 1465-20th cent., including much correspondence of Thomas Wynn, 1st Lord Newborough, 1761-1805. This group remains in NLW.

Schedule (1980), viii + 138pp. *AR 1948-49*, p.41.

GLYNNE OF HAWARDEN

Papers of the Glynne family of Hawarden Castle, co. Flint, 17th-19th cent., and records of the estate, 1304-1880. See also **Hawarden**. Other records in Clwyd R O (Hawarden).

Schedule (1940), vol. I (diaries, correspondence, etc), 219pp. vol. II (deeds etc), 138pp. Also **Maps**. *AR 1934-35*, p.44. *NLWJ*, 2 (1941-2), pp.23-5.

WILLIAM GLYNNE-JONES see JONES

GOGERDDAN

Records of the Pryse family of Gogerddan, co. Cardigan, and the associated families of Lewes of Abernantbychan, co. Cardigan, and Hean Castle, co. Pembroke, Lewis of Llangors, co. Brecon, Lloyd of Aberllefenni, co. Merioneth, and Loveden of Buscot Park, Berkshire. Include deeds from 14th cent., manorial records, 17th-19th cent., and silver and lead-mining records, 17th-20th cent. The main body of the archive remains uncatalogued, but see 1994 box-list. The manuscript 'Old Schedule' provides access to the early deeds of the Gogerddan estate itself.

Schedules: *Lead-mine Records* (1950), 50 pp.; *Rentals and Valuations* (1989), 11pp.; rough box-list (1994), 7pp. Also **Maps**. *AR 1948-49*, pp. 55-8. See also *AR 1982-83*, p.48.

GOUGH

Records (deposited by Mrs Gough) of the Holland family of Pennant, parish of Eglwys-bach, co. Denbigh, including deeds, 1458-1810, and correspondence, 1560-1826.

Preliminary report (1941), 4pp. *AR 1940-41*, p.27.

GRAY

Deeds and documents (received *per* Irvine E. Gray) relating to property in various Welsh counties, 1555-1875.

Schedule [*c*. 1951], 16pp. *AR 1950-51*, pp.22 and 37.

ARCHBISHOP GREEN

Papers of Charles Alfred Howell Green (1864-1944), bishop of Bangor and archbishop of Wales. See also NLW MSS 4838-41. Other papers in St Deiniol's Library, Hawarden.

AR 1943-44, p.18.

FRANCIS GREEN

Deeds acquired from Francis Green (1854-1942), lawyer and antiquary, mostly relating to co. Pembroke, 17th-19th cent., including some relating to the Green family, 1806-80, and papers from the office of James Summers, solicitor, Haverfordwest, 1826-67.

Francis Green Deeds (1981), ii + 137pp. *AR 1925-26*, p.11; *1934-35*, p.32; @.

Facsimiles of the Francis Green MSS in Haverfordwest public library, an invaluable source for the genealogy of south west Wales families. These facsimiles are kept on open shelves in the NLW manuscript catalogue room and are listed and indexed in the following schedule:

Francis Green MSS (1986), i + 75pp.

GREGYNOG

Rentals and other estate office books of the Gregynog estates of Arthur Weaver, Arthur Blaney and Lord Sudeley, in co. Montgomery, 1752-1893. See also **Davies, Gregynog**.

Schedule [c. 1957], 4pp. *AR 1956-57*, p.43.

GREGYNOG PRESS

Archives of the Gregynog Press, 1922-62. See also **Thomas Jones**.

Gregynog Press Archives (1992), 21pp.

CHARLES GRIFFIN

Deeds and documents (deposited by Charles Griffin), 1635-1869, mostly relating to cos Monmouth and Hereford, particularly to the Griffin family, Newton House, Dixton, co. Monmouth. See also **Sir L. Twiston Davies**.

Schedule (1949), 23pp. *AR 1949-50*, p.41.

EDWARD GRIFFITH

Deeds and documents collected by Edward Griffith (1832-1918), antiquary, mainly relating to the Dolgellau area, co. Merioneth, 1511-1905. See also NLW MSS 2691-2754.

Schedule (1977), ii + 77pp.

ELLIS-GRIFFITH
Papers of Sir Ellis Jones Ellis-Griffith (1860-1926), politician, including material collected for his biography.

Schedule (1956), 18pp. *AR 1955-56*, p.26. See also *1964-65*, p.27.

J. E. GRIFFITH
Manuscripts collected by and papers of John Edwards Griffith (1843-1933), antiquary and botanist. (*NLW MSS 19058-96*). See **E. G. Wright**.

Schedule (1983), [i] + 28pp. *AR 1971-72*, pp. 58-60.

JOHN GRIFFITH
Deeds (donated by John Griffith), 1701-1891, relating to the parish of Dolgellau, co. Merioneth. (*NLW Deeds 554-73*).

Schedule (1952), 6pp. *AR 1952-53*, p.24.

LL. WYN GRIFFITH
Papers of Llewelyn Wyn Griffith (1890-1977), author.

AR 1962-63, p.27; *1963-64*, pp.27-8. Working list available.

MOSES GRIFFITH
Papers of Moses Griffith (1893-1973), agriculturalist, relating in particular to grassland management and the breeding of Welsh Black cattle and Welsh ponies and cobs.

AR 1978-79, p.45; *1979-80*, p.50; *1992-93*, p.54.

SAMUEL GRIFFITH
Deeds and documents (donated by Lt.-Col. Samuel Griffith), 1508-1706, relating to the parishes of Llanbedr and Llandecwyn, co. Merioneth.

Schedule (1973), 3pp. *AR 1946-47*, p.25.

JAMES GRIFFITHS
Papers of James Griffiths (1890-1975), first Secretary of State for Wales. Other papers are in Coleg Harlech.

Schedule (1979), iii + 194pp. *AR 1975-76*, pp. 39-40; *1977-78*, p.42.

JOHN GRIFFITHS (BOMBAY)
Papers of John Griffiths (1837-1918), Principal of the Bombay School of Art. (*NLW MS 15331*).

Schedule (1950), 6pp. *AR 1949-50*, p.27.

JOHN GRIFFITHS (LLANYRE)
Deeds (deposited by Dr John Griffiths, Llanyre), relating to the parishes of Diserth, Llansanffraid-yn-Elfael, Llandeglau and Glasgwm, co. Radnor, and Llanfechain, co. Montgomery, 1630-1886.

Schedule [c. 1932], 17pp. *AR 1931-32*, p.52.

WILLIAM GRIFFITHS
Papers of William Griffiths (1788-1861), Calvinistic Methodist minister in Gower, co. Glamorgan, 1816-61.

Schedule (1975), 6pp. *AR 1974-75*, p.33; *1975-76*, pp.33-5.

W. J. GRUFFYDD
Papers of William John Gruffydd (1881-1954), poet and Celtic scholar.

Schedules (1976), [iii] + 29pp.; (1985), [i] + 230pp. *AR 1954-55*, p.27.

GUNLEY
Records of the Pryce and Campbell family of Gunley, co. Montgomery, 1578-1923.

AR 1949-50, pp.45-6. Also **Maps.**

GWARCWM
Deeds relating to Gwarcwm, parish of Llanbadarn Fawr, co. Cardigan, 1771-1888.

Schedule [c. 1947], 3pp. *AR 1946-47*, p.27.

GWAUNCAEGURWEN AND PENLLERFEDWEN COMMONERS ASSOCIATION
Records of the Association, 1894-1983. *Returned to the Association.*

Schedule (1983), iii + 16pp.

GWENALLT
Papers of David James Jones ('Gwenallt', 1899-1968), poet and scholar. *Conditional access.*

Schedule (1980), iii + 69pp. *AR 1972-73*, pp.38-9.

GWERNYFED
Records of the estate of the Williams family of Gwernyfed, co. Brecon, mostly in that county, including the Llangors estate, 1461-1924.

Preliminary schedule (1955), 34pp. *AR 1955-56*, pp.38-9.

GWILI
Papers of John Gwili Jenkins ('Gwili', 1872-1936), theologian and author.

AR 1936-37, p.26; *1971-72*, p.54; *1976-77*, p.48.

A. J. GWILLIM
Deeds and papers (deposited by A.J. Gwillim) relating to the parish of Ystradfellte, co. Brecon, 1703 - 20th cent.

Schedule (1973), 5pp. *AR 1973-74*, p.72.

GWRYCH CASTLE
Records of the Gwrych Castle estate and the families of Lloyd, Bamford and Hesketh, later the earls of Dundonald, in cos Denbigh, Caernarfon and Flint, and Cheshire, Lancashire and Derbyshire, 1535-1920.

Preliminary schedule (1942), 37pp. Also **Maps**. *AR 1942-43*, p.32.

GWYDIR (B.R.A.)
Records of the Gwydir estates, of the Wynn family, mainly in cos Caernarfon, Denbigh and Merioneth, 1625-1886. See also **Wynn (of Gwydir)** and NLW MSS 9719-27. Other records in Gwynedd R O (Caernarfon).

Schedule (1993) v + 35pp. *AR 1940-41*, p.18.

GWYNFRYN
Records of the estate of the Jones family of Gwynfryn, parish of Llangynfelyn, co. Cardigan, 1600-1920, including documents relating to William Basil Jones (1822-97), bishop of St Davids. See also **Evans & Griffin**.

Schedule (1955), 84pp.

GWYSANEY
Family papers and estate records of Davies, Puleston, Cooke and Davies-Cooke of Llannerch and Gwysaney, cos Denbigh and Flint, c. 1300-1880. The records deposited in NLW have been transferred to Clwyd R O (Hawarden) where they have joined other portions of the Gwysaney archive. The Gwysaney MSS on the other hand (described in the 1953 schedule) were scattered by auction at Sothebys on 15 June 1959, though most of the Welsh material had previously been bought for NLW, now *NLW MSS 17110-62*; for location of others see *Guide to the Location of Collections* (Royal Commission on Historical Manuscripts, London, 1982), p.17. The records listed in the first two volumes of the schedules and some

of those listed in the 1948 volume are available in NLW on microfilm and in NLW Facs 371. See also **Kinmel**.

Schedules [n.d. ?1920s], 4pp.; (1942), 160pp.; (1947) 212pp. (transcripts of letters and papers); (1948), 109pp.; (1953) 107pp. (manuscripts). *AR 1941-42*, p.27; *1946-47*, pp.39-40; *1958-59*, pp.41-2. *NLWJ*, 7 (1951-2), pp.326-43.

HAMILTON AND GREVILLE
Letters and papers, 1581-1805, relating to Sir William Hamilton's estates in co. Pembroke; and to improvement schemes by the Greville family at Milford Haven, 1794-1813.

Schedule [*c.* 1930], 12pp. *AR 1929-30*, p.20.

JAMES HANLEY
Papers of James Hanley (1901-85), novelist. (*NLW 23122-32*).

AR 1988-89, p.66; *1990-91*, p.60.

HARPTON COURT
Records of the Harpton Court estate, cos Radnor and Brecon, 16th-20th cent., and papers of the associated families of Lewis, Frankland, Cornewall and Duff Gordon, 18th-19th cent.; include the papers of Sir George Cornewall Lewis (1806-63), politician. See also **Minor Lists 1992**.

Schedules: vol. I (1964, records, Sir George Cornewall Lewis papers), 216pp.; vol. II (1972, early correspondence), 161pp.; vols III and IV (1987, mainly correspondence of Sir George Cornewall Lewis), 414pp.; vol. V (1987, deeds, 1564-1908), 313pp. Also **Maps**. *AR 1952-53*, p.41.

MESSRS HARRISON & SONS
Records from the office of Messrs Harrison & Sons, Welshpool, solicitors, relating mostly to cos Denbigh, Montgomery and Salop, 15th-20th cent. Include records of the estates of the Jones family of Llanlloddian and Llanfair Caereinion, co. Montgomery, and of Llandysilio, co. Denbigh; the Harrison family in co. Montgomery; the estates of Brynllywarch and Leighton Hall acquired by the Leyland and Naylor families; the Pugh family of Llanerchydol, Welshpool; the Lloyd, Humphreys and Lloyd-Humphreys family of Forden and Chirbury (the Woodlands estate); the Bank House estate of the Fairlies-Humphreys family of Montgomery. See also **Minor Lists 1992**.

Preliminary schedules (1976), 106pp.; (1980), 23pp. Also **Maps**. *AR 1974-75*, pp. 66-70; *1979-80*, pp.75-6.

HARRISON FAMILY PAPERS

Papers, mainly correspondence, 1771-1840, of the Jones and Harrison family of Llantysilio Hall, Llangollen. (*Minor Deposit 623*).

Schedule (1957), 24pp. *AR 1957-58*, p.38.

G. R. D. HARRISON

Deeds (donated by Col. G.R.D. Harrison) relating to the manor of Overgorther, cos Montgomery and Salop, 1571-1768.

Schedule (1947), 3pp. *AR 1946-47*, p.25.

HAVERFORDWEST

Records of the borough of Haverfordwest, late 13th cent-1901. *Transferred to Dyfed R O (Haverfordwest)*. Available in NLW on microfilm (NLW Film 355-63).

Schedules (1948), 94pp.; (1960), 289pp. B.G. Charles, *Calendar of the Records of the Borough of Haverfordwest, 1539-1660* (Cardiff, 1967). *AR 1947-48*, p.37-8.

HAVERFORDWEST (EATON EVANS & WILLIAMS)

Records, mostly deeds, from the office of Eaton Evans & Williams, Haverfordwest, 17th-19th cent. See also **Haverfordwest (Williams & Williams)**, **Eaton Evans & Williams** and **Eaton Evans & Morris**.

Schedule [*c.* 1920], 83pp., in manuscript, an outsize volume shelved at the end of the schedules.

HAVERFORDWEST (WILLIAMS & WILLIAMS)

Records from the office of Williams & Williams, Haverfordwest, solicitors, largely deeds and draft deeds, mostly 19th cent. and relating to the Haverfordwest area of Pembrokeshire. See also NLW MSS 2921-3018 and **Haverfordwest (Eaton Evans & Williams)**.

Schedules [*c.* 1920], 928pp., in manuscript, in three outsize volumes shelved at the end of the schedules. Also **Maps** *s.n.* Williams & Williams.

HAWARDEN

Deeds and documents relating to the castle and manor of Hawarden and to the families of Glynne of Hawarden and Ravenscroft of Broadlane Hall, co. Flint, and their estates, 13th-20th cent. See also **Glynne of Hawarden**.

Calendar of Deeds & Documents. Vol. III The Hawarden Deeds (Aberystwyth 1931), 477pp. *NLWJ*, 2 (1941-2), pp.23-5.

HELYGOG
Deeds relating to the Helygog estate, near Dolgellau, co. Merioneth, 1616-1954.

Schedules (1933), 11pp.; (1986), i + 18pp. *AR 1932-33*, p.42, *1935-36*, p.54; *1981-82*, p.53.

ROPARZ HEMON
Twenty two Breton manuscripts, 18th-19th cent., the collection of Louis P.Nemo ('Roparz Hemon', 1900-78), Breton writer and scholar.

Schedule (1982), ii + 24pp. *AR 1980-81*, p.75.

Papers of Roparz Hemon.

Schedule (1986), ii + 14pp.; (1992), vol. II, 11pp. *AR 1985-86*, p.54; @.

W. J. HEMP
Deeds (donated by Wilfred James Hemp, antiquary) relating to properties in several Welsh counties, 1557-1808.

Schedule [n.d. and 1933], 15pp. *AR 1933-34*, p.30. For papers of W. J. Hemp see *AR 1965-66*, pp. 31-2; *1967-78*, p.26; *1972-73*, p.39; also in Clwyd R O (Hawarden) and at the Royal Commission on Ancient Monuments in Wales, Aberystwyth.

HENDREFELEN
Deeds and documents relating mainly to property of the families of Herbert and Hughes of Hendrefelen, parish of Ysbyty Ystwyth, co. Cardigan, 1546-1885.

Schedule (1961), 67pp. *AR 1948-49*, p.26.

D. D. HERBERT
Papers of David Daniel Herbert of Resolven (1905-59), local historian, including material on the history and literary history of the Resolven area, some of it archival material collected by him.

AR 1964-65, p.30; *1965-66*, pp.32-3. Also **Maps**.

T. G. G. HERBERT
Records collected by Thomas G. G. Herbert of Aberaeron. They include the papers of Daniel Lewis Lloyd (1843-99), bishop of Bangor; and records of the family of Pryse and Saunders of Tŷ Mawr, co. Cardigan, and Glanrhydw, co. Carmarthen, 1609-20th cent. For Herbert's personal papers see **Minor Lists, 1990**.

AR 1969-70, pp.54-6; *1970-71*, p.68; *1972-73*, p.69.

HEREFORD CATHEDRAL

The medieval chapter records of Hereford Cathedral. *Returned to Hereford Cathedral.*

A Calendar of the earlier Hereford Cathedral Muniments (1955), 1389pp.in three vols; *A List of Hereford Cathedral account rolls, court rolls, rentals and surveys* (1955), 128pp.Indexes to these volumes, compiled later, at Hereford, are available in two further volumes. *NLWJ*, 9 (1955-6), pp.401-12.

HESGIN

Papers of Thomas Owen ('Hesgin', 1872-1956), author.

Schedule (1956), 32pp. *AR 1956-57*, p.23.

HIGHMEAD

Estate and family records of Evans and Davies-Evans of Highmead, co. Cardigan, 1548-1903, relating mainly to those parts of cos Cardigan and Carmarthen in the neighbourhood of Llanybydder. Other records in Dyfed R O (Carmarthen) *s.n.* Davies-Evans.

AR 1940-41, p.27; *1942-43*, p.31. Working list available.

HIND AND ELLEN (NEW QUAY)

Records of the ships *Hind* and *Ellen* of New Quay, owned by Captain William Phillips, 1873-88, with other shipping records, 1853-98.

AR 1956-57, p.34.

HOLLAND

Deeds and documents (donated by Frederick Holland), 1398-1793, relating mainly to co. Monmouth, some to the families of Thomas, Kemeys, and Gardner (later Gardner-Kemeys) of Bertholey, parish of Llantrissent, 16th-18th cent.

Schedule (1979), 33pp.

LORD HOOSON

Papers of Emlyn Hooson (1925-   ), MP for Montgomeryshire, 1962-79, later Lord Hooson. *Conditional access.*

Schedule (1980 + suppls), ii + 17pp. *AR 1978-79*, p.79; *1979-80*, p.76; *1980-81*, p.77; *1988-89*, p.62; *1993-4*.

HUGHES A'I FAB

Archives of Hughes a'i Fab (Hughes & Son), Wrexham, publishers, 1889-1977.

AR 1978-79, pp.76-7; *1981-82*, p.81.

CLEDWYN HUGHES
Manuscripts and typescripts of works by Cledwyn Hughes (1920-78), novelist and topographical writer. (*NLW MSS 20764-9, 20891-4, 21635-62*). See also **Minor Lists 1983**.

Schedule (1980), v + 9pp. *AR 1971-72*, p.62; *1978-79*, p.63.

D. G. LLOYD HUGHES
Research material of D. G. Lloyd Hughes relating to the history of Burry Port and Pembrey, co. Carmarthen, and Pwllheli.

Schedule (1992), 31pp. *AR 1992-93*, p.54.

D. R. HUGHES
Papers of Welsh literary interest collected by David Rowland Hughes of London and Old Colwyn (1874-1953), eisteddfod administrator, 19th-20th cent.

Schedule (1955), 6pp.

H. HAROLD HUGHES
Deeds (donated by H. Harold Hughes) relating to the parishes of Llanfihangel Genau'r-glyn, Llangynfelyn and Llanbadarn Fawr, co. Cardigan, 1577-1852.

Schedule [1932], 22pp. *AR 1931-32*, p.36.

H. M. HUGHES
Papers of Hugh Michael Hughes (1858-1933), Congregational minister.

Schedule (1958), 6pp. *AR 1958-59*, p.30.

J. R. HUGHES
Manuscripts and documents collected by and research papers of John Roberts Hughes, Tre-Taliesin (1886-1962), antiquary and historian of the Quakers in Wales, 18th-20th cent. See also NLW MSS 16053-75.

Schedules (1963), 29pp. (manuscripts and papers); (1963), 31pp. (deeds); *AR 1962-63*, pp.38-9.

J. R. HUGHES DEEDS
Deeds and legal papers (purchased from J. R. Hughes) relating mainly to cos Glamorgan and Monmouth, 1672-1919, deriving largely from Cardiff solicitors' offices.

AR 1948-49, pp.40-1.

O. P.HUGHES

Papers of O. P.Hughes relating to gold mining in co. Merioneth, 1918-36.

Schedule (1947), 12pp. *AR 1946-47*, p.40.

C. L. J. HUMPHREYS

Deeds (deposited by C.L.J. Humphreys) relating to the parishes of Betws, Berriew, Llandyssil, Llanmerewig, Newtown, and Llanllwchaearn, co. Montgomery, 1647-1802. See also **Minor Lists 1982**.

Schedule (1973), 11pp. *AR 1972-73*, p.69.

E. MORGAN HUMPHREYS

Papers of Edward Morgan Humphreys (1882-1955), journalist and author.

Working list available.

HURCOMB

Deeds and documents (purchased from W.E. Hurcomb), 1441-1832, relating to the estates of the Jones family of Pen y Bryn, Ruabon, co. Denbigh, and the Maddocks family of Prees Henlle, Whittington, co. Salop.

Schedule (1978), vi + 62pp.

IOLO MORGANWG

The very full and rich archive of Edward Williams ('Iolo Morganwg', 1747-1826), poet and antiquary, and his son, Taliesin Williams ('Taliesin ab Iolo', 1787-1847). The main group of Iolo's collection of manuscripts together with most of his notebooks constitute the 'Llanover MSS', now NLW MSS 13061-184. The rest of the archive is described here. The remainder of the collection of manuscripts, the 'Iolo Aneurin Williams MSS', is described in the 1978 schedule (*NLW MSS 21287-386*). The second part of the 1978 schedule describes a series of volumes made up at NLW from loose papers (*NLW 21387-433*). Iolo's own correspondence is listed in the 1957 schedule (the letters now bound in *NLW 21280-6*) and that of Taliesin in the 1959 schedule (*NLW MSS 21271-9*). Other papers, including papers, 1762-91, of John Bedford (d. 1791), writer on the iron industry, remain uncatalogued (1994).

Schedule (1955), 43pp. (a small group, partly re-numbered and incorporated in the 1957 and 1978 schedules); (1957), [ii] + 455pp. (Iolo correspondence); (1959), [viii] + 308pp. (Taliesin correspondence); (1978), [i] + 291 + [iv]pp., bound in two vols (pp.1-35, manuscripts, pp.36-291, papers). *AR 1953-54*, pp.34-5; *1954-55*, pp.33 and 39-40. On John Bedford see Philip Riden, *John Bedford and the Ironworks at Cefn Cribwr* (Cardiff, 1993); a working list of Bedford's papers is available.

JACKSON & AWDRY
Deeds (deposited by Messrs Jackson & Awdry) relating to properties in cos Pembroke and Carmarthen, 1699-1748.

Schedule (1955), 6pp. *AR 1954-55*, p.50.

MATHER-JACKSON
Deeds (donated by Sir H. Mather-Jackson) relating mainly to the family of Lewis of Llantilio Crossenny, co. Monmouth, *c.* 1753-1912.

Schedule [retyped *c.* 1960 from earlier schedules of *c.* 1922 and *c.* 1924], 20pp. *AR 1922 (Oct.)*, p.9; @.

NEWTON JACKSON
Deeds and documents (donated by Mrs Newton Jackson), 16th-19th cent., relating to properties in co. Monmouth, mainly in the hundred of Skenfrith.

Schedule [pre-1928], 47pp. *AR 1924 (May)*, p.10.

FRANÇOIS JAFFRENNOU
Papers of François Jaffrennou ('Taldir', 1879-1956), Breton poet and scholar.

AR 1966-67, p.29.

EVAN JAMES
Manuscripts of Evan James ('Ieuan ab Iago', 1809-78) and James James ('Iago ab Iago', 1833-1902), author and composer of *Hen Wlad fy Nhadau.*

List (1969), 3pp. See *NLWJ*, 16 (1969-70), pp.172-84. *AR 1937-38*, p.70; *1968-69*, p.52.

THOMAS LEWIS JAMES
Documents, mainly 19th-cent. transcripts by Thomas Lewis James, relating to the history of Haverfordwest. (*NLW MSS 9671-3*).

Schedule (1934), 6pp. *AR 1934-35*, p.32.

WARREN JANE
Deeds and documents (deposited by Mr Warren Jane), relating to co. Monmouth, 1568-1825, with two manuscripts relating to the Roberts family of Wooton, co. Gloucester, 18th cent.

Schedule (1933), 19pp. Transcript (of two Roberts MSS) (1933), 14pp. *AR 1932-33*, p.38; *1933-34*, p.40.

JEFFREYS & POWELL
Deeds and documents from the office of Jeffreys & Powell, solicitors, Brecon, relating to cos Brecon, Glamorgan, Monmouth, Radnor, Carmarthen and Hereford, 1557-1926; include records relating to the Pant Griffith estate, co. Brecon, and Court Rhyd-hir estate, co. Glamorgan. Other records in Powys R O.

Schedules (1958), 10pp.; (1959), 6pp.; (1960), 8pp.; (1962), 8pp.; (1964), 19pp.; (1966), 7pp.; (1968), 33pp.; (1970), 26pp. Also **Maps**. *AR 1958-59*, p.54; *1960-61*, p.56; *1962-63*, p.55; *1964-65*, p.58; *1966-67*, p.55; *1967-68*, p.50; *1968-69*, p.51; *1970-71*, p.69.

DAVID JENKINS
Music manuscripts of David Jenkins (1848-1915), composer.

Schedule (1944), 3pp. *AR 1943-44*, p.20.

DAVIES-JENKINS
Deeds and papers (deposited by Brigadier E. M. Davies-Jenkins) relating mainly to co. Montgomery, notably to Llanidloes, 1685-1943.

AR 1973-74, pp.70-1. Also **Maps**.

JOHN JENKINS
Manuscripts and records collected by John Jenkins of Resolven (d.1953), mineral surveyor and antiquary. Include records of the manor of Neath Ultra and Cilybebyll, 1632-1831; deeds, largely relating to mineral rights, cos Glamorgan and Brecon, 1546-1886; and literary manuscripts, including some owned by Philip Williams of Plas Dyffryn Clydach (d. 1717).

Schedules (1955, manuscripts and documents), 67pp.; (1955, printed books, maps etc), 22pp. Also **Maps**. *AR 1954-55*, pp.28-30.

H. S. JEVONS
Papers of Herbert Stanley Jevons (1875-1955), economist, including papers relating to his advisory work in India, mostly 1918-30, and Abyssinia, 1935-53.

Schedules (1963), 19pp.; (1965), 7pp. *AR 1962-63*, p.56; *1964-65*, pp.58-9.

JOHN Y GWAS
Papers of John William Evans, Felindre ('John Y Gwas', c.1880-c.1960), local historian, with much biographical data relating to cos Cardigan and Carmarthen.

AR 1960-61, p.40.

AUGUSTUS JOHN
Papers of Augustus Edwin John (1878-1961), artist. (*NLW MSS 22775-803*).

Augustus John Papers (1991), 240pp. *AR 1987-88*, p.61; *1988-89*, p.66.

E. T. JOHN
Papers of Edward Thomas John (1857-1931), MP for East Denbighshire, 1910-18, and political activist; few papers are earlier than 1910.

Schedule (1979), iv + 936pp., in three vols, and (vol. IV) 283pp. *AR 1930-31*, p.48; *1976-77*, p.68.

GRIFFITH JOHN
Papers of Griffith John (1831-1912), missionary in China.

AR 1969-70, p.36.

GWEN JOHN
Papers of Gwen John (1876-1939), artist, including some papers of her nephew Edwin John. (*NLW MSS 22276-318*).

Gwen John Papers (1988), 83pp. *Gwen John Papers at the National Library of Wales* (Aberystwyth, 1988), also printed in *NLWJ*, 25 (1987-8), pp.191-240. *AR 1984-85*, pp.39-40.

JAMES R. JOHN
Deeds (donated by James R. John), relating to Aberystwyth, co. Cardigan, 1810-92.

Schedule (1981), i + 7pp. *AR 1960-61*, p.29.

HERBERT LLOYD-JOHNES
Papers of Herbert Johnes Lloyd-Johnes (1900-83), Senior British Liaison Officer to the Polish Forces, 1940-6, and antiquary. See also **Dolaucothi**.

Numerous donations, references to *AR* not detailed here.

JONES CHARITY
Records relating to the charity established by John Jones of Carmarthen, physician (d. 1697), for the benefit of the poor of several Pembrokeshire parishes, 1699-1941, including deeds from 1571.

AR 1948-49, p.45. Also **Maps.**

A. G. PRYS-JONES
Papers of Arthur Glyn Prys-Jones (1888-1987), writer.

A. G. Prys Jones Papers (1992), i + 37pp. *AR 1990-91*, p.63.

SIR C. BRYNER JONES
Papers of Sir Cadwaladr Bryner Jones (1872-1954), agriculturalist, many relating to Welsh cattle; a few earlier manuscripts and documents, 17th-19th cent.

Schedule (1985), 9pp.

D. PARRY-JONES
Papers of Canon Daniel Parry-Jones (1891-1981), author and recorder of country tradition.

AR 1967-68, p.27; *1978-79*, p.52; *1984-85*, p.34.

D. T. M. JONES
Records from the office of D.T.M. Jones, Llandovery, solicitor, the business founded about 1775 by Edward Jones. Include office correspondence from 1775 and records relating to the south Welsh counties, 16th-20th cent., including the estates of Dinas, co. Brecon, Abermarlais, Briwnant, Cynghordy, Glansefin, Glanyrannell, Llwyncelyn and Ton, co. Carmarthen, Glan-brân, co. Glamorgan, and Honeyborough, co. Pembroke.

Schedule (1978), 865pp., in two vols; (1980), 1126 pp., in three vols. Also **Maps** (schedule). *AR 1956-57*, p.43; *1958-59*, pp.55-6; *1959-60*, pp. 51-3; *1960-61*, pp. 56-7; *1961-62*, p.48.

DAVID JONES
Papers of David Jones (1895-1974), artist and writer. His whole written archive was acquired in four groups, two in 1978 and two in 1985, one of the latter previously deposited in Cambridge University Library.

Schedule ('1978 Deposit'), ii + 53pp. A draft catalogue of the worksheets of *In Parenthesis* and *The Anathemata* ('1978 Purchase') is available as are working lists of the two 1985 groups. *AR 1978-79*, pp.62 and 79-80; *1985-86*, p.60.

DAVID GLANAMAN JONES
Papers of David Glanaman Jones, Pontardawe (1867-1951), minister and writer, and of his brothers, *c.* 1887-1925. (*NLW MSS 16687-97*).

Schedule (1956), 8pp. *AR 1955-56*, p.42.

DOUGLAS A. JONES

Papers (deposited by Douglas A. Jones), relating to the history of Neath and collected or compiled by Donald H. Jones, 18th-20th cent., including papers, 1755-1835, relating to the Mackworth family and the Gnoll estate.

Schedule [c. 1945], 8pp. *AR 1944-45*, p.31.

E. D. JONES AND M. E. JONES

Deeds (deposited by E.D. Jones and Mrs M.E. Jones), relating to the parish of Llangeler, co. Carmarthen, 1769-1891.

Schedule (1964), 3pp. *AR 1964-65*, p.58.

E. K. JONES

Papers of Evan Kenffig Jones (1863-1950), Baptist minister, including records collected by him relating to Baptism in Wales, 19th cent., and papers of the Welsh Baptist Union.

Preliminary list [c. 1951], 8pp. Box-list (1962), 7pp. These two lists to be used in conjunction. *AR 1950-51*, p.31; *1969-70*, p.27.

E. W. CEMLYN JONES

Deeds (deposited by E.W. Cemlyn Jones), relating to the Conwy area of co. Caernarfon, 1617-1853, and other documents relating to north Wales, 18th-19th cent.

Schedule [c. 1935], 10pp.

EDWARD JONES ('IORWERTH DDU')

Papers of Edward Jones ('Iorwerth Ddu'), 1866-1924.

Schedule [1959], 3pp. *AR 1958-59*, p.29.

LORD ELWYN-JONES

The political papers of Elwyn Jones, later Lord Elwyn-Jones (1909-89), MP, 1945-74, Lord Chancellor, 1974-9.

Lord Elwyn-Jones Papers (1992), ii + 33pp. *AR 1989-90*, p.59.

SIR EVAN D. JONES

Deeds (from the collection of Sir Evan D. Jones), relating to properties in cos Cardigan and Pembroke, 1675-1720.

Schedule (1977), 3pp. *AR 1938-39*, p.41.

GLYN JONES
Manuscripts and worksheets of Glyn Jones (1905-), writer. (*NLW MSS 20705-18, 20744*). Correspondence acquired in 1993.

Schedule (1971), 4pp. *AR 1971-72*, p.62. See also *AR 1993-94*.

GWENAN JONES
Papers of Gwenan Jones (1889-1971), Welsh scholar and educationalist.

AR 1970-71, p.25.

GWYN JONES
Papers of Gwyn Jones (1907-), writer and scholar, including archives of his editorship of *The Welsh Review*.

Gwyn Jones Papers (1994), ii + 67pp. *AR 1992-93*, p.55.

HAROLD JONES
Papers of Harold Jones of Tredegar relating to the establishment of a Trades Union Congress for Wales, 1965-74.

Schedule (1975), [iii] + 143pp. *AR 1974-75*, p.70.

IDWAL JONES
Papers of Richard Idwal Merfyn Jones (1895-1937), poet and playwright. See also **Minor Lists, 1992** *s.n.* Dai Williams (Tregaron).

AR 1959-60, pp.29-30.

DR IORWERTH HUGHES JONES
Papers of Dr Iorwerth Hughes Jones (c. 1902-1972), patriot and friend of artists. Include papers relating to public affairs in the Swansea area and papers of the Rev. W. Glasnant Jones ('Glasnant', 1869-1951), his father.

AR 1970-71, p.33; *1977-78*, pp.44-5.

SIR HAYDN JONES
Papers of Sir Henry Haydn Jones (1863-1950), MP for Merionethshire, 1910-45; include music manuscripts of his father, Joseph David Jones (1827-70) and some records of Merioneth estates, 19th cent.

Schedule (1982), 272pp. *AR 1954-55*, pp.30-1.

ITHEL W. JONES
Deeds (deposited by Ithel W. Jones), relating to the parishes of Llangynfelyn, Llanfihangel Genau'r-glyn and Llanbadarn Fawr, co. Cardigan, 1583-1772.

Schedule (1969 and suppl.), 5pp. *AR 1968-69*, p.51; *1970-71*, p.69.

J. R. JONES
Papers of John Robert Jones (1911-70), philosopher.

AR 1977-78, p.70.

J. W. JONES
Papers collected by John William Jones, Blaenau Ffestiniog (1883-1954), including valuable papers of Welsh writers, 19th-20th cent., and material of local interest.

Papurau J. W. Jones (1992), vol. I, iii + 196pp.; vol. II, 83pp. Frequent donations from 1926 onwards, references to *AR* not detailed here.

JACK JONES
Manuscripts and typescripts of the works of Jack Jones (1884-1970), novelist.

Schedule (1961 and suppls), 31pp. *AR 1961-62*, pp.28-9; *1963-64*, p.30; *1964-65*, p.32; *1965-66*, p.35; *1966-67*, p.31; *1967-68*, pp.28-9; *1968-69*, p.27; *1969-70*, p.31.

KITTY IDWAL JONES
Papers of Kitty Idwal Jones (1898-1984), daughter of Sir John Herbert Lewis, including letters to her from Morfydd Llwyn Owen (1891-1918), composer, 1914-17.

Schedule (1991), i + 4pp. *AR 1989-90*, p.64.

MARTIN JONES
Papers of Martin Jones (1897-1979), agricultural botanist.

AR 1980-81, p.49.

O. T. JONES
Papers of Owen Thomas Jones (1878-1967), geologist, 1903-43; include research notes on north Cardiganshire and west Montgomeryshire lead mines. Another group of O.T. Jones papers is in the Institute of Geological Science.

Schedule (1968 + suppl.), 20pp. Also **Maps**. *AR 1968-69*, p.27; *1969-70*, p.31; *1971-72*, p.45; *1974-75*, p.40.

R. O. JONES
Documents collected by Robert Owen Jones of Llanfwrog (d.1959), local historian, relating to Ruthin and surrounding parts of co. Denbigh, 1500-19th cent.

AR 1959-60, pp.30-31.

R. VAUGHAN JONES
Papers of Robert Vaughan Jones (1873-1943) and his father, John Jones, relating mainly to the Welsh cultural life of Liverpool, 1871-1939.

AR 1943-44, p.21.

REES JENKIN JONES
Papers of Rees Jenkin Jones (1835-1924), preacher and author, with manuscripts collected by him and a small group of deeds, co. Cardigan, 1620-1801. The papers and manuscripts are now *NLW 14147-213*. See also NLW MSS 4361-70.

Schedule [pre-1934], 10pp. *AR 1925-26*, p.12. See also *AR 1966-67*, p.32.

T. GWYNN JONES
Papers of Thomas Gwynn Jones (1871-1949), poet and scholar.

Schedules (1949), 148pp.; (1992), [i] + 10pp.; (1993), i + 41pp.; i + 18pp.; i + 12pp.; ii + 14pp. *AR 1942-43*, p.22; *1959-60*, p.31; *1960-61*, p.31; *1961-62*, pp.29-30.

T. L. JONES
Deeds (deposited by T.L. Jones) relating to co. Carmarthen, 1759-1862.

Schedule [1971], 4pp. *AR 1971-72*, p.78.

T. LLECHID JONES
Manuscripts collected by and papers of the Rev. Thomas Llechid Jones (1867-1946), local historian with north Wales interests; include pedigrees, genealogical material and correspondence of H.R. Hughes, Kinmel (1827-1911).

Schedule [? 1950s], 39pp.

THOMAS JONES
The papers of Thomas Jones, C.H. (1870-1955), confidant of prime ministers, especially Lloyd George and Baldwin, a notably full archive. Includes important papers relating to Coleg Harlech, *The Observer* newspaper, the Gregynog Press and Sir Henry Jones.

Schedules [c. 1960], 593pp.; (1993), iii + 122pp. *AR 1983-84*, p.46. See Thomas Jones, *Whitehall Diary*, 3 vols (London, 1969-71), and *A Diary with Letters 1931-1950* (London, 1954); E.L. Ellis, *T.J.: a Life of Thomas Jones C.H.* (Cardiff, 1992).

W. BRADWEN JONES
Music manuscripts of W. Bradwen Jones (1892-1976), composer.

Schedule (1973 + suppl.), 7pp. *AR 1972-73*, p.52; *1977-78*, p.44.

W. R. JONES ('GWENITH GWYN')
Papers of William Rhys Jones ('Gwenith Gwyn', 1868-1937), Baptist minister and folklorist.

Schedules (1976), ix + 133pp.; (1984), [i] + 12pp. *AR 1976-77*, p.72; *1984-85*, p.38.

WILLIAM GLYNNE-JONES
Papers of William Glyn Jones ('William Glynne-Jones', 1907-77), novelist. *NLW MSS 20759-63, 21230-2.*

Schedule [1974], 3pp. *AR 1971-72*, p.62; *1974-75*, p.47.

KEMEYS-TYNTE see TYNTE

KENFIG
Records of the borough of Kenfig, co. Glamorgan, 1397-1879. *Transferred to West Glamorgan R O.*

Schedule [1944], 13pp. *AR 1943-44*, p.30.

KENSINGTON
Papers relating to the family of Edwardes, barons Kensington, of St Brides, Little Haven, co. Pembroke, 1791-1914. See also **Lucas**.

Schedule (1954), 12pp.

H. B. KENT
Deeds (donated by Hugh B. Kent) mostly relating to Cheshire and Shropshire, 1702-1809.

Schedule [1934], 5pp. *AR 1934-35*, p.34, represents another donation.

KENTCHURCH COURT
Records of the family of Scudamore of Kentchurch Court, co. Hereford, 1299-1900; include the papers of Sir Harford Jones, later Jones Bridges (1764-1847), British ambassador to Persia. *Transferred to Hereford R O.* See also NLW MSS 4901-12.

Schedules (1957), 575pp., in two vols; (1964, Sir Harford Jones correspondence), [i] + 394pp.; (1973, supplementary records and papers), vi + 272pp. *AR 1942-43*, pp.32-3; *1965-66*, pp.54-5.

KINMEL
Deeds (aquired from Kinmel Park) from the collection of Angharad Llwyd (1779-1866), antiquary, including deeds relating to the families of Salusbury

116

of Lleweni, 1313-1727, Myddelton of Chirk, 1637-18th cent., and Davies of Llannerch and Gwysaney, 1610-1767. Some of these deeds are bound up in Angharad Llwyd's MSS, NLW MSS 1551-1608.

Schedule (1982), [ix] + 157pp.

KYLE
Deeds (donated by Mrs M. Kyle), largely relating to the Cardigan area, 16th-17th cent., and the Swansea area, 19th cent.

Schedule (1983), [i] + 28pp. *AR 1971-72*, p.46.

LABOUR PARTY WALES
Records of the Labour Party Wales (South Wales Regional Council of Labour from 1937, Welsh Regional Council of Labour from 1959, Labour Party Wales from 1975), including minutes, correspondence and papers, 1937-87. *Conditional access.*

Labour Party Wales Archives (1991), ii + 37pp. *AR 1984-85*, p.43. @.

LADIES OF LLANGOLLEN
Papers of Lady Eleanor Butler (1739-1829) and Sarah Ponsonby (1755-1831), 'The Ladies of Llangollen'. These are 'The Hamwood Papers'. *(NLW MSS 22967-96).*

AR 1990-91, p.63. See Eva Mary Bell, *The Hamwood Papers of the Ladies of Llangollen and Caroline Hamilton* (London, 1930), where some of the papers are printed.

J. LAMB
Deeds (purchased from J. Lamb), 1661-1808.

Schedule (1964), 7pp. *AR 1963-64*, p.45.

LANCYCH
Estate and family records of Griffiths, Jones and Jones-Lloyd of Lancych, parish of Clydau, co. Pembroke, mostly in cos Pembroke and Carmarthen, 1738-1949.

Schedules (1962), 23pp.; (1972), 13pp. paginated 24-36. *AR 1961-62*, p.49; *1971-72*, p.78.

ABBÉ LE CALVEZ
Papers of Abbé Armand Le Calvez ('Armañs ar C'halvez', 1921-72), Breton educationalist.

AR 1980-81, pp.49-50.

LEESWOOD
Estate and family records of Eyton and Wynne-Eyton of Leeswood Hall, Mold, 1520-1894. *Transferred to Clwyd R O (Hawarden).*

Schedule (1961), 359pp. *AR 1939-40*, p.33.

LE HARDY
Deeds (purchased through Col. Le Hardy) relating predominantly to co. Carmarthen, 1532-1862.

AR 1946-47, p.34. Working list available.

EVELYN LEWES
Papers of Evelyn Lewes (d. 1961), author.

AR 1960-61, p.34.

LEWIS, LLANRHYSTYD
Papers and music manuscripts of John Lewis ('Eos Glan Wyre'), Llanrhystud, co. Cardigan, and his brother David Lewis (1828-1908), composer. *(NLW MSS 8177-277).* See also **D. Wyre Lewis**.

Schedule [*c.* 1929], 37pp. *AR 1928-29*, pp.23-4.

ALUN LEWIS
Papers of Alun Lewis (1915-44), poet.

Alun Lewis Papers (1990), i + 39pp. *AR 1987-88*, p.58.

D. MORGAN LEWIS
Manuscripts of David Morgan Lewis (1851-1937), professor of physics and Congregational minister, incorporating small groups of the manuscripts of his father, Evan Lewis, Brynberian (1813-96), of J. Lloyd James ('Clwydwenfro', 1835-1919), and of other Congregational ministers. *(NLW MSS 11614-97).*

Schedule (1938), 86pp. *AR 1937-38*, p.27.

D. WYRE LEWIS
Papers of David Wyre Lewis (1872-1966), Baptist minister, including papers of the Lewis family of Llanrhystud, 19th-20th cent., and papers relating to Timothy Richard (1845-1919), missionary in China. See also **Lewis, Llanrhystyd**.

AR 1963-64, pp.31-2;*1968-69*, pp.28-9; *1975-76*, p.45.

E. A. LEWIS
Papers of Edward Aneurin Lewis (1880-1942), historian, including extensive abstracts from public records concerning Wales.

Schedule (1962), 8pp. *AR 1961-62*, pp.23-4. See also *AR 1933-34*, p.32, and *1942-43*, pp.22-3.

SIR HENRY LEWIS
Papers of Sir Henry Lewis (1889-1968), Celtic scholar.

AR 1969-70, p.32; *1975-76*, pp.44-5; *1978-79*, p.49.

HYWEL D. LEWIS
Papers of Hywel David Lewis (1910-92), philosopher.

Schedule (1993), iii + 42pp. *AR 1992-93*, p.53.

SIR JOHN HERBERT LEWIS
Papers of Sir John Herbert Lewis (1858-1933), politician and associate of T.E. Ellis and Lloyd George. Other papers in Clwyd R O (Hawarden).

Sir John Herbert Lewis Papers (1991), i + 185pp., superseding earlier schedules of 1943 and 1963. *AR 1960-61*, p.57; *1963-64*, p.52; *1974-75*, p.70-1; *1975-76*, p.79; *1989-90*, p.64.

SAUNDERS LEWIS
Literary papers of John Saunders Lewis (1893-1985). His political papers do not survive. (*NLW MSS 22723-7, 22951-64, 23015-27, 23224-33*).

AR 1980-81, p.50; *1991-92*, p.60.

TIMOTHY LEWIS
Papers of Timothy Lewis (1877-1958), Welsh scholar, including many transcripts of manuscripts of Welsh literature and Welsh law; including also substantial groups of the papers of J. Gwenogvryn Evans (1852-1930) and Beriah Gwynfe Evans (1848-1927), journalist and playwright.

Schedule (1962), 35pp. *AR 1957-58*, p.24; *1958-59*, p.33.

LIVERPOOL LIBRARIES
Deeds (donated by the Liverpool City Libraries Committee), 1602-1900, relating to the estate of the Burchinshaw family and other property in co. Denbigh, and to the Tremadog estate of the Roche family and other property in co. Caernarfon.

Schedule [pre-1934], 16pp. *AR 1930-31*, p.37.

119

LLAN
Records relating to Cwmni'r Llan a'r Wasg Eglwysig Gymreig (The Llan and Welsh Church Press Co.), 1923-60.

Schedule (1960), 4pp. Supplementary groups described in *AR 1961-62*, p.47, and *1963-64*, p.50.

LLANBADARN FAWR
Letters from the Llanbadarn Fawr parish chest, 1842-55, mostly relating to ecclesiastical appointments in Wales and the need for Welsh-speaking incumbents. (*Llanbadarn Fawr parochial records 10*).

Transcripts [? 1950s], 233pp. *AR 1949-50*, p.42.

LLANDINAM
Papers relating to the commercial and industrial interests of David Davies (1818-90) and Edward Davies, his son, of Llandinam; include records of railway construction, the Ocean Coal Co. and Barry Dock and Railway.

Schedule (1933 + suppl.), 46pp. Also **Maps** (schedule, *s.n.* M. S. Davies). *AR 1933-34*, p.38; *1934-35*, p.43.

Papers of David Davies, 1st Baron Davies of Llandinam (1880-1944), philanthropist; include papers relating to the King Edward VII Welsh National Memorial Association, from 1911, University College of Wales, Aberystwyth, the Welsh Branch of the League of Nations Union, and the New Commonwealth Movement, from 1933.

AR 1970-71, p.59. Working lists available.

LLANELIDAN
Records of the Denbighshire manors of Llanelidan and Llanfair Dyffryn Clwyd; Rhos, Llanhychan and Rhiwbebyll; and Llech, Llan and Meifod, 1647-1872.

Schedule [pre-1934], 11pp. *AR 1932-33*, p.38.

LLANERCHFROCHWEL
Records of the Llannerchfrochwel estate in co. Montgomery, 1689-1883.

Schedule (1947), 30pp. *AR 1947-48*, p.36.

LLANFAIR AND BRYNODOL
Estate and family records of Griffith of Porthamal, Anglesey, and Llanfair, co. Caernarfon, Griffith of Brynodol, co. Caernarfon, and the associated families of Rowlands of Nant, co. Caernarfon, and Wynn of Taltreuddyn,

co. Merioneth. Include a few ministers' accounts for cos Caernarfon and Anglesey, mid 14th-15th cent., and some literary and historical MSS, 17th-18th cent. Other records in Gwynedd R O (Caernarfon).

Schedule (1984), [vi] + 778pp., in three vols, superseding earlier 30pp. preliminary schedule. Also **Maps** *s.n.* Brynodol. *AR 1940-41*, p.28. *NLWJ*, 2 (1941-2), pp.76-8.

LLANGIBBY CASTLE
Records of the Llangibby estate and other properties mainly in cos Monmouth, Glamorgan and Pembroke, 13th-20th cent.; manorial records, co. Monmouth, 13th-19th cent.; correspondence, mainly of the families of Powell and Addams-Williams, 17th-20th cent; a collection of literary and historical manuscripts (the manuscripts now *NLW MSS 16962-17109*).

Schedules (1939), 430pp. (deeds and documents); (1939), 139pp. (MSS, letters and manorial records). *AR 1938-39*, p.50. *NLWJ*, 1 (1939-40), pp.47-9.

LLANIDLOES BOROUGH
Records, 1835-1974, of the borough of Llanidloes, including council minute books, 1835-1955.

Schedule (1979), 10pp. *AR 1979-80*, pp.77-8.

LLANLLYR
Records of the Llanllyr estate, cos Cardigan and Carmarthen, and the Lewes family, 1631-1861; include records of Tal-y-sarn fair, 1631-1837.

Schedule (1955), 30pp. *AR 1957-58*, p.38.

LLANOVER MSS
The Llanover MSS, the manuscripts collected or compiled by Edward Williams ('Iolo Morganwg'), are NLW MSS 13061-185, described in volume IV of the *Handlist*. The only remaining value of the 1914 list is that it is based on an earlier catalogue, compiled at Llanover, and includes the MSS 'not found' in 1914, some of them now 'Iolo Aneurin Williams MSS' (see **Iolo Morganwg**), others presumed lost.

List (1914), 24pp. *AR 1916 (Oct.)*, pp.5-6. *NLWJ*, 1 (1939-40), pp.39-40.

LLANOVER PAPERS
Correspondence and papers of the Waddington, Hall and Herbert family of Llanover and Llanarth Court, co. Monmouth, 1786-1940, notably of Augusta Hall, later Lady Llanover (1802-96). See also NLW MSS 15370 and 16381 and **Bunsen**. Other papers in Gwent R O.

AR 1967-68, pp.40-2; *1973-74*, p.51. Also **Maps**.

LLEWELLIN-TAYLOUR see **TAYLOUR**

LLEWENI
Records of the Lleweni estate, co. Denbigh, late 13th cent.-1769, and correspondence of the Salusbury family, mid 16th cent.-1645. Other records in Clwyd R O (Hawarden).

Schedule (1971), 210pp. (estate records); for the correspondence see *Calendar of Salusbury Correspondence 1553 - circa 1700,* ed. W.J. Smith (Cardiff, 1954). *AR 1925-26,* p.10.

LLIDIARDAU
Estate and family records of Parry of Llidiardau, parish of Llanilar, co. Cardigan, and the associated families of Hughes of Glanrheidol and Hughes of Allt-lwyd, mainly 18th-20th cent. See also **Roberts & Evans** and **Allt-lwyd.**

Preliminary report (1956), 19pp. In process of cataloguing (1994). Also **Maps.** *AR 1955-56,* pp.51-7.

D. LLOYD & SON
Records from the office of D. Lloyd & Son, Lampeter, solicitors, including general letter-books of the firm, 1853-1920, and letter-books of Lampeter Union 1842-1930, Lampeter Borough Council, 1892-1922, Lampeter and Llanybydder Rural District Councils, 1895-1922.

Schedule [*c.* 1970], 3pp.

D. FRANCIS LLOYD
Deeds (deposited by D. Francis Lloyd) relating to the parishes of Betws Bledrws and Llanddewibrefi, co. Cardigan, 1807-62.

Schedule [1938], 6pp. *AR 1937-38,* p.68.

E.A. LLOYD
Deeds (deposited by E.A. Lloyd) relating to co. Radnor, 1593-1948.

Schedule (1963), 7pp. *AR 1962-63,* p.32.

ETHEL LLOYD
Deeds (deposited by Ethel Lloyd) relating mainly to the Herbert family of Cilybebyll, co. Glamorgan, 1614-1775. See also **Cilybebyll.**

Schedule [*c.* 1941], 6pp.

J. D. K. LLOYD

Deeds (deposited by J.D.K. Lloyd) relating mainly to the Montgomery area, 1597-1887.

Schedule (1961), 52pp. Also **Maps**. *AR 1938-39*, p.47. See also *AR 1972-73*, p.72; *1975-76*, p.45; *1977-78*, p.72; *1978-79*, pp.39-40.

JOHN LLOYD

Documents collected by Col. Sir John Conway Lloyd of Dinas, Brecon (1878-1954), mainly relating to cos Brecon, Glamorgan and Monmouth, 1588-1864; include records relating to industry, notably the Clydach, Hirwaun and Beaufort ironworks and the Bute and Dowlais iron companies; also Lloyd family papers. See also **Maybery**.

Schedule (1968, vol. I, records of industrial interest), 52pp. The remainder, the greater part, uncatalogued (1994). *AR 1937-38*, pp.68-9.

ROGER LLOYD

Deeds and documents (deposited by Roger Lloyd) relating to properties mainly in north Wales, including the Gesailgyfarch estate, co. Caernarfon, 13th-19th cent.

Schedules (1945), 7pp.; (1952 + suppl.), 68pp. *AR 1937-38*, p.69; *1944-45*, p.31; @.

LLOYD GEORGE see GEORGE

LLOYD-JOHNES see JOHNES

LLWYN

Deeds and documents, 17th-20th cent., relating to the estate of the Humffreys and Dugdale families of Llwyn, parish of Llanfyllin, and to properties elsewhere.

Schedules (1970), 180pp.; (1973), 108pp. *AR 1951-52*, p.33; *1966-67*, p.54.

LLWYNDYRYS

Deeds and documents relating to the Llwyndyrys estate and other properties in the parish of Llandygwydd, co. Cardigan, 1730-1923.

Schedule (1941), 28pp. Also **Maps**.

LLWYNGWAIR

Estate and family records, 16th-20th cent., of Bowen of Llwyngwair, co. Pembroke, with records of associated estates, particularly that of Bevan of Laugharne, cos Pembroke and Carmarthen.

Schedules (1953), 385pp.; (1961), 45pp. Also **Maps**. *AR 1942-43*, p.31; *1943-44*, p.29; *1961-62*, pp.45-6; @. *NLWJ*, 7 (1951-2), pp.376-8.

LLWYN-Y-BRAIN
Records of the Llwyn-y-brain estate, co. Carmarthen, and the family of Pryse-Rice, 1564-20th cent.

AR 1949-50, p.46; *1962-63*, pp.59-60. Also **Maps**.

LLYSDINAM
Papers, 17th-20th cent., of the Venables family of Llysdinam, Newbridge-on-Wye, co. Radnor, including in particular diaries, journals and correspondence of Richard Venables (1775-1858) and his sons Richard Lister Venables (1809-94) and George Stovin Venables (1810-88). Estate records in Powys R O.

Schedule (1979), v + 627pp., in two vols. *AR 1970-71*, pp.61-3. See also *1979-80*, p.81; *1988-89*, p.67.

LLYSNEWYDD
Estate and family records of Lewes of Llysnewydd, parish of Llangeler, and Dyffryn, parish of Llandybïe, co. Carmarthen, mainly 16th - 20th cent. Other records in Dyfed R O (Carmarthen).

Schedule (1974 + suppls), 100pp. *AR 1957-58*, pp.44-7; @.

LOCAL GOVERNMENT BOUNDARY COMMISSION
Papers of the Local Government Boundary Commission relating to boundary reviews in Wales, 1945-9.

Schedule [1959], 7pp. *AR 1958-59*, p.59.

LOCHTURFFIN
Deeds and documents (deposited by T.H. Thomas of Lochturffin) relating to property of the John and Thomas families of Trehale, parish of St Edrins, co. Pembroke, 1618-1912.

Schedule [*c.* 1938], 8pp. *AR 1938-39*, p.50.

LOCKWOOD
Records of the estates of the families of Wood and Lockwood, largely in cos Monmouth and Glamorgan, 1564-1905.

AR 1939-40, p.34. Also **Maps**.

LONDON, MIDLAND & SCOTTISH RAILWAY CO.

Registers of shareholders, etc, of railway and canal companies in Wales and the Borders which became incorporated in the LMS Railway Co., from 1847.

Schedule (1993), 5pp. *AR 1945-46*, p.31.

LONDONDERRY

Records of the Welsh estates of the marquesses of Londonderry, mostly in the Machynlleth area, 17th-19th cent. See also **Plas Machynlleth**.

Schedule (1952), 84pp. *AR 1951-52*, p.35.

LONGUEVILLE

A large archive from the offices of Messrs Longueville & Co., Oswestry, a firm which acted for many major north Wales estates. One substantial deposit is covered by the 1960 schedule; later ones have been sorted and are largely covered by working lists. Estates include Chirk Castle; Rhug; Nannau and Hengwrt; Wynnstay; Ruthin, the family West and Cornwallis-West; Penbedw Hall; Aston Hall; Llanrhaiadr Hall; Whitehall-Davies of Broughton; records mainly 17th-20th cent. Also records relating to enclosures, railways and mining, 19th cent.; office records, 19th-20th cent.

Schedule (1960), 136 pp.; (1993, wills and probates), i + 15pp.Also **Maps**. *AR 1941-42*, p.28; *1947-48*, p.39; *1958-59*, p.56; *1959-60*, pp. 53-62; *1969-70*, p.56; *1980-81*, p.78; *1981-82*, p.83; *1986-87*, p.65; *1988-89*, p.67.

LOVESGROVE

Estate and family records of Evans of Lovesgrove, near Aberystwyth, mainly 1850-1950; include papers deriving from the service in India of Sir Griffith Humphrey Pugh Evans (1840-1902), papers of Brig.-Gen. Lewis Pugh Evans (1881-1962) and deeds, 1774-1907. Other records in Dyfed R O (Aberystwyth).

AR 1981-82, p.81.

LOWLESS

Deeds (deposited by Owen F. Lowless) relating to co. Pembroke including the Holyland estate of the Adams family, Pembroke, 1856-1946.

Schedule (1959 + suppl.), 21pp. *AR 1959-60*, p.62; *1965-66*, p.54.

LUCAS

Records (deposited by R.K. Lucas), mainly 17th-20th cent., from the office of Messrs John Harvey & Sons, later Messrs James Thomas & Sons, land estate agents, Haverfordwest, chiefly relating to the estates of the bishop of St Davids (including some official diocesan records); of Lord Kensington; of the family of Scourfield of New Moat and Williamston; of the family of Barham of Trecwn; of the family of Brooks of Noyadd, Llannarth, co. Cardigan; of Captain H.J.P.Thomas in Gadlys, Aberdare, co. Glamorgan. Other records in Dyfed R O (Haverfordwest).

Schedule (1960), 318pp. Also **Maps**. *AR 1939-40*, p.34.

TOM MACDONALD
Papers of Tom Macdonald (1900-80), author.

Schedule (1993) ii + 29pp. *AR 1989-90*, p.64.

McEWEN
Deeds (purchased from Mr McEwen) relating to north Wales, mostly the Abergele area, 1574-1917.

Schedule [c. 1923], 11pp. *AR 1923* (May), p.8.

MACHYNLLETH DEEDS
Deeds from a Machynlleth solicitor's office relating mainly to those parts of cos Montgomery, Merioneth and Cardigan closest to Machynlleth, 1642-1911; records of numerous slate quarrying companies, 1848-1905, and other local industries; some local government records, 1855-1909.

AR 1937-38, p.73.

MACHYNLLETH SALVAGE
Records collected in a salvage campaign, during the Second World War, mostly deriving from the offices of Machynlleth Urban District Council, 1861-1927.

Schedule (1980), [i] + 13pp. *AR 1943-44*, p.22.

MAENOL
Records of the associated families of Evans, Hayward, and Phillips of Maenol, near Llanidloes, co. Montgomery, and especially of Thomas Hayward, solicitor, Llanidloes, including deeds relating to cos Montgomery, Pembroke and Radnor, 18th-20th cent.

Preliminary schedule (1956), 27pp. *AR 1955-56*, pp.49-50.

MAENORDEIFI
Deeds relating to Maenordeifi, co. Pembroke, and neighbouring parishes, 1553-20th cent.

Schedule (1987), [i] + 11pp. *AR 1981-82*, p.49.

MAESANNOD AND RHYDONNEN

Deeds relating to the estates of Lloyd of Maesannod, parish of Llanynys, and Rhydonnen, parish of Llandysilio-yn-Iâl, co. Denbigh, 1592-20th cent.

Schedule (1987), i + 12pp. *AR 1982-83*, p.49.

MAESGWYNNE

Records of the Howell and Powell family relating to the Maesgwynne estate and other properties in cos Carmarthen and Pembroke, 1565-1888.

Schedule (1956), 88pp. *AR 1944-45*, p.32.

MAES-MAWR

Estate and family records of Davies of Maes-mawr Hall, parish of Llandinam, co. Montgomery, 1583-1938.

AR 1969-70, pp.51-2; *1971-72*, p.76.

MAESNEWYDD

Deeds relating to the Morgan family of Maesnewydd, parish of Llanfihangel Genau'r-glyn, and properties in cos Cardigan, Merioneth, and Montgomery, 1550-1879.

Schedule (1940), 49 + 14pp. *AR 1937-38*, p.69.

W. H. MAINWARING

Papers of William Henry Mainwaring (1884-1971), Labour MP for Rhondda East, 1933-59.

W. H. Mainwaring Papers (1994), i + 3pp. *AR 1974-75*, pp.74-75.

MATHER-JACKSON see JACKSON

IDRIS MATHIAS

Records (donated by Idris Mathias) largely relating to the Swansea Old Brewery & Davies (Cardigan) Bonded Stores Ltd, Cardigan, 1872-1921.

Idris Mathias Papers (1992), i + 8pp. *AR 1990-91*, p.60.

ROLAND MATHIAS

Papers of Roland Mathias (1915-   ), poet. See also **Minor Lists 1982**.

AR 1993-94.

WILLIAM MATHIAS
Music manuscripts of William Mathias (1934-92), composer

Catalogue of William Mathias Music Manuscripts (1994), 60pp. *AR 1993-94.*

MAUDE & TUNNICLIFFE
Deeds (deposited by Messrs Maude & Tunnicliffe) relating to the Waters family of Chester and Tenby and to properties in several Welsh counties, 1792-1913.

Schedule (1958), 10pp. *AR 1957-58*, pp.38-9.

MAYBERY
Records of the Maybery family of co. Brecon, industrialists and lawyers, largely deriving from the legal practice established by Walter and John Powell, employed by the early ironmasters, to which Henry Maybery succeeded. Include deeds, mostly co. Brecon and adjacent counties, mostly 16th-19th cent, but also an estate in Ravenstone, co. Leicester, 1290-1583; manorial records, mostly co. Brecon, 16th-19th cent.; extensive industrial records, especially the iron industry, 1790-1861; stray official county records, co. Brecon, 18th-19th cent.; many terriers for the archdeaconry of Brecon, 17th-18th cent.; papers of John Lloyd (1833-1915), historian of the South Wales iron industry. See also **John Lloyd.**

Schedules (1970), 465pp.; (1971), 444pp.; (1971), 494pp. Also **Maps.** *AR 1952-53*, pp.46-50; *1956-57*, p.42; *1960-61*, p.54; *1963-64*, pp.50-2. A large part of the archive remains uncatalogued (1994).

LEILA MEGANE
Papers of Margaret Jones ('Leila Megane', 1891-1960), singer, with papers of her husband, T. Osborne Roberts (1879-1948), composer.

AR 1979-80, p.63.

MEMORIAL COLLEGE, SWANSEA
Archives of the Memorial College, Swansea, 1793-1973, including papers of several Congregational ministers and college professors.

AR 1980-81, p.60.

HUW MENAI
Papers of Huw Menai Williams ('Huw Menai', 1887-1961), poet.

AR 1981-82, p.83.

C.W. MEREDITH
Deeds and documents (donated by C.W. Meredith) relating to cos Radnor and Hereford, 1624-1751.

Schedule (1962), 5pp *AR 1961-62*, p.32.

LORD MERTHYR
Deeds relating to south Wales counties, 1584-1921, including some relating to the Baskerville family of Aberedw, co. Radnor; a few papers, mainly of industrial interest, of William Thomas Lewis, 1st baron Merthyr (1837-1914).

Schedules (1934) 7pp.; (1947), 75pp. *AR 1933-34*, p.33; *1946-47*, p.42.

MICHAELCHURCH
Records of the manor of Michaelchurch, co. Radnor, 1754-1849.

Schedule (1952), 8pp. *AR 1952-53*, p.51.

MIERS
Deeds and documents relating to the Mackworth family of Gnoll Castle and the Miers family of Ynys-pen-llwch, co. Glamorgan, and to properties in cos Glamorgan and Somerset, 1735-1882.

Schedule (1955), 26pp.

MILBORNE
Estate and family records of Gunter of the Priory, Abergavenny, and Milborne of Wonastow, co. Monmouth, earlier of Milborne Port, co. Somerset, estates mainly in cos Monmouth, Brecon and Hereford, 13th-19th cent., mainly 1450-1750; manorial records, mainly co. Monmouth, 15th-17th cent.; correspondence, mainly 18th cent.

Schedule (1948), 513pp. *AR 1929-30*, p.40. *NLWJ*, 5 (1947-8), pp.295-6.

MINOR LISTS AND SUMMARIES. *Shelved at the end of the schedules.*
On this series of annual volumes see above, p.14. Each volume may contain as many as fifty lists or summaries, each list or summary representing a small archive or group or collection; only the more distinctive or significant are included in the following synopses of the contents of each volume. Groups supplementary to archives mentioned elsewhere in the Guide are not indicated here, but are cross-referenced elsewhere. Corresponding descriptions will be found in the *Annual Report*: for **1982** in *AR 1981-82* etc. A free-text database of post-1985 Minor Lists and Summaries may be searched in the Catalogue Room.

1982.
Breconshire parliamentary election papers, 1874-80.

Papers of William Crwys Williams ('Crwys', 1875-1968), poet, also **1991, 1992.**

Cymdeithas yr Iaith Gymraeg, archives, from 1974, also **1983 - 1993** *passim. Conditional access.*

Papers of Sir Alfred Thomas Davies (1861-1949), Permanent Secretary to the Welsh Department of the Board of Education, 1907-25.

Records of the Wernllwyd estate, Welshpool, 1747-20th cent.

Material for a biography of Peggy Eileen Whistler ('Margiad Evans', 1909-58), writer.

Papers of Mrs P.Joyce Evans (1890-1987), missionary in Madagascar, 1914-39, also **1984.**

Records of David Hughes & Sons, tailors and drapers, Aberdovey, 1870-1946.

Records of the Humphreys family of Montgomery and Berriew, co. Montgomery, 18th-20th cent.

Papers of Lewis Lewis ('Awenfab o Wynfe', ?1838-1906), poet, and his family in co. Carmarthen, 1777-1920, also **1984-1986.**

Papers of David Myrddin Lloyd (1909-81), librarian and scholar, also **1993.**

Records of David Owen & Son of Newtown, threshing machine contractors, 1860-1958.

Papers of Llywelyn Phillips (1914-81), agriculturalist and author.

Papers of Thomas Jones Pierce (1905-64), historian.

Deeds of the estates of the Priestley family of Hirdrefaig, Anglesey, 1758-1921.

Papers of the Rev. J.M. Lloyd Thomas, Llannarth, co. Cardigan (1868-1955), minister of the Old Meeting Church, Birmingham, and active member of the Society of Free Catholics.

Archives of the Welsh Folk Song Society, from 1908, also **1983, 1984, 1986, 1989.**

Archives of the Welsh Library Association from 1961, also **1983, 1989** and see *AR 1971-72,* p.80.

Papers of Ffowc Williams, Llandudno (1889-1985), teacher and naturalist.

1983

Deeds, parishes of Dorstone, co. Hereford, and Llanigon, co. Brecon, 1754-1967.

Records of the estate of the Crewe Read family of Llandinam Hall, co. Montgomery, 1870-1907.

Papers of the Rev. Thomas George Davies (1900-77), Baptist minister, including records of the Presbyterian College, Carmarthen, 1846-63.

Deeds relating to the parishes of Old Radnor and Presteigne, co. Radnor, 1631-1970.

Papers of Howell T. Evans (1877-1950), schoolmaster and historian, also **1984**.

Papers of Peggy Eileen Whistler ('Margiad Evans', 1909-58), writer.

Records of the family of Evans of Neuadd-fawr and Rhydyronnen, parish of Llanfihangel Genau'r-glyn, co. Cardigan, 1843-1955.

Papers of the Rev. William Roberts (1830-86), Calvinistic Methodist minister, Abergele.

Papers of Helen and Philip Suggett, including papers relating to the translation into English of the works of Teilhard de Chardin and the history of Mountain Ash and Aberdare, 1940-70s.

Records of the King Edward VII Welsh National Memorial Association, established in 1912 to promote the cure of tuberculosis, to its dissolution in 1948.

Papers of Gwyn Williams, Trefenter (1904-90), writer.

Papers of John Lloyd Williams, Labour MP for Kelvingrove, Glasgow, 1945-50.

1984

Papers of Jacob Davies ('Alaw Cowyn', c. 1887-1973), blacksmith and author.

Papers of Emrys G. Bowen (1900-83), geographer, also **1987**.

Papers of the Wales and Monmouth Branch of the Council for British Archaeology, from 1961, also **1986, 1991**.

Records of Crucadarn and other manors in co. Brecon, 16th-20th cent.

Cyngor Ysgolion Sul Cymru, records, 1915-80, also **1985**.

Papers of Dr Noëlle Davies (d. 1983) relating to Plaid Cymru and to the Welsh economy, 1935-57, also **1987, 1988**.

Manuscripts of W. T. Pennar Davies (1911-), writer.

131

Deeds relating to the Lloyd Jack estate, co. Cardigan, 1764-1865.

Papers of Selwyn Jones (1906-81), journalist and writer on music, also **1985**.

Papers of Ben Morgan relating to the Welsh community in the Workington area, 1924-83.

Records of the Royal Welsh Agricultural Society, 1904-55.

Papers of Frederick Charles Richards (1878-1932), artist.

Deeds relating to the Trewern Hall estate, parish of Buttington, co. Montgomery, 1728-1938, also **1985-1987, 1989**.

Papers of Cecily Williams-Ellis relating to the work of the Council for the Preservation of Rural Wales, 1941-81.

1985
Deeds, parishes of Clodock and Michaelchurch Escley, co. Hereford, 1701-1874.

Papers of David Thomas Davies (1876-1962), dramatist.

Papers of Ellis William Davies (1871-1939), Liberal MP for South Caernarfonshire, 1908-18, and Denbigh, 1923-9.

Papers of S. Islwyn Evans, journalist and press officer, relating to the South Wales Coalfield, 1929-70.

Deeds relating mainly to the Ffrwdgrech estate, co. Brecon, 1709-1900.

Papers of Victor Hampson-Jones (1909-77), educationalist.

Papers of Gerallt Jones (1907-84), poet.

Papers of the family of Naylor of Leighton Hall and Brynllywarch, co. Montgomery, 1839-1931. See also **Harrison**.

Papers of L. Haydn Lewis (1903-85), poet.

Papers of Gwenfron Moss (1898-   ), missionary in China, 1928-51, and India, 1953-64, also **1990**.

Papers of the Ottley family of the West Indies, 18th-20th cent.

Papers of Reginald Francis Treharne (1901-67), historian.

Papers of Lewis E. Valentine (1893-1986), nationalist.

Records of Wrexham Conservative Party Association, 1913-67.

Records of the Ystradgynlais and Swansea Colliery Co., 1803-1936.

1986

Records of Conservative Party associations in north Wales, 1953-85, also **1993, 1994.** *Conditional access.*

Papers relating to the Brymbo area, co. Denbigh, 1841-1960s.

Papers of David Evans (1875-1951), industrial journalist and author.

Papers of Leslie Wynne Evans (1911-85), historian of south Wales industry and of education in Wales.

Papers of David Greenslade relating to the Welsh in the USA and Canada, 1940-85.

Family records of Griffiths and Lewis of Glanhafren, Newtown, later of Milford Hall, 1833-1984.

Papers of William Thomas Morgan ('Gwilym Alaw', 1844-1917), poet.

Papers of Richard Williams ('Gwydderig', 1842-1917), poet.

Papers of Frank Price Jones (1920-75), historian and broadcaster.

Papers of the 'No Assembly Campaign' prior to the Devolution Referendum, 1979.

Records of the South Wales Baptist College, founded in 1807, 1838-1968, also **1987, 1990, 1992.**

Papers of the 'Wales for the Assembly Campaign' prior to the Devolution Referendum, 1979, also **1991.** *Conditional access.*

Papers of Tudor Elwyn Watkins, later Lord Watkins (1903-83), Labour MP for Brecon and Radnor, 1945-70.

1987

Papers of Richard I. Aaron (1901-87), professor of philosophy.

Papers of the family of Anwyl, 1848-1983, including letters to Edward Anwyl (1866-1914), Welsh scholar.

Records of Cardiff Conservative Associations, 1918-83, also **1988, 1991.** *Conditional access.*

Papers relating to 'Theatr Fach Garthewin', 1946-85, also **1989.**

Papers of René Hague (1905-81) relating to David Jones.

Papers relating to the Jones family of Henblas, Caersws, co. Montgomery, 1700-1933, also **1990** and **1994.**

133

Papers of Gareth Vaughan Jones (1905-35), journalist, murdered in China, also **1992**.

Papers of John Tysul Jones (1902-86), local historian, including papers of Thomas Jacob Thomas ('Sarnicol', 1873-1945), poet.

Papers of Thomas Mervyn Jones (1910-89), chairman of Wales Gas Board, 1948-70.

Papers of Owain Llewelyn Owain (1878-1956), journalist, editor of *Y Genedl Gymreig*, also **1990**.

Papers of W. Emrys Pride (1904-   ), civil servant and author, also **1988**.

Papers of Shadrach Pryce (1833-1914), dean of St Asaph, 1899-1910, and Lewis Pryce (1873-1930), archdeacon of Wrexham, and their family, also **1992-1994**.

Papers of John Roberts, Llanfwrog (1910-84), Calvinistic Methodist minister and poet.

Papers of the Spurrell family of Carmarthen, including William Spurrell (1813-89), founder of the House of Spurrell, printers and publishers.

Minutes of the Welsh Tourist Board, from foundation to dissolution, 1948-70.

Records of Western Mail & Echo Ltd and previous owners of the *Western Mail* and *South Wales Echo*, 1869-1980.

1988
Papers of Cassie Davies (1898-1988), inspector of schools, also **1992**.

Papers of Lord Edmund-Davies (1906-92), judge, also **1990, 1991**.

Papers of Clifford Evans (1912-85), actor, also **1990**.

Papers of Tom Hooson (1933-85), Conservative MP for Brecon and Radnor, 1979-85. *Conditional access.*

Papers of John Legonna (1918-78), nationalist, also **1990**.

Records of the Montgomeryshire Liberal Association, 1895-1987, also **1989, 1992**. *Conditional access.*

Papers of and papers concerning Dr William Price, Llantrisant (1800-93), pioneer of cremation.

1989
Records of the Caerphilly Constituency Labour Party, 1960-87.

Papers relating to Cardiganshire lead mines, 1847-1937.

Papers of David Charles Davies (1901-53), writer and scholar.

Records of the family of Havard of Newport and Milford, co. Pembroke, 1760-1914, including records of ship-building and shipping.

Papers of Dr Thomas James Jenkin (1885-1965), botanist.

Papers of Rose Mabel Lewis ('Lewis Armytage', 1853-1928), author.

Manuscripts of David Moule-Evans (1905-88), composer.

Papers of Alun Oldfield-Davies (1905-88) relating to David Jones, artist and writer.

Papers of Ffransis G. Payne (1901-92), folk historian and author, also **1991**.

Papers of Elwyn Roberts (1904-88), General Secretary of Plaid Cymru, 1964-71.

Papers of D. Emlyn Thomas (1892-1954), Labour MP for Aberdare, 1946-54, also **1991**.

Papers of Dr William Thomas (1890-1974), Chief Inspector of Schools in Wales.

1990
Papers of Beata Brookes (1931-   ) as MEP for North Wales, 1979-89. *Conditional access.*

Papers of Ithel Davies (1894-1989), political activist.

Papers of David Emrys James ('Dewi Emrys', 1881-1952), poet.

Papers of Colin Gresham (1913-89), antiquary.

Papers of Brynmor John (1934-88), MP for Pontypridd, 1970-88. *Conditional access.*

Records of Monmouth Conservative Association, 1903-88. *Conditional access.*

Papers of David Rees Rees-Williams, Lord Ogmore (1903-76), politician.

Papers of Emrys Roberts (1910-90), Liberal MP for Merioneth, 1945-51, and public servant.

1991
Papers of Euros Bowen (1904-88), poet.

Papers of Constance Bullock-Davies (d. 1989), medievalist.

Papers of Idris Cox (1899-1989), Communist Party activist.

Records of the 'Glanamman Lodge' of the True Ivorites, Ammanford, 1840-1946.

Papers of Ben G. Jones (1914-89), Liberal politician and London Welshman. *Conditional access.*

Papers of John Collwyn Rees (1919-80), political theorist.

Papers of William Leslie Richards (1916-89), author.

Papers of Jeffrey Thomas (1933-89), MP for Abertillery, 1970-83. *Conditional access.*

Papers of Wynford Vaughan-Thomas (1908-87), broadcaster and author.

Papers of Eunice Bryn Williams (d. 1991), including a collection of 19th-cent. Welsh tune books.

1992
A collection of manuscripts of children's literature in Welsh made by Canolfan Llenyddiaeth Plant Cymru, also **1994**.

Records of the Burghill estate, co. Hereford, 1849-62, later part of the Chirk Castle estate.

Records of Cymdeithas Telynau Cymru (Welsh harp society) from establishment in 1962 to dissolution in 1983.

Records of the estate of the Mesham family of Ewloe Hall, co. Flint, 1734-1893.

Records of Gŵyl Fawr Aberteifi, 1952-90.

Papers of Dr Deian Hopkin including records of Llanelly Trades Council and Divisional Labour Party, 1917-67.

Papers of Jack Raymond Jones (1922-93) writer and artist.

Papers of John Henry Jones (1909-85), Director of Education for Cardiganshire, 1944-72, and author.

Papers (*s.n.* Philip H. Lawson) on the history of the Anwyl family.

Papers relating to the 1852 election candidature of Sir George Cornewall Lewis in Herefordshire.

Papers of Ted Rowlands (1940-), MP for Merthyr Tydfil, from 1972.

Music manuscripts from the Department of Music, University College of Wales, by various composers, mostly 20th cent., including papers of Charles Clements (1898-1983).

1993

Papers of Glyn Mills Ashton ('Wil Cwch Angau', 1910-91), librarian and author.

Records of the Llanaeron estate, co. Cardigan, and the Lewis family, 1571-1969.

Papers of Alun Tudor Lewis (1905-86), author.

Papers of Dyddgu Owen (1906-92), author.

Papers of the Owen family of Summerhill, co. Pembroke, 1771-1989.

Papers of Dorothy Sylvester (1906-   ), geographer.

1994

Papers of Sir Alun Talfan Davies (1913-   ), lawyer.

Papers of D. P.Garbett-Edwards, public servant.

Records of the antiquarian bookshop of Tom Lloyd-Roberts, Caerwys, 1968-93.

Papers of Gomer Morgan Roberts (1904-93), Calvinistic Methodist minister and historian.

Records of the Royal Cambrian Academy of Art, Conway, from its establishment, 1881-1991.

Papers of Mansel Thomas (1912-79), writer.

MISCELLANEOUS

During the 1920s and 1930s some lists or schedules which comprised no more than a few pages were bound up in volumes titled 'Miscellaneous'. There are five such volumes, numbered I to V. The contents of the more distinctive groups listed in these volumes are indicated below. Some groups have been incorporated in NLW Deeds, or other series; some retain their identity as groups.

I

Deeds, Carmarthen town and Dyer of Aberglasney, 1709-1851.

Glamorgan manorial surveys, 17th cent., and deeds, 1384-1591, including the foundation deed of Cowley chantry, Swinford, co. Leicester.

Deeds, Tal-y-garn, co. Glamorgan, 1570-1695.

Deeds, co. Denbigh, 1581-1755.

Deeds, Wrexham area, 1618-1850.

Deeds, Aberystwyth, 1834-1902.

Deeds, Clodock, co. Hereford, 1594-1772.

Deeds, Llysfaen, co. Caernarfon, 1546-1860.

II

Deeds, Lampeter Velfrey, co. Pembroke, 1735-1930.

Documents relating to the manor of Maesmynan, co. Denbigh, 1663-18th cent.

Deeds, Llanfair Caereinion, co. Montgomery, 1774-1877.

Nanteos estate records, co. Cardigan, 19th cent.

Deeds, Dymock, co. Gloucester, 1656-1788.

Deeds, co. Denbigh, 1575-1686, including lead mines, the Wyche family.

Deeds and papers, Jones of Nantmel, co. Radnor, 1774-1840, and Radnorshire Militia, 1762-78.

III

Deeds, mainly Llanbadarn Fawr and Aberystwyth, co. Cardigan, 1762-1848, including co-partnership in a bank, 1806.

Deeds and papers, Dickson family, lands in co. Cavan and elsewhere in Ireland, 1671-1922.

Deeds, Eglwysilan, co. Glamorgan, 1417-1568.

Deeds relating to Hadnock, parish of Dixton, co. Monmouth, 1641-1775.

Documents relating to shipping at Aberystwyth, 1816-63.

IV

Poor-law papers, parish of Llanfihangel-y-traethau, 1790-1863.

Records of Llanfwrog Baptist Church, Ruthin, 1791-1907.

Papers of the James family, Tynrhos, Llanfihangel Genau'r-glyn, co. Cardigan, 1753-1899.

Deeds, Middletown, co. Montgomery, 1601-92.

Deeds, mostly in Swineshead, co. Lincoln, 1310-1427.

V

No distinctive groups.

MOCCAS

Estate and family records of the Cornewall family of Moccas Court, co. Hereford, mostly 18th-19th cent. *Transferred to Hereford R O.*

Preliminary schedule [*c.* 1961], 14pp. *AR 1960-61.* pp.52-3.

MOELFFERNA

Records of Moelfferna Quarries, co. Merioneth, 1871-1960. Other records in Gwynedd R O (Dolgellau).

AR 1961-62, pp.22-3.

MONMOUTH MANOR

Records of the manor of Monmouth, 1610-1919.

Schedule [1936 + suppl.], 11pp. *AR 1935-36,* p.47. @.

MONMOUTHSHIRE COUNTY COUNCIL

Records of the Magor and St Mellons Rural District Council, from 1895; Poor-law Guardians records for the unions of Chepstow, from 1870, Monmouth, from 1900, and Newport, from 1899. *Transferred to Gwent R O.*

Schedule [1940], 8pp. *AR 1938-39,* p.48; @.

MONTGOMERY BOROUGH

Records of the borough of Montgomery, 1486-1885, mostly 17th-19th cent.

Schedule (from *Montgomeryshire Collections,* 45 (1937-8), pp.19-43). *AR 1936-37,* p.24.

MONTGOMERYSHIRE COUNTY RECORDS

Records of Quarter Sessions for co. Montgomery, 1719-1971, with a few records of the Lieutenancy, Petty Sessions, coroners and the county court. Records of Boards of Guardians, 1837-1930 (from 1795 for the Montgomery and Pool Union); Highway Boards, 1874-95; the Montgomeryshire Second District Turnpike Trust, 1768-1876; early County Council records. *Transferred to Powys R O.* Microfilm is available in NLW of the Quarter Sessions Order Books, enclosure awards and deposited plans.

Montgomeryshire County Records [*c.* 1970], 47pp. *Montgomeryshire Public Records* (1970), 7pp. (a summary list); *Montgomeryshire enclosure awards and maps* (1957), 21pp. *Montgomeryshire deposited plans* (1974), 11pp. *AR 1934-35,* p.46; pp.48-50; *1954-55,* p.51; *1955-56,* p.50; *1964-65,* pp.59-60; *1968-69,* p.52; *1972-73,* p.74. The early County Council records were covered only by a working list while in NLW.

Records for most of the pre-1974 Rural and Urban District Councils of Montgomeryshire. These remain in NLW (1994), sorted but not listed. Some Petty Sessions records also remain (see below, *AR 1981-82*).

AR 1979-80, pp.78-9; *1980-81*, pp.78-9; *1981-82*, p.84; *1983-84*, p.55. For Petty Sessions records see *AR 1981-82*, p.87 *s.n.* Williams, Gittins & Tomley.

MONTGOMERYSHIRE YEOMANRY CAVALRY
Correspondence relating to the Montgomeryshire Yeomanry Cavalry, 1809-41. *Withdrawn*. See also **Powis**.

Calendar (1949), 12pp.

DAVID G. MORGAN
Papers of Dr David G. Morgan (1903-65), medical administrator in the Cardiff area.

AR 1977-78, p.47.

ARCHBISHOP JOHN MORGAN
Papers of John Morgan (1886-1957), bishop of Llandaff and archbishop of Wales, including papers of his father John Morgan (1840-1924), archdeacon of Bangor, and of Alfred Ollivant (1798-1882), bishop of Llandaff.

AR 1974-75, pp.76-7; *1982-83*, p.54.

ROBERT MORGAN
Papers of Robert Morgan (1921-94), writer and artist.

Schedule (1993), ii + 16pp. *AR 1991-92*, p.61.

T. J. MORGAN
Papers of Thomas John Morgan (1907-86), Welsh scholar and author, including papers of Ben Davies, Panteg (1864-1937), poet, Llewellyn Llewellyn ('Llewelyn Ddu o Lan Tawe') and Robert Griffith Berry (1869-1945), author.

AR 1986-87, p.60.

MORRIS & SON, BARMOUTH
Records of Messrs Morris & Son, Barmouth, drapers, tailors and dressmakers, 1847-1939. Other records in Gwynedd R O (Dolgellau).

Schedule (1994), i + 2pp. *AR 1972-73*, p.43.

LORD MORRIS OF BORTH-Y-GEST

Papers of John William Morris, later Baron Morris of Borth-y-gest (1896-1979), judge.

AR 1979-80, pp.41-3.

JOHN MORRIS

Papers of John Morris (1931-), MP, for Aberafan from 1959, Secretary of State for Wales, 1974-79. *Conditional access.*

AR 1993-94.

SIR RHYS HOPKIN MORRIS

Papers of Sir Rhys Hopkin Morris (1888-1956), MP, relating to Tanganyika, 1928, and Palestine, 1929.

AR 1956-57, p.32.

T.E. MORRIS

Deeds (deposited by T. E. Morris) relating mostly to the Ruthin area, co. Denbigh, and Maentwrog area, co. Merioneth, 1723-1889.

Schedule [1937], 5pp. *AR 1936-37*, p.30.

MOSTYN

Medieval and other manuscripts, some in Welsh, bought at the 1974 Mostyn sale (*NLW MSS 21238-54*). For the main group of Mostyn manuscripts see *NLW MSS 3021-76*. Other Mostyn manuscripts are at UW, Bangor, together with the archives of the Mostyn family.

Catalogue (1975), iii + 166pp. *AR 1974-75*, p.46. *NLWJ*, 19 (1975-6), pp.209-16.

The 'Mostyn Talacre' manuscript of Welsh poetry (*NLW 21582*).

Catalogue (1977), 11pp. *NLWJ*, 20 (1977-8), pp.207-8.

J. MOSTYN

Deeds and papers (donated by Major J. Mostyn) relating mainly to cos Brecon, Radnor and Hereford, 1565-1893, including the Hamilton family, 19th cent.

AR 1960-61, pp.35-6; *1961-62*, pp.32-3.

MUDDLESCOMBE

Estate and family records of Mansell of Muddlescombe, co. Carmarthen, relating to cos Carmarthen and Glamorgan, 13th-17th cent. Other records in Dyfed R O (Carmarthen) *s.n.* British Records Association.

Schedule (1950), 530pp. *AR 1937-38*, p.56. *NLWJ*, 9 (1955-6), pp.106-8.

MUDIAD YSGOLION MEITHRIN
Archives of Mudiad Ysgolion Meithrin (the National Association of Welsh-medium Nursery Schools and Play-groups), 1971-86.

Archifau Mudiad Ysgolion Meithrin (1993), i + 11pp. *AR 1989-90*, p.61.

MYNACHTY
Estate and family records of Gwynne of Mynachty, co. Cardigan, 1642-1882.

Schedule (1953), 42pp.

MYNDE
Estate and family records of Pye of the Mynd, co. Hereford, and Symons of Clowerwall, co. Gloucester, later of the Mynd, lands mainly in cos Hereford and Monmouth, 13th-20th cent.; manorial records include those of the manor of Kilpeck, 1442-1747.

Schedule (1960 + suppls), 366pp. (outsize, shelved at end of series). *AR 1958-59*, pp.25-7; *1969-70*, p.26; *1983-84*, p.39.

MYSEVIN
Papers of William Owen[-Pughe] of Mysevin (1759-1835), antiquary and lexicographer, and manuscripts collected by him; include papers relating to the Gwyneddigion, Cymreigyddion and Cymmrodorion societies (*NLW MSS 13221-63*).

Schedule (1939 + suppl.), 149 + 16pp. *AR 1940-41*, p.25. *NLWJ*, 2 (1941-2), pp.90-2.

NANHORON
Estate and family records of Edwards of Nanhoron, co. Caernarfon, and, associated families: Vaughan of Bronheulog, co. Denbigh, Lloyd of Rhosbeirio and Hirdrefaig, Anglesey, Robinson of Monachty, Anglesey, and Gwersyllt, co. Denbigh, Jones of Gelliwig, co. Caernarfon, and Browning of London; 15th - 19th cent. Other records in Gwynedd R O (Caernarfon).

Schedules [1934], 170pp.; [1945], 6pp. *AR 1934-35*, p.43; *1944-45*, p.31. *NLWJ*, 2 (1941-2), pp.78-9.

NANTEOS

Estate and family records of Powell of Nanteos, previously of Llechwedd-ddyrys, co. Cardigan, mainly 17th-20th cent. Includes correspondence, 17th-19th cent., and records relating to lead-mining in north Cardiganshire. See also **Cwrt Mawr, Roberts & Evans** and **Miscellaneous II**.

Preliminary schedule (1957), 51pp. *Nanteos Estate Records* (1989), [iv] + 407pp. in two vols. The latter vols supersede the preliminary schedule with regard to rentals, accounts and correspondence. Also **Maps** (schedule). *AR 1957-58*, pp.39-43.

NATIONAL EISTEDDFOD OF WALES

Compositions submitted to the National Eisteddfod, with adjudications, 1887-1947. See also **Eisteddfod Genedlaethol Cymru**.

Schedule [1949], 314pp. *AR 1922 (May)*, p.3; *1932-33*, p.41; *1935-36*, p.51; *1938-39*, p.48; *1939-40*, p.34. *NLWJ*, 2 (1941-2), p.84.

NATIONAL SAVINGS (CARDIGANSHIRE AND PEMBROKE-SHIRE)

Records of Local Savings Committees in Cardiganshire and Pembrokeshire, 1931-73.

Schedule (1981), 3pp. *AR 1977-78*, p.72.

NATIONAL SAVINGS MOVEMENT

Records of the National Savings Movement in Wales, including records of local savings committees, 1919-78.

Schedule (1978), [ii] + 68pp. *AR 1977-78*, pp.72-3.

NEFYDD

Historical and literary manuscripts collected by William Roberts ('Nefydd', 1813-72), Baptist minister and author, including papers of his own, manuscripts relating to Baptist history in Wales, the establishment of British Schools in Wales, and some papers of Edmund Jones, The Tranch, Pontypool (1702-93), Ben Jones ('P.A. Môn', 1788-1841), Daniel Jones, Liverpool (1788-1862) and Christmas Evans (1766-1838). (*NLW MSS 7011-189* except for some deeds).

Schedule [1935], 70pp. *AR 1930-31*, pp.34-6, 39-40.

NEUADD-FAWR

Deeds and documents of the Jones and Davys families relating to the Neuadd-fawr estate in cos. Cardigan and Carmarthen and the Dôl-coed estate in co. Brecon, 1554-1915.

Schedule (1958 + suppl.), xii + 169pp. Also **Maps**. *AR 1941-42*, p.27; *1975-76*, p.76.

NEUADDLWYD AND ABERAERON
Deeds and documents, 1545-1848, relating to the parishes of Henfynyw and Llannarth, co. Cardigan, and papers relating to Neuaddlwyd and other Congregational churches, 1791-1896 (now *NLW MSS 19154-7* and *NLW Deeds 433-73*).

Schedule (1949), 19pp. *AR 1949-50*, p.25.

NEVILL
Records of the business concerns of Charles Nevill and his son, Richard Janion Nevill, notably the Swansea Copper Works and the Llanelly Copper Works and collieries in co. Carmarthen, 1797-1910. See also **Parker**. Other records in Dyfed R O (Carmarthen).

Schedule (1939), 320pp. *AR 1935-36*, p.51.

NEW RADNOR
Charters of the borough of New Radnor, co. Radnor, 1562 and 1739.

Calendar [*c.* 1931], 6pp. *AR 1931-32*, p.55.

NEWMAN PAYNTER
Deeds (deposited by Messrs Newman, Paynter & Co.) relating to various Welsh counties, 1668-1882.

Schedule (1937), 53pp. *AR 1937-38*, p.70.

NORTH WALES EMPLOYERS' MUTUAL INDEMNITY CO.
Records of the North Wales Employers' Mutual Indemnity Co. and of the United Westminster and Wrexham Collieries, 1898-1952, with some records of other industrial firms in the Wrexham area.

AR 1969-70, p.53.

NOYADD TREFAWR
Estate and family records of Parry, later Webley-Parry, later Webley-Parry-Pryse, of Noyadd Trefawr, co. Cardigan, and Lewes of Abernantbychan, co. Cardigan, and Gellidywyll, co. Carmarthen, 14th-20th cent., mainly 1530-1860. Include papers of Thomas Lewes (1742-95) as secretary to diplomats.

Schedule (1962), xxi + 361pp. in three vols. Also **Maps**. *AR 1954-55*, pp.51-5; *1956-57*, p.46. *NLWJ*, 12 (1961-2), pp.379-87.

ODDFELLOWS

Records of the Independent Order of Oddfellows Manchester Unity Friendly Society, for numerous mid-Wales lodges, 1825-1971.

AR 1949-50, p.25; *1963-64*, pp. 25-6; *1965-66*, p.26; *1969-70*, p.28; *1976-77*, p.68. *Llafur*, 1 (1972), p.29.

OLDFIELD

Estate and family records of Oldfield of The Farm, Betws-yn-Rhos, co. Denbigh, 14th-19th cent., including industrial records, 18th-19th cent.

AR 1962-63, pp.36-8.

ONSLOW

Terriers, parish of Llanllwchaearn, co. Montgomery, 1665-1749, and deeds, parish of Cil-y-cwm, co. Carmarthen, 1709-58 (donated by A.R. Onslow).

Schedule [1937], 3pp. *AR 1936-37*, p.30.

ORIELTON

Estate and family records of Owen of Orielton, co. Pembroke, and of Bodeon, Anglesey; estates mainly in cos Pembroke, Anglesey and Caernarfon, 15th-19th cent. See also **Owen and Colby**. Other papers of the Anglesey estate in Gwynedd R O (Caernarfon).

Preliminary schedule [1950s], 13pp.

ORMATHWAITE

Estate and family records of the family of Walsh (also Benn, Benn-Walsh), later barons Ormathwaite, of Pen-y-bont, co. Radnor. The estate was created by John Walsh, nabob and associate of Lord Clive; deeds, co. Radnor, 16th-20th cent.; estate records, 18th-20th cent.; family papers, 18th-20th cent., including diaries of Sir John Benn Walsh, 1st baron Ormathwaite (1798-1881), politician, 1811-77. Other papers in the India Office Library.

Ormathwaite Papers (1990), xvii + 91pp., superseding an earlier schedule 'Pen-y-bont Deeds and Documents'. Also **Maps**. *AR 1972-73*, pp.72-3; *1983-84*, p.57.

OTTLEY

Papers of the family of Ottley of Pitchford Hall, co. Salop, later Charles Cecil Cope Jenkinson, 3rd Earl of Liverpool (1784-1851), later Cotes. Extensive correspondence, mostly centred on Adam Ottley (1653-1723), bishop of St Davids, and Adam Ottley (1685-1752), registrar of St Davids,

145

including a long series of letters from Browne Willis (1682-1760), 1716-23. Also Civil War correspondence and some literary papers, 16th - 18th cent. For the deeds and estate records (part of the same archive) see **Pitchford**.

The Ottley Papers [1933], 102pp. *Ottley correspondence* (1981), [iii] + 786pp. in three vols. Also **Maps**. *AR 1932-33*, p.37; *1933-34*, pp.38-9; *1934-35*, p.45; *1935-36*, p.50. *AR 1983-84*, pp.48-9, describes a supplementary group for which a working list is available. The literary papers, Civil War correspondence and the Jenkinson and Cotes papers of the 1930s groups are uncatalogued (1994). On the correspondence of the bishop and the registrar, see *NLWJ*, 4 (1945-6), pp.61-74. The Civil War correspondence is published in *Transactions of the Shropshire Archaeological and National History Soc., 2nd series, VI-VIII (1894-6).*

OWEN AND COLBY
Estate and family records of Owen of Orielton and Colby of Ffynone; deeds, mainly 16th-19th cent., predominantly cos Pembroke and Anglesey; correspondence, 1679-1897; Pembrokeshire militia papers, 1778-1805. See also **Orielton** and **Spence-Colby**.

Schedule (1954 + suppl.), 221 + 1pp. *AR 1948-49*, p.58; *1965-66*, p.52. *NLWJ*, 9 (1955-6) pp.106-8.

OWEN AND PORTSMOUTH
Deeds (donated by Miss E.M. Owen and Mrs G.A. Portsmouth) relating to the parish of Dolgellau, co. Merioneth, 1632-1798.

Schedule (1971), 5pp. *AR 1971-72*, p.47.

BOB OWEN, CROESOR
Papers of Robert Owen ('Bob Owen, Croesor', 1885-1962), book collector and local historian. For manuscripts from his collection see NLW MSS 7355-98, 7900-1, 16148-50, 16306-14, 16322-3, 19160-349. Other papers in UW, Bangor, and Gwynedd R O (Caernarfon).

Papurau Bob Owen, Croesor (1993), i + 109pp., superseding an earlier schedule of 5pp. *s.n.* Robert Owen. *AR 1958-59*, pp.42-3; *1959-60*, pp.39-42; *1960-61*, pp.43-4; *1963-64*, pp.43-4.

C. E. VAUGHAN OWEN
Research papers of Cecil E. Vaughan Owen (1901-81), local historian, relating mainly to the history of Montgomeryshire, especially Arwystli and Llanidloes.

Box list (1981), 15pp. Also **Maps**. *AR 1981-82*, p.56.

146

EDWARD OWEN
Papers of Edward Owen (1853-1943), antiquary, including useful transcripts of Welsh records in the Public Record Office (*NLW MSS 17974-18102*); deeds and documents relating mainly to the estates of Edwards of Plas Newydd, Chirk, and Puleston of Emral, cos Denbigh and Flint, 1463-1769.

Schedule (1948), 86pp. *AR 1943-44*, p.16.

GRIFFITH E. OWEN
Records from the offices of Barker, Morris & Owen, Carmarthen, solicitors, in which Griffith Einion Owen was a partner, 18th-19th cent. Include records relating to the following estates and families: Cwmgwili, Gwynne of Garth, Scurlocke of Carmarthen, Johnes of Hafod, Lloyd of Mabws and Penty Park, Phillips of Laugharne, Lloyd Jack, Hughes of Tre-gib, Rees of New Inn, Morgan of Carmarthen (ironmasters), Morris of Carmarthen (bankers), Lloyd of Abertrinant, the Brigstocke family, Edwardes of Trefgarn, Jones and Griffiths of Alltyferin and Llwyn-y-brain, parish of Llanegwad. Include also manorial records, 18th-19th cent.; office records, 19th cent.; records of Carmarthen borough and records of iron and tinplate industry, all late 18th-19th cent. See also **D.M.C. Charles**.

AR 1943-44, pp.23-5. Working list available for a large part of the archive.

HUGH OWEN
Papers of Hugh Owen (1880-1953), Anglesey antiquary.

AR 1978-79, pp.41-3.

J. C. OWEN
Papers (donated by the Rev. J.C. Owen) relating to tithes and other ecclesiastical matters in parishes in cos Cardigan and Brecon, 1859-1921.

Schedule (1933), 8pp. *AR 1932-33*, p.30.

J. DYFNALLT OWEN
Papers of J. Dyfnallt Owen (1873-1956), Congregational minister and poet.

Schedule (1957), 40pp.

BISHOP JOHN OWEN
Papers of John Owen (1854-1926), bishop of St Davids, 1897-1926. *Under embargo until 2002*.

AR 1971-72, p.79.

O. EILIAN OWEN
Papers of O. Eilian Owen (1865-1938), lexicographer, Calvinistic Methodist minister and historian.

Schedule [after 1938], 23pp. *AR 1938-39*, p.27.

ROBERT OWEN see **Bob Owen**

THOMAS EDWARD OWEN
Papers of Thomas Edward Owen and Thomas Owen, his father, permanent way inspectors for the Manchester and Milford Railway, 1820-1905.

Thomas Edward Owen Papers (1983), ii + 8pp. *AR 1945-46*, p.19.

TREVOR OWEN
Manuscripts and papers collected by Canon Trevor Owen (d. 1916). They include a group of papers of Sir William Williams ('Speaker Williams', 1634-1700), papers of John Williams (1700-87), attorney-general of the Chester Circuit and Chief Justice of the Brecon Circuit, and papers of John Roberts, Maes-y-porth, deputy registrar of the diocese of Bangor, 1773-1827. See also NLW MSS 2771-88 and **Coedymaen**.

Schedule (1983), [ii] + 91pp.

VAUGHAN OWEN
Deeds relating to properties mainly in cos Merioneth and Montgomery, including the estate of Owen of Dolgoed, parish of Tal-y-llyn, co. Merioneth, and Bennett of Glanyrafon, parish of Trefeglwys, co. Montgomery, 1546-1946.

Schedules (1962), 9pp.; (1965), 7pp.; (1966 + suppl.), 31pp. *AR 1961-62*, p.50; *1965-66*, pp.55, 62; *1971-72*, p.82.

WILLIAM OWEN, PRYSGOL
Music manuscripts of William Owen, Prysgol (1813-93), containing anthems and hymn tunes composed by him (*NLW MSS 21547-51*).

Schedule (1973), 4pp.

PANTLLUDW
Deeds and documents (donated by Mrs Ruck, Pantlludw) relating mainly to cos Merioneth and Caernarfon, notably the Garnons family of Rhiwgoch, co. Merioneth, 1653-1782.

Schedule [1928], 36pp. *AR 1928-29*, p.30.

PANTON

Family records of Paul Panton (1727-97), antiquary, and his son Paul Panton (1758-1822), together with documents collected by them, 1432-1818. Notable among the collected material is a group of Wynn of Gwydir records, 1546-1669. For other Panton family records see **Plas Gwyn** and **Esgair and Pantperthog**; for the Panton MSS see NLW MSS 1970-2068 (above, p.5) and for other Panton (Gwydir) MSS see NLW MSS 9051-69 and **Wynn**.

Panton Deeds (1981), xi + 59pp.

PARKER

Papers of and concerning Thomas Parker (1761-*c.* 1818) and Louisa, his wife (d. *c.* 1833), of Kidwelly, relating mainly to property in Kidwelly and to the Allihies copper mine in co. Cork, Ireland, 1698-1844.

Schedule (1936), 29pp.

LORD PARRY

Papers of Gordon Samuel David Parry, later Lord Parry of Neyland (1925-   ), chairman of the Welsh Tourist Board.

AR 1993-94.

SIR DAVID HUGHES PARRY

Papers of Sir David Hughes Parry (1893-1973), professor of law and university administrator.

AR 1974-75, pp.75-6; *1976-77,* p.73; *1977-78,* p.76; *1983-84,* p.57.

MORRIS PARRY

Papers of Morris Parry of Chester (d. 1943), bibliographer.

AR 1942-43, p.27.

OWEN PARRY

Papers of Owen Parry, Llanegryn, antiquary, including a group of papers of William John Roberts ('Gwilym Cowlyd', 1827-1904).

Schedule (1958 + suppl.), 7pp. *AR 1957-58,* p.25; *1958-59,* p.37.

R. WILLIAMS PARRY

Papers of Robert Williams Parry (1884-1956), poet.

Papurau R. Williams Parry (1979), ii + 108pp. *AR 1977-78,* p.52.

WINNIE PARRY
Papers of Sarah Winifred Parry ('Winnie Parry', 1870-1953), author.

AR 1961-62, p.46.

H. T. PAYNE
Manuscripts of Henry Thomas Payne (?1760-1832), archdeacon of Carmarthen and antiquary. One group is now *Minor Deposits 184-9*.

AR 1936-37, p.27. Other manuscripts are with the archives of the Church in Wales. See *NLWJ*, 4 (1945-6), pp.210-4.

IORWERTH PEATE
Papers of Iorwerth Cyfeiliog Peate (1901-82), first curator of the Welsh Folk Museum and poet.

AR 1983-84, p.44; *1987-88*, p.59.

PEMBROKESHIRE COUNTY RECORDS
Pembrokeshire Quarter Sessions, County Council and other county records, 18th-20th cent. *Transferred to Dyfed R O (Haverfordwest)*.

Shelf-list (1936), 17pp. *AR 1938-39*, p.48.

PENALLY
Deeds (donated by Major Saurin, Penally) relating mainly to co. Pembroke, especially Jones of Cilwendeg and the Saurin family, 1625-1883; include documents relating to the Skerries lighthouse, Anglesey, 1730-1847.

Schedule (1942), 14pp. *AR 1941-42*, p.22.

PENCERRIG
Deeds and documents, mainly 17th-19th cent., of the Jones family of Pencerrig, parish of Llanelwedd, (including Thomas Jones (1742-1803), the artist), relating to the estate in co. Radnor.

Schedule (1953), 60pp. *AR 1951-52*, p.34; *1952-53*, p.46.

PENCRUG
Deeds relating to Pencrug and other properties in the parishes of Llanafan Fawr and Llanafan Fechan, co. Brecon, 1587-1863.

Schedule [1952], 15pp.

PENGELLY
Deeds and documents relating to Pengelly, parish of Troed-yr-aur, co.

Cardigan, and to other properties in cos Cardigan and Pembroke, 1564-1865.

Schedule (1953 + suppl.), 26 + 3pp. *AR 1952-53*, p.46; *1968-69*, p.49.

PENIARTII

Estate records and family papers of Owen and Wynne of Peniarth, co. Merioneth, 15th-19th cent., including groups relating to Mostyn of Nant and Mostyn and Williams of Penbedw, co. Flint, to Maurice of Lloran, co. Denbigh, and to Corbet of Ynysmaengwyn, co. Merioneth, estates also in cos Caernarfon, Montgomery and Salop. Include the papers of Mrs Elizabeth Baker (*c.* 1720-89). For the Peniarth MSS see above, p.4. Some later estate records in Gwynedd R O (Dolgellau).

Peniarth Deeds [1920s], 144pp.; *Peniarth manuscripts and documents* [1959], 264pp. Also **Maps**. Working lists available of a revised schedule of 'Peniarth Deeds' and of the Penbedw group. The Ynysmaengwyn group remains unlisted (1994). *AR 1920 (Oct.)*, pp.5-6; *1925 (May)*, p.20; *1954-55*, p.57; *1955-56*, p.57; *1980-81*, p.60.

PENLLE'RGAER

Estate and family records of Price of Penlle'rgaer, Llewelyn of Ynysgerwyn, later of Penlle'rgaer, and Dillwyn of Penlle'rgaer, co. Glamorgan, 15th-20th cent. Estates in cos Glamorgan, Brecon and Carmarthen. Include early coal-mining records. See also **Lewis Weston Dillwyn, William Dillwyn** and **Llysdinam**. Other papers in UW, Swansea.

Schedules (1927, Group A, Brecknockshire), 181pp.; (1933, Group B, Glamorgan and Carmarthenshire), 323pp.; (1991, supplementary), 13pp. *AR 1927-28*, pp.46-7; *1990-91*, p.64. See also *AR 1939-40*, p.33; *1942-43*, p.34 (these two groups uncatalogued 1994).

PENNAL TOWERS

Estate and family records of Price of Esgairweddan and Edwards and Thruston of Talgarth Hall and Pennal Towers, Pennal, co. Merioneth, 1501-20th cent.

AR 1959-60, p.24.

PENPONT

Estate and family records of Williams of Penpont, co. Brecon, mostly relating to co. Brecon, 14th-19th cent. Other records in Powys R O.

Schedules (1936), 341pp.; (1975), 589pp. *AR 1936-37*, pp.24-5; *1969-70*, p.57. See also *AR 1975-76*, p.53.

PENRALLEY

Records of the James and Williams families of Penralley, Rhaeadr, co. Radnor, 1650-1969, including naval records, 18th-19th cent., and papers of Stephen William Williams (1837-99), surveyor and antiquary. See also **Birmingham Corporation**.

Penralley Papers (1992), ii + 68pp. *AR 1991-92*, p.61.

PENRICE AND MARGAM

Estate and family records of Mansel, later Talbot, of Penrice, in Gower, Glamorgan, and, from the 16th cent., of Margam Abbey, 12th-19th cent. The Margam Abbey archive is one of the fullest surviving British monastic archives. There are substantial early archives for Penrice, and other estates, mostly in Glamorgan; manorial records for the manor of Margam Abbey and others; early records of the coal industry. The early records, with the exception of the correspondence, are for the great part included in W. de Gray Birch's six published volumes. Other records in West Glamorgan R O and BL Harleian Charters 75A1-75D25..

A Descriptive Catalogue of the Penrice and Margam Manuscripts, ed. W. de Gray Birch (6 vols, London, 1893-1905); schedules (1942, vol. I, including Williams of Plas Dyffryn Clydach papers, largely literary, 17th - 18th cent., and supplementary Margam records), 53pp.; (1942, vol. II, Mansel correspondence, 1565-1848), 230pp.; (1942, 'Appendix', by W. de Gray Birch, supplementing *A Descriptive Catalogue*, mostly post-1750 records), 343pp.; (1946, 'Appendix vol. II', further supplementary records), 218pp. *AR 1941-42*, pp.26-7..

PENTRE MAWR

Estate records of the families of Williams, Jones, and Jones-Bateman of Pentre Mawr, parish of Abergele, co. Denbigh, 1575-1867.

Schedule [1947], 42pp. *AR 1946-47*, p.36.

PENTY PARK

Estate and family records of Lloyd of Mabws, co. Cardigan, Philipps of Hafodneddyn, co. Carmarthen, and Lloyd of Penty Park, co. Pembroke, mostly relating to cos Pembroke and Carmarthen, 1590-1916. See also **Griffith E. Owen** and **Roberts & Evans**.

Schedule (1962), 36pp. *AR 1943-44*, p.30.

PEN-Y-BONT

A 23-page schedule under this title has been superseded, see **Ormathwaite**.

PENYRWRLODD

Deeds relating mainly to the parishes of Hay and Llanigon, co. Brecon, notably to Penyrwrlodd Hall, 1674-1897.

Penyrwrlodd Deeds (1982 + suppl.), i + 9pp. *AR 1982-83*, p.47.

PETERWELL

Records of the estate of Lloyd, later Adams, later Harford, of Peterwell, Lampeter, co. Cardigan; deeds 1696-1871, estate papers, 19th-20th cent. See also **Falcondale**.

Peterwell Estate Papers (1987), ii + 60pp. superseding an earlier schedule. *AR 1928-29*, pp.39-40; *1984-85*, p.42.

JOHN PETTS

Papers of John Petts (1914-91), artist *(NLW MSS 23207-13)*.

AR 1993-94.

GRISMOND PHILIPPS

Deeds (donated by Grismond Philipps) relating to Cilbronnau and other property in the parishes of Llangoedmor and Ciliau Aeron, co. Cardigan, 1553-1731.

Schedule [pre-1934], 5pp. *AR 1932-33*, p.31.

EGERTON PHILLIMORE

Papers of Egerton Grenville Bagot Phillimore (1856-1937), Welsh scholar.

Uncatalogued (1994).

PHILLIPS (TAL-Y-BONT)

Farming records of the Phillips family of Tre-faes Isaf, Llangwyryfon, and Erglodd and Llwyn-glas, Tal-y-bont, co. Cardigan, 19th-20th cent.

Schedule (1978), ii + 15pp. *AR 1977-78*, p.43.

D. RHYS PHILLIPS

Papers of David Rhys Phillips (1862-1952), librarian and local historian, relating to librarianship in Wales, Welsh bibliography and the history of the Vale of Neath; include documents and papers collected by him, 18th-19th cent. See also NLW MSS 14362-73.

Schedule (1976, vol. I, manuscripts and papers), vii + 62pp.; (1977, vol. II, correspondence), 362pp. *AR 1952-53*, pp.32-4.

MARGARET PHILLIPS

Deeds (deposited by Margaret Phillips) relating to the parish of Llanrhidian, co. Glamorgan, 1718-67 (*Minor Deposit 619*).

Schedule (1959), 3pp. *AR 1958-59*, p.56.

RICHARD AND EIDDWEN PHILLIPS

Papers of Richard Phillips (1891-1983), agriculturalist, and Eiddwen Phillips (1901-72), his wife.

AR 1984-85, p.33. Also **Maps**.

W. D. PHILLIPS

Deeds (donated by W.D. Phillips) relating to the parish of Walford, co. Hereford, and Penheolferthyr, Merthyr Tudful, co. Glamorgan, 1788-1859.

Schedule (1931), 3pp. *AR 1930-31*, p.38.

PICTON CASTLE

Estate and family records of Philipps of Picton Castle, co. Pembroke, 13th-20th cent.; estates mainly in co. Pembroke, also cos Carmarthen and Glamorgan; manorial records and coal-mining records, 17th-19th cent. Other records in Dyfed R O (Haverfordwest).

Schedule (1970), 404pp.; (1993), ii + 14pp.; *Manorbier Court Rolls* [1980s, an expanded description of Picton Castle 225 containing court rolls 1687-98], 6pp. Also **Maps** (schedule). *AR 1948-49*, pp. 51-3; *1985-86*, p.61.

PICTON FAMILY

Records of the Picton family of Poyston, co. Pembroke, and Iscoed, co. Carmarthen, and of its estates in cos Carmarthen, Pembroke and Glamorgan, 18th - 20th cent.

Schedule (1956), 39pp. *AR 1955-56*, p.42.

HARRY PIERCE

Papers (deposited by Harry Pierce) of the Pierce family of Meriadog, later of Cwybyr, co. Flint, 19th - 20th cent., with a few other documents 1596-1764.

Schedule (1944), 5pp. *AR 1943-44*, p.30.

BENJAMIN PIERCY

Papers of Benjamin Piercy (1827-88), railway engineer, relating to railways, especially in north-east Wales, river Dee conservancy and the Piercy

154

estate in cos Flint and Denbigh. (The manuscripts now *NLW MSS 9745-847*).

Schedule (1934), 187pp. Also **Maps** (schedules). *AR 1933-34*, p.29; *1934-35*, p.57.

J. R. F. PIETTE
Papers of Jean Raymond François Piette ('Arzel Even', 1920-71), Breton scholar. *Conditional access.*

AR 1972-73, p.53.

PINSENT & CO.
Records (deposited by Pinsent & Co) relating mainly to co. Radnor, 1634-1917, in particular to the Newcastle Court estate.

AR 1965-66, pp.55-6.

PITCHFORD
Deeds relating to the estates of the Ottley family of Pitchford Hall, co. Salop, mainly in the areas of Bridgnorth and Pitchford, with some lands in adjoining counties, 12th-19th cent., including almost a thousand medieval deeds. For the remainder of the archive of which this is a part, see **Ottley**.

Schedule (1942), 564pp. Also **Maps**.

PLAID CYMRU
Archives of Plaid Cymru from its foundation as Plaid Genedlaethol Cymru (The Welsh Nationalist Party) in 1925. *Conditional access.*

Frequent deposits recorded in *AR* from 1954, not detailed here. Working list available.

PLANET
Archives of the journal *Planet*, 1970-9, including manuscripts of contributors and editor's correspondence (editor, Ned Thomas, literary editor, John Tripp).

Planet archives (1991), 6pp. *AR 1974-75*, p.73; *1976-77*, p.73; *1987-88*, p.62; *1991-92*, p.58.

PLAS BLAENDDÔL
Deeds and documents of the families of Vaughan and Jones relating to the Tanymanod and Gelli estates, parish of Ffestiniog, co. Merioneth, 1799-1932.

Schedule (1960), 65pp. *AR 1960-61*, p.61.

PLAS BOWMAN

Deeds and documents (deposited by Mrs Thomas, Plas Bowman) of the Williams family of Bodelwyddan, co. Flint, relating to the Bodelwyddan, Bodidris and Pengwern estates in cos Flint and Denbigh, 1788-1898.

Schedule (1947), 18pp. *AR 1946-47*, p.43.

PLAS BRONDANW

Estate and family records of Williams and Ellis of Plas Brondanw, parish of Llanfrothen, co. Merioneth, 17th-19th cent.

Schedule (1941), 18pp.

PLAS GWYN

Estate and family records of Panton of Bagillt, co. Flint, and Plas Gwyn, Anglesey, 1507-1847. They comprise deeds, north Wales counties, 1507-1844; Panton family correspondence (notably Paul Panton, father and son), 1752-1847; papers of John Jones (1650-1727), dean of Bangor, including valuable ecclesiastical and antiquarian correspondence. See also **Panton** and **Esgair and Pantperthog**. Other records in Clwyd R O (Hawarden) and UW, Bangor.

Schedules (1924), 25pp. (John Jones papers); (1928), 23pp. (Panton correspondence); (1929 + suppl.), 52 + 2pp. (deeds). *AR 1928-29*, p.40; @.

PLAS HEATON

Estate and family records of Heaton of Plas Heaton, estates in cos Denbigh, Flint, Norfolk, and in the city of Chester, 1380-1908. Other records in Clwyd R O (Ruthin).

Schedule (1948), 52pp. Also **Maps**. *AR 1947-48*, p.38.

PLAS LLANGOEDMORE

Estate records relating to the families of Vaughan of Crosswood and Millingchamp and Vaughan of Plas Llangoedmor, co. Cardigan, and to properties mainly in cos Cardigan and Carmarthen, 1630-1898. See also **Morgan Richardson**.

Schedule [after 1945], 25pp. Also **Maps**. *AR 1924 (May)*, p.11.

PLAS MACHYNLLETH

Rentals and other records relating to the Plas Machynlleth estate of the marquesses of Londonderry, mainly in cos Montgomery and Merioneth, 1843-1921, including records of lead-mining companies, notably the Van mines, 1865-1923. See also **Londonderry**.

Schedule (1941), 7pp. Also **Maps**. *AR 1940-41*, p.28.

PLAS NANTGLYN

Estate and family records of Wynne and Edwards of Plas Nantglyn, co. Denbigh, 16th-19th cent., including Welsh literary manuscripts, 17th-18th cent. Other records in Clwyd R O (Ruthin).

Schedule (1949), 43pp. *AR 1947-48*, pp 42-3; *1948-49*, p.61.

PLAS POWER

Estate and family records of Myddelton, Lloyd and Fitzhugh of Plas Power, Wrexham, including also records of the Chirk Castle estate, 14th-20th cent. but mainly 17th-18th. Include industrial records, 1627-1822, extensive correspondence, 17th-19th cent., and some papers of Thomas Lloyd (*c*. 1673-1734), lexicographer. See also NLW MSS 716-36. Other records in Clwyd R O (Ruthin).

AR 1970-71, pp.64-7. Several small supplementary groups of Plas Power records were subsequently acquired in salerooms. They have been added to the archive. See *AR 1979-80*, p.62; *1984-85*, p.40; *1985-86*, p.59; *1988-89*, p.65; *1989-90*, p.63; *1990-91*, p.62. Also **Maps**.

PLAS WYN

Deeds and documents relating to the Wynne family of Tŷ Gwyn and New Hall (Plas Wyn), Llansanffraid Glynceiriog, and properties in cos Denbigh, Merioneth and Salop, 1753-1878.

Schedule (1969), 28pp. *AR 1968-69*, p.34.

PLAS-YN-CEFN

Estate and family records of Lloyd of Cefn, co. Denbigh, 15th-19th cent.; estates in cos Caernarfon, Denbigh and Flint; include records of lead and copper mining, 18th-19th cent.; include also a substantial group of papers of Humphrey Humphreys (1848-1712) for his period as bishop of Hereford, 1701-12. See also **Bodewryd**.

Schedule (1958), 586 pp. in two vols. *AR 1938-39*, p. 51. *NLWJ*, 12 (1961-2), 292-7. See also *AR 1970-71*, pp.74-5, and *1971-72*, pp. 81-2 (uncatalogued 1994).

PLAS YOLYN

Estate and family records of Edwards and Morrall of Cilhendre and Plas Yolyn in Dudleston, Shropshire, 13th - 19th cent.; they include manuscripts and papers of Morgan Llwyd (1619-59), writer and mystic; papers of Colonel John Jones, Maesygarnedd (?1597-1660) and of his family, 17th - 18th cent.; estate records, mainly in cos Salop, Denbigh and Merioneth, 13th-19th cent. (The manuscripts and papers now *NLW MSS 11430-81*).

Schedule [1938], 193pp. *AR 1937-38*, pp.50-1.

PLYMOUTH

Records of Welsh estates of the earls of Plymouth, 14th - 18th cent.; the two most notable groups relate to the families of Ellis of Alrhey, co. Flint, and Lewis of Van, co. Glamorgan, both representing estates acquired through marriage in the 18th cent., both including early deeds. Other records in Glamorgan R O (Cardiff).

Schedule (1939), 300pp. Also **Maps**. *AR 1934-35*, p.46.

PORTMADOC

Records from the office of Messrs Breese, Jones & Casson, solicitors, and from the Harbour Office, Porthmadog; they include the papers of William Alexander Madocks (1773-1828), and records relating to Porthmadog harbour, 1824-1917, the Ffestiniog and Blaenau Railway Co., 1866-83, the Caernarvonshire Volunteers, 1860-83. Other records in Gwynedd R O (Caernarfon and Dolgellau).

Schedule [1950], 19pp. Also **Maps**. *AR 1937-38*, p.72.

G.C.B. POULTER

Deeds and documents (donated by G.C.B. Poulter) relating to the Groydd estate in the parish of Cerrigydrudion and other properties in cos Denbigh and Merioneth, 1706-1886.

Schedule [after 1967], 16pp. *AR 1961-62*, p.34; *1967-68*, p.22.

POWIS CASTLE

Records of the Herbert family of Montgomery, Chirbury and Powis Castle, later earls of Powis, and Clive of Walcott, 13th-20th cent. Include estate records, mainly in co. Montgomery and adjacent counties, notably Salop, 13th-20th cent., records of lead and silver mining, co. Cardigan, 18th-19th cent.; records of the Castle Island estate, Ireland, 16th-19th cent.; manorial records for the barony of Powis, from 1549, the lordship of Oswestry, from 1577 (but no series), the manors of Cydewain, Halcetor and Montgomery, from 1525, Chirbury, from 1373, Pool, from 1653, the borough of Llanfyllin, from 1653, and many others; correspondence, mainly 17th-19th cent.; manuscripts and papers of Edward Herbert, 1st baron Herbert of Cherbury (1583-1648); papers of Robert Clive, 1st baron Clive (1725-74) and Brigadier-General John Carnac (c. 1716-1800), relating to India. See also **Chartism, Clive, Montgomeryshire Yeoman Cavalry** and NLW MSS 5295-313. Other estate records in Shropshire R O. Other Clive papers in the India Office Library.

Schedules: *Manuscripts and documents* (1959), 7pp.; *Manuscripts* (1965), 2pp. (these two list manuscripts and political papers of Edward Lord Herbert); *Powis*

Castle correspondence (1970), 1065pp. in two vols; *Powis Castle deeds and documents* (1971-3), vol. I, 300pp., vol. II, 328pp. vol. III, 332pp. vol. IV, 320pp., vol. V, 291pp.; *Powis manorial records: group I* (revised 1986), [i] + 22pp. (substantially the same as 'Powis manorial records, group I', *Montgomeryshire Collections*, 48 (1943-4), pp. 53-85); *Powis manorial records, group II* (1970), ii + 179pp.; *Political and other letters* (1941), 48pp. (correspondence, 1742-1890); *Letters and documents relating to the proposed union of the dioceses of St Asaph and Bangor* (1941), 245pp. (a calendar of papers, 1835-49); *Powis Castle Archives* (1982-83 deposit), vol. I (1986), 36pp. (rentals); vol. II (1986), i + 19pp. (maps); *Powis (1990 deposit): Clive of India papers* (1990), 5pp. (a summary list). A schedule of deeds relating to the Barony of Powis (1982-83 deposit) awaits typing (1994). Also **Maps** (schedule). *AR 1932-33*, pp.41-2; *1934-35*, p.46; *1936-37*, p.30; *1939-40*, p.35; *1944-45*, pp.31-2; *1946-47*, p.42; *1958-59*, pp.57-8; *1978-79*, pp.82-3; *1981-82*, p.84; *1982-83*, p.54; *1989-90*, p.65. Royal Commission on Historical Manuscripts, 10th Report (1885), pp.378-99; *Montgomeryshire Collections*, 20 (1886), pp.1-282 (Herbert Papers); *NLWJ*, 3 (1943-4), pp.36-43 (on the legal papers); *Index of English Literary Manuscripts*, vol. I (1450-1625), ed. P. Beal (London, 1980), part 2, pp.167-84 (on the manuscripts of Edward, Lord Herbert of Cherbury). Much of the 1980s deposits remains uncatalogued (1994).

JOHN COWPER POWYS

Parts of the scattered literary archive of John Cowper Powys (1872-1963), novelist, including his diaries (*NLW MSS 21775-84, 21869-73, 21928-40, 22206-41, 22373-9, 22506-13, 22807-14* and others un-numbered (1994)).

AR 1981-82, p.63; *1982-83*, p.47; *1983-84*, p.51; *1984-85*, p.40; *1985-86*, p.60; *1986-87*, p.64; *1987-88*, p.62; *1990-91*, p.63.

POWYSLAND CLUB

Records of all sorts relating to Montgomeryshire, sometimes to adjacent counties, notably Shropshire, collected by the Powysland Club. Include deeds, mainly 16th-19th cent.; Land Tax returns, 1826-31; turnpike trust records (1st Division of the Montgomeryshire Trust), 1756-1893; some vestry books and other parochial records, 18th-19th cent.; genealogical material; papers relating to Robert Owen (1771-1858), the socialist; documents relating to Welshpool borough council, 17th-19th cent.; manorial records, including Halcetor, 1599-1715; papers of Roderick Urwick Sayce (1890-1970), anthropologist.

Preliminary schedule (1965 + suppl.), 13 + 3pp.; box-list (1982), i + 52pp.; box-list (1985), [i] + 10pp.; (1993), i + 7pp. *AR 1965-66*, pp.57-8; *1966-67*, p.57; *1977-78*, p.73-4; *1982-83*, p.51; *1985-86*, p.62. *1993-94*. See also *AR 1977-78*, pp. 73-4, not included in the above lists.

POYSTON

Deeds and documents (bequeathed by Henry Owen of Poyston) relating to the Vaughan and Laugharne families of Pontfaen, co. Pembroke, mainly 16th-19th cent.

Schedule (1939), 126pp. *AR 1919* (Oct.), pp.4-5.

PRESBYTERIAN COLLEGE, CARMARTHEN

Records of the Presbyterian College, Carmarthen, 1820-1951. See also **Minor Lists 1983**.

AR 1963-64, pp.49-50.

PRESS BENEFIT AND SUPERANNUATION SOCIETY

Records of the Press Benefit and Superannuation Society for South Wales and Monmouthshire from foundation to dissolution, 1882-1967.

AR 1969-70, p.35.

PRESTEIGNE

Deeds relating to Presteigne, co. Radnor, 1657-1914.

Schedule (1973), 13pp. *AR 1972-73*, p.50.

PRICE OF NORTON

Deeds associated with the family of Price of Norton, co. Radnor, 1674-1831, mostly relating to that county. Other records in Powys R O.

Schedule (1957), 36pp. *AR 1957-58*, pp. 2-3.

ARTHUR MORGAN PRICE

Deeds and documents (deposited by Arthur Morgan Price) relating to the parish of Llanfihangel Cwm Du, co. Brecon, 1672-1872.

Schedule (1973), 16pp. *AR 1973-74*, p.75.

W. W. PRICE

Papers of Watkin William Price of Aberdare (1873-1967), local historian.

AR 1961-62, p.40; *1968-69*, p.40; *1975-76*, p.80. The Welsh biographical index of W. W. Price (the most comprehensive one available for the period mid-19th to mid-20th cent.) has been photocopied and bound in thirty vols, available on the open shelves of the Printed Books reading room.

CARADOG PRICHARD

Papers of Caradog Prichard (1904-80), poet.

Papurau Caradog Prichard (1984), [i] + 13pp. *AR 1983-84*, p.51.

160

PROBYN

Deeds, 1547-1788, relating mainly to the family of Howell, parish of Amroth, co. Pembroke, 17th cent., and Lloyd of Clochfaen, co. Montgomery, 18th cent. The deeds purportedly derive from the muniments of the Probyn family.

Schedule [? 1950s], 17pp. *AR 1939-40*, p.24. See also *AR 1948-49*, p.25.

ARCHBISHOP PROSSER

Papers of David Lewis Prosser (1868-1950), bishop of St Davids and archbishop of Wales.

AR 1949-50, p.32; *1954-55*, p.35; *1955-56*, p.41; *1956-57*, p.32.

DANIEL PROTHEROE AND RHYS MORGAN

Music manuscripts and papers of Daniel Protheroe (1866-1934), composer, and Rhys Morgan ('The Welsh Tenor', 1892-1961).

Schedule (1983), iii + 27pp. *AR 1982-83*, p.47.

A. IVOR PRYCE

A collection of deeds and documents made by Arthur Ivor Pryce (d. 1940), antiquary, mostly 16th-20th cent. and relating to cos Anglesey, Caernarfon and Merioneth; includes court rolls of Caernarfon borough, 1392-3 (see **Caernarvon Court Rolls**).

Schedule (1961), 123pp.

PULESTON

Estate and family records of Puleston of Emral, co. Flint, 14th-19th cent., estates mainly in cos Flint and Denbigh; various minister's accounts, 1485-1510; records for Irish estates, 1580-1795. See also NLW MSS 423, 3561-88, 6704, 22844 and BL Add. MSS 46397-400, 46846 and Add. Charters 74370-435.

Schedule [pre-1928], 153pp. *AR 1920-21*, p.12. See Royal Commission on Historical Manuscripts, 2nd Report (1871), pp.65-8. The subsequent partial scattering of the archive is reflected in the references given above.

QUARITCH

Estate records (purchased from Bernard Quaritch Ltd) of Williams of Screen, co. Radnor, and Felin Newydd, co. Brecon, 1361-1874.

Schedule [pre-1934], 166pp. *AR 1922 (Oct.)*, p.10.

161

'S.R.' AND 'J.R.'

Papers of Samuel Roberts ('S.R.', 1800-85) and John Roberts ('J.R.', 1804-84), of Llanbrynmair, ministers and reformers. (*NLW MSS 9511-98*). See also **J. Luther Thomas**.

Schedule [pre-1934], 10pp. *AR 1931-32*, p.39.

RADCLIFFE

Deeds and documents (deposited by D. C. Radcliffe) relating to cos Flint and Denbigh, mainly the Rhyl area, 1788-1904; include documents relating to estates of the diocese of St Asaph.

Schedule (1938), 38pp. *AR 1933-34*, p.44.

RADNORSHIRE QUARTER SESSIONS

Quarter Sessions records for co. Radnor, 1753-1971. *Transferred to Powys R O*. Microfilm copies of the Order Books and deposited plans enclosure awards are available in NLW.

Schedules (1963), [ii] + 193pp.; (1971), 19pp. *AR 1962-63*, pp.56-8; *1973-74*, p.75; @.

KEITH RAFFAN

Papers of Keith Raffan (1949-   ), Conservative MP for Delyn, 1983-92. *Conditional access.*

Keith Raffan Papers (1992), ii + 27pp. *AR 1991-92*, p.57.

RATGOED

Records relating to slate quarries in Machynlleth, co. Montgomery, and Corris, Llanuwchllyn, Tal-y-llyn (among them Ratgoed quarries) and Tywyn, co. Merioneth, 1853-99.

Schedule (1980), i + 4pp. *AR 1941-42*, p.20.

RAWLEY

Deeds (purchased from Robert Rawley) relating to various Welsh counties, 1626-1830, including a group relating to Parry of Llanrhaiadr Hall, co. Denbigh, 1698-1830.

Schedule (1932), 12pp.

ALWYN D. REES

Papers of Alwyn David Rees (1911-74), sociologist and editor of *Barn*, 1966-74.

AR 1977-78, pp.74-5; *1992-3,* p.55.

J. SEYMOUR REES
Papers of John Seymour Rees, Seven Sisters (1888-1963), author and Congregational minister, including work by many other Welsh writers, 19th-20th cent. (*NLW MSS 18628-707, 18764-866, 19383-7, NLW Deed 801*).

Schedule (1964 + suppl.), 126 + 58pp. *AR 1963-64*, p.38; *1964-65*, p.37.

J. T. REES
Music manuscripts of John Thomas Rees (1857-1949), composer (*NLW MSS 16841-50, 19923-76, 20974-6*). See also Minor Deposits 779-80 and NLW MS 22019.

J. T. Rees Music MSS (1968 + suppl.), 10pp. *AR 1949-50*, p.33; *1951-52*, p.29; *1967-68*, pp.32-3; *1972-73*, p.44. See also *AR 1962-63*, p.60.

T. MARDY REES
Papers of Thomas Mardy Rees (1861-1953), Congregational minister and author.

AR 1977-78, pp.48-9; *1978-79*, p.54.

TERENCE REES
Manuscript and printed scores and librettos of operas, not exclusively British, 19th-20th cent., collected by Dr Terence Rees; also some ephemera of the theatre.

Schedule [1983], 6pp. *AR 1982-83*, p.53; @.

WILLIAM REES
Papers of William Rees (1887-1978), historian.

AR 1978-79, p.53.

WILLIAM REES ('ARIANGLAWDD')
Papers of the William Rees ('Arianglawdd', 1854-1934), Baptist minister and author; of Pembrokeshire interest.

Schedule (Welsh), [1971], 8pp. *AR 1971-72*, pp.48-49.

RENDEL
Papers of Stuart Rendel, 1st Baron Rendel (1834-1913), MP for Montgomeryshire, 1880-94, friend of Gladstone, and of others of the Rendel family, from 1841, notably those of Sir George William Rendel (1889-1979), diplomat. The archive derives from several sources, represented by the several schedules. The 1955 schedule and vols II and

III relate solely to the papers of Lord Rendel; vol. IV includes a further group together with papers of others of the family. The papers listed in the 1955 schedule are now *NLW MSS 19440-67*, those in vol III are *NLW MSS 20569-72*. See also **Minor Lists 1986** and NLW MSS 23028-35. *Conditional access* (papers of Sir George William Rendel).

Schedules (1955), 140pp.; (1971, vol. II), 379pp.; (1971, vol. III), [i] + 127pp.; (1974, vol. II 'Appendix'), [i] + 15pp.; (1986 + suppls, vol. IV), iv + 45pp. *AR 1959-60*, p.64; *1966-67*, pp.58-9; *1969-70*, p.43; *1980-81*, p.80; *1981-82*, p.86; *1982-83*, p.53; *1984-85*, p.44; *1985-86*, p.62; *1987-88*, p.63; *1988-89*, p.68; @. See *Personal Papers of Lord Rendel*, ed. F.E. Hamer (London, 1931).

RENT TRIBUNAL RECORDS
Records (presented by the Welsh Office) relating to Rent Tribunals, 1946-60. They arise from the housing and rent Acts of 1946, 1949 and 1954 and comprise cases for all Welsh Tribunals other than Cardiff and East Glamorgan (which are in Glamorgan R O).

Summary list [1968], 5pp. *AR 1967-68*, p.35.

REYNE
Deeds (purchased from Lt.-Col. Reyne) mainly relating to co. Brecon, 1641-1925, mostly 18th cent.

AR 1974-75, p.47.

RHEOLA
Family and estate records of Edwards-Vaughan of Rheola, Resolven, co. Glamorgan, 1483-1929, mainly late 18th-20th cent., including industrial records.

AR 1964-65, pp.24-5

RHIWLAS
Estate and family records of Price of Rhiwlas, co. Merioneth, 1609-1921. Other records in Gwynedd R O (Dolgellau).

AR 1948-49, pp.54-5. Working list available.

OWEN RHOSCOMYL
Papers of Robert Scourfield Mills ('Arthur Owen Vaughan', 'Owen Rhoscomyl', 1863-1919) adventurer and author. See also NLW MS 22008.

AR 1959-60, p.38; *1968-69*, p.34; *1969-70*, p.38.

RHUAL
Estate and family records of Edwards, Griffith and Philips of Rhual, Mold, co. Flint, 1331-19th cent. *Transferred to Clwyd R O (Hawarden).*

Schedule (1949), 132pp. *AR 1948-49*, pp.46-7.

RHYDOLDOG
Deeds relating mainly to co. Radnor, notably to the Oliver family of Rhydoldog, parish of Llansanffraid Cwmteuddwr, 1598-1904.

AR 1969-70, p.54. Working list available.

SIR JOHN RHŶS
Papers of Sir John Rhŷs (1840-1915), Celtic scholar and Principal of Jesus College, Oxford.

AR 1978-79, pp.77-8. Working list available.

RICHARD FAMILY
Letters to Henry Richard (1812-88), 'The Apostle of Peace', and to others of his family, 1808-1904 (*NLW MSS 14020-4*). See also NLW MSS 5503-11 and 10196-208.

Schedule (1937), 26pp.

BRINLEY RICHARDS
Papers of Brinley Richards (1904-81), solicitor and author, many relating to administration of the National Eisteddfod, Congregationalism and local government in the Maesteg area; include groups of papers of William Evans ('Wil Ifan', 1882-1968), Lewis Davies, Y Cymer (1863-1951) and Edgar Phillips ('Trefin', 1889-1962).

Schedule (Welsh) (1968), iii + 61pp. *AR 1981-82*, p.58.

CERI RICHARDS
Papers of Ceri Richards (1903-71), artist. (*NLW MSS 23005-14*).

AR 1991-92, p.61.

DAVID RICHARDS
Letters and journals of David Richards, mining agent, of Harlech, co. Merioneth, written during a visit to Patagonia to search for gold, 1891-94 (*NLW MSS 21197-200*).

Schedule (1974), 40pp. *AR 1973-74*, p.46.

GWYNFRYN RICHARDS

Papers of Gwynfryn Richards (1902-92), dean of Bangor, including a few earlier documents relating to the diocese.

Schedule [1973 + suppl.], 6pp. *AR 1973-74*, pp.45-6; *1975-76*, pp.80-1; *1976-77*, p.45; *1983-84*, p.45.

ROBERT RICHARDS

Papers of Robert Richards (1884-1954), Labour MP for Wrexham, 1922-54, and historian.

Schedule [after 1954], 19pp.

MORGAN RICHARDSON

Records from the office of Morgan & Richardson, later Morgan Richardson, solicitors, Cardigan, 16th-20th cent., with family papers of Thomas Morgan, solicitor, 19th cent. Estates include those of Phillips of Haverfordwest, Lort and Lort-Phillips of Lawrenny, co. Pembroke; Lewes, Parry and Tyler of Gernos, co. Cardigan; Saunders Davies of Pentre, co. Pembroke; Thomas and Beynon of Llanfair and Dôl-llan and Beynon of Llaethliw, cos Cardigan and Carmarthen; Vaughan and Millingchamp of Plas Llangoedmor, co. Cardigan; Pigeonsford and Brynog, co. Cardigan; Posty, co. Pembroke. See also NLW MSS 12533-57.

Schedule (1965), ii + 555pp. in two vols. Also **Maps**. *AR 1935-36*, p.51; *1939-40*, pp.28, 35; *1943-44*, p.31; *1956-57*, p.46; *1959-60*, pp.64-5; *1960-61*, p.59.

ROBERTS & EVANS

Records from the office of Roberts & Evans, solicitors, Aberystwyth, mostly 18th-20th cent. They include records of many north Cardiganshire estates, notably Aber-mad, Allt-lwyd, Crosswood, Ffosrhydgaled, Fronfraith, Glan-paith, Llidiardau, Mabws, Nanteos and Pen-glais; of the Gilbertson family, 18th-20th cent.; stray Cardiganshire Quarter Sessions records, 1790-19th cent.; Cardiganshire Road Board records, 19th cent.; office records, 19th-20th cent.

AR 1988-89, p.67. Working list available.

D. FRANCIS ROBERTS

Papers of David Francis Roberts (1882-1945), Calvinistic Methodist minister and theologian.

AR 1945-46, p.27; @.

EVAN ROBERTS

Papers of Evan Roberts, Llandderfel (1877-1958), local historian, friend of John Cowper Powys.

Schedule (Welsh) (1987), 72pp.

G. V. ROBERTS

Literary manuscripts, autographs and documents collected by G.V. Roberts (*NLW MSS 18428-34*).

Schedule (1963), 16pp. *AR 1962-63*, p.39.

HUGH ROBERTS

Manuscripts of Hugh Roberts ('Yr Hen Idris', 1832-1907) of Abergynolwyn, co. Merioneth, antiquary.

Papurau Hugh Roberts ('Yr Hen Idris'), Abergynolwyn (1993), i + 2pp.

J. BRYN ROBERTS

Papers of John Bryn Roberts (1848-1931), Liberal MP for South Caernarfonshire, 1885-1906, and judge.

Schedule (1975), [ii] + 242pp. *AR 1931-32*, p.51.

KATE ROBERTS

Papers of Kate Roberts (1891-1985), writer. They include papers of Morris T. Williams (1900-46), her husband, and Edward Prosser Rhys (1901-45), poet and editor, with associated papers relating to Gwasg Aberystwyth, 1942-4, and Gwasg Gee, 1934-52, publishers. See also **Gee**. Further Morris T. Williams papers in Clwyd R O (Ruthin).

Papurau Kate Roberts (1990-91), 471pp. in three vols (vol. I, correspondence, vol. II, manuscripts, vol. III, Morris T. Williams and Prosser Rhys). *AR 1972-73*, p.73; *1977-78*, p.75; *1978-79*, p.83; *1984-85*, p.33; *1985-86*, p.58.

RICHARD ROBERTS & SONS

Records of Messrs Thomas & Roberts, later Richard Roberts & Sons, timber merchants, Aberystwyth, 1855-1916.

AR 1947-48, p.22.

SILYN ROBERTS

Papers of Robert Silyn Roberts (1871-1930), poet and worker for social reform, and of his wife, Mary Silyn Roberts. Other papers in UW, Bangor.

Schedule [1965 + suppl.], 7pp. *AR 1965-66*, p.59; *1967-68*, p.52.

HENRY ROBERTSON

Records of Henry Robertson of Palé, Llandderfel, co. Merioneth (1816-1888), railway engineer. See also **Minor Lists 1993** *s.n.* Palé. Other records in Clwyd R O (Ruthin) *s.n.* Llantysilio Hall and Gwynedd R O (Dolgellau).

AR 1948-49, p.55. Also **Maps**.

ROBYNS OWEN & SON

Deeds (donated by Messrs Robyns Owen & Son) relating to Hendre Bach, parish of Aberdaron, co. Caernarfon, 1671-1863.

Schedule (1973), 5pp.

RODDICK

Records (deposited by Mrs J. Roddick) of the Phillips family of Kilbarth, parish of Rudbaxton, co. Pembroke, 1650-1892, and papers of John William Phillips, senior (1824-88) and junior (1864-1934), solicitors, Haverfordwest. Include antiquarian papers of Pembrokeshire interest, 19th-20th cent., and other records relating to the Haverfordwest area, 1575-1913.

AR 1945-46, pp.31-2.

ROGERS

Records of the families of Rogers of Gelli and Edwards of Abermeurig, co. Cardigan, 1552-1924.

AR 1970-71, p.72.

EMLYN ROGERS

Papers of Emlyn Rogers (1895-1954), historian of Trade Unionism in the coal mining industry of north Wales.

AR 1968-69, p.32. Working list available.

RÛG

Estate records of the Vaughan family of Rûg (Rhug), mainly in cos Merioneth and Denbigh, 1329-1862. *Transferred to Gwynedd R O.*

Schedules (1934), [i] + 264pp.; 7pp.; (1947), 11pp. *AR 1933-34*, p.48; *1935-36*, p.55; *1946-47*, p.46.

RUTHIN

Records of the lordship of Ruthin and associated estates, mainly in co. Denbigh, 14th cent.-1854, mainly relating to the period of ownership by the

Myddelton family of Chirk Castle, 16th-19th cent.; include court records of the lordship, 1718-1850, with a few earlier (the main group of early records is in the PRO) and correspondence, 17th cent.-1848. For other Ruthin records, including those of the later ownership by the West and Cornwallis-West family see **Longueville**. Other records in Clwyd R O (Ruthin).

Schedule (1964), 565pp. *AR 1920 (May)*, p.5; *1920 (Oct.)*, p.6; *1922 (Oct.)*, pp.9-10; *1928-29*, p.34.

ST PIERRE
Deeds relating to the family of Lewis of St Pierre, co. Monmouth, 14th-18th cent.; manorial records, cos Monmouth and Gloucester, 16th-17th cent. Other records in Gwent R O.

Schedule [pre-1934], 26pp. *AR 1931-32*, p.48.

D. S. SAVOURS
Deeds (donated by D.S. Savours) relating to Llancarfan and elsewhere in co. Glamorgan, 1604-1705.

Schedule [1934], 3pp. *AR 1934-35*, p.38.

R. U. SAYCE
Papers of Roderick Urwick Sayce (1890-1970), anthropologist. See also **Powysland Club**.

Papers of R. U. Sayce (1994), i + 8pp.

SEALYHAM
Deeds relating to the family of Tucker of Sealyham, co. Pembroke, 1746-1843.

Schedule [1938], 6pp. *AR 1938-39*, p.30.

NASSAU SENIOR
Papers of Nassau William Senior (1790-1864), economist, including his journals, 1848-63.

Nassau Senior Papers (1979), xxiii + 566pp. in two vols. *AR 1941-42*, p.28; *1948-49*, pp.33-4. *NLWJ*, 21 (1979-80), pp.76-84. See also *AR 1976-77*, p.44.

SEVERN ROAD
Records of Severn Road Welsh Congregational Church, Canton, Cardiff, 1868-1980.

Schedule (Welsh) (1981), 7pp. *AR 1980-81*, p.81.

GLYN SIMON
Papers of William Glyn Hughes Simon (1903-72), bishop of Llandaff and archbishop of Wales.

AR 1971-72, p.52.

SINNETT
Deeds (donated by J.L.M. Sinnett) relating to the parishes of Llanerfyl and Llangadfan, co. Montgomery, and Aberystwyth, co. Cardigan, 1719-1812 (*NLW Deeds 283-311*).

Schedule (1947), 9pp. *AR 1946-47*, p.31.

SLEBECH
Estate and family records of Barlow, Phillips and de Rutzen of Slebech, co. Pembroke, 13th-20th cent.; include records of the Knights Hospitallers of the Commandery of Slebech, 14th cent.; ministers' accounts, 1355-1485; manorial records 16th-19th cent. The estate was bought by Nathaniel Phillips in 1792; there are records of the Phillips' Jamaican sugar plantations, 1760-1812. Other records in Dyfed R O (Haverfordwest).

Schedule (1948), 322pp. *AR 1938-39*, p.45. *NLWJ*, 5 (1947-8), pp.179-98.

SMALLWOOD
Papers of R.H. Gough Smallwood of Wrexham (1864-1943), local historian and authority on shorthand, together with deeds and documents collected by him, mainly relating to the Wrexham area and mainly 17th-19th cent.

Schedule (1978), [v] + 300pp. *AR 1944-45*, p.28.

GILBERT SMITH
Deeds and documents (purchased from Gilbert Smith) relating to the parish of St Asaph, co. Flint, 1365-1677.

Schedule [1936], 25pp. *AR 1936-37*, p.32.

J. F. SMITH
Deeds and documents (donated by J.F. Smith) relating to properties in co. Flint, 1657-1873 (*NLW Deeds 495-533*).

Schedule [1951], 8pp.

SNELL
Manuscripts of the work of Welsh composers of late 19th and early 20th cent., mostly autograph, acquired from the office of Snell & Sons, Swansea,

music publishers; include many works by John Thomas ('Pencerdd Gwalia', 1826-1913), Joseph Parry (1841-1903) and David Jenkins (1848-1915). (*NLW MSS 19761-896*). See also **Minor Lists 1994**.

Schedule (1967), 16pp. *AR 1966-67*, pp.44-5. For business records of Snell & Sons see *AR 1966-67*, pp.45, 54, not catalogued (1994).

SOLVA
Papers of Hugh Jones of Solva ('Cromwel o Went', 1800-1872), Congregational minister (*NLW 10275-94*).

Schedule [pre-1934], 23pp. *AR 1931-32*, p.35; *1932-33*, p.27.

SOTHEBY
Manuscripts, deeds and documents (deposited by A.F. Sotheby) relating to the Wynne family of Bodewryd (part of the same archive as **Bodewryd**). Includes literary manuscripts, 16th-18th cent., deeds and documents, 1317-1761, some relating to the families of Lewis of Chwaen and Owen of Penrhos Bradwen, Anglesey.

Schedule [pre-1934], 144pp. *AR 1930-31*, pp.48-9.

SOUTH WALES WOMEN'S TEMPERANCE UNION
Records of the South Wales Women's Temperance Union, 1901-66.

Schedule (1994), i + 5pp. *AR 1969-70*, p.30.

SPENCE-COLBY see COLBY

C. THOMAS-STANFORD
Deeds and documents (donated by C. Thomas-Stanford) relating to the rectory of Llanegryn and to other properties in cos Merioneth and Montgomery, 1538-1826.

Schedule [1927], 6pp. *AR 1926-27*, p.41.

SWEENEY HALL
Estate and family records of Baker and Browne of Sweeney Hall, Oswestry, Leighton of Loton Park, co. Salop, Parker of Whitehouse, co. Worcester, and Charlton of Ludford, co. Hereford, 1563-1876. Include the papers of Edward Lloyd of Llanforda, *c.* 1660-81, and letter-books of Sir Henry Watkin Williams-Wynn (1783-1856), British Ambassador to Denmark, 1831-51. Other records in Shropshire R O.

Schedule [pre-1934 + suppl.], 65pp. *AR 1932-33*, pp.38-9; *1949-50*, p.41. *NLWJ,*

6 (1949-50), pp.299-300. See also *AR 1934-35*, p.45, additional deeds not yet catalogued (1994). See also *AR 1958-59*, p.32 (*NLW MSS 18248-56*) and *1969-70*, p.42.

A. J. SYLVESTER
Papers of Albert James Sylvester (1889-1989), principal private secretary to Lloyd George, 1923-45, including his diaries.

AR 1990-91, p.63. Working list available.

SZLUMPER
Papers collected by Sir James Weeks Szlumper (1834-1926), engineer, relating to railways in Glamorgan and the south of England, 1878-1901. (*NLW MSS 9241-7*).

Schedule [after 1930], 16pp. *AR 1930-31*, pp.45-6.

TALBOT OF HENSOL
Records of the Jenkins and Talbot families of Hensol, co. Glamorgan, relating to estates mainly in cos Glamorgan and Monmouth, 1429-1789. Other records in Glamorgan R O (Cardiff).

Schedule (1957), 272pp. *AR 1939-40*, p.32.

TANYBWLCH MS
A volume of Welsh poetry, from Plas Tan-y-bwlch, mostly transcribed in the early 18th cent. (*Minor Deposit 1206B*).

Catalogue of the contents [1932], 42pp. *AR 1961-62*, pp.51-2.

TANYBWLCH (LLANLLECHID)
Deeds and documents relating mainly to the Tan-y-bwlch estate in the parishes of Llanllechid and Bethesda, co. Caernarfon, 1650-1922.

Schedules [1933], 17pp.; (1986), i + 7pp. *AR 1932-33*, p.31; *1981-82*, p.53.

GLEN A. TAYLOR
Deeds (donated by Glen A. Taylor) relating to cos Glamorgan and Monmouth, notably to the families of Morgan of Pencreeg, co. Monmouth, and Mackworth of Neath, 1528-1833.

Schedules [1933], 3 + 4pp.; [1934], 8pp. *AR 1931-32*, p.38; *1932-33*, p.44; @. See also *AR 1936-37*, p.30.

HENRY TAYLOR DEEDS
Deeds collected by Henry Taylor (1845-1927), Flintshire antiquary. See NLW MSS 6267-331 for associated manuscripts. Other deeds and papers in Clwyd R O (Hawarden).

Uncatalogued (1994).

LLEWELLIN-TAYLOUR
Deeds and documents collected by A.R. Llewellin-Taylor, mostly relating to England, 1237-1898.

Schedule (1963), 43pp. *AR 1962-63*, pp.30-2. See also *AR 1964-65*, pp.33-5, another varied group of this collection (uncatalogued 1994).

TEDDINGTON
Deeds (donated by Mrs M. Davies of Teddington) relating to cos Denbigh and Salop, 1564-1865, in particular to Tregeiriog, parish of Llangadwaladr, co. Denbigh.

Schedule [1929], 19pp. *AR 1929-30*, p.39; *1936-37*, p.30.

W. COOMBE TENNANT
Papers of Winifred Coombe Tennant ('Mam o Nedd', d. 1956), 1917-55, mainly relating to 'Gorsedd y Beirdd' and the National Eisteddfod.

Schedule (1958), 18pp. *AR 1957-58*, p.20; *1958-59*, p.23.

THELWALL
Papers (donated by Col. G.E.H. Thelwall) relating to the Williams family of Treffos, Anglesey, 1745-1900.

AR 1980-81, p.55.

THOMAS (SAUNDERSFOOT)
Deeds (deposited by Miss N. Thomas, Saundersfoot) relating to properties in cos. Pembroke, Carmarthen and Cardigan, 1553-1877.

Schedule (1938), 28pp. Also **Maps**. *AR 1937-38*, p.72.

SIR BEN BOWEN THOMAS
Papers of Sir Ben Bowen Thomas (1899-1977), educationalist and public servant.

Sir Ben Bowen Thomas Papers (1994), i + 15pp. *AR 1977-78*, pp.39-40.

C. TAWELFRYN THOMAS
Papers of C. Tawelfryn Thomas (1840-1939), including a collection of the poetry of William Cosslett ('Gwilym Eilian', 1831-1904) (*NLW MSS 9712-15*).

Schedule [1935], 41pp. *AR 1934-35*, p.38.

D. AFAN THOMAS
Music manuscripts and papers of David John 'Afan' Thomas (1881-1928), composer.

Schedule (1980), iii + 82pp. *AR 1949-50*, p.26; *1952-53*, p.51; *1961-62*, p.36; *1965-66*, p.41; *1972-73*, p.67.

SIR D. LLEUFER THOMAS
Papers of Sir Daniel Lleufer Thomas (1863-1940), public servant. See also NLW MSS 3601-40.

AR 1942-43, p.16; *1952-53*, pp.29-31.

D. VAUGHAN THOMAS
Music manuscripts and papers of David Vaughan Thomas (1873-1934), composer.

Schedule (1970 + suppls), 12pp. *AR 1970-71*, p.73; *1982-83*, p.44; @.

DAVID THOMAS
Papers of David Thomas (1866-1940), inspector of schools and folklorist; include a valuable collection of folk-lore made by Cardiganshire schools, 1921-6.

Schedule (1980), v + 154pp.

DAVID THOMAS (BANGOR)
Papers of David Thomas, Bangor (1880-1967), Labour party activist and writer, 1907-29. Other papers at UW, Bangor.

Schedule [after 1968], 4pp. *AR 1968-69*, p.33.

EDWARD AND HELEN THOMAS
Diaries and manuscripts of Edward Thomas (1878-1917), poet, and correspondence with Helen Thomas (1877-1967). (*NLW MSS 22900-21, 23077*). Further correspondence in UW, Cardiff (copies available in NLW).

Edward and Helen Thomas manuscripts (1993), 23pp. *AR 1991-92*, pp.58, 60; *1992-93*, p.56.

LORD ELIS-THOMAS
Political papers of Dafydd Elis Thomas, later Lord Elis-Thomas of Nant Conwy (1946-), MP, 1974-92, president of Plaid Cymru, 1984-91. *Conditional access.*

AR 1992-93, p.56.

GWYN THOMAS
Papers of Gwyn Thomas (1913-81), novelist.

Gwyn Thomas Manuscripts and Papers [1988], iv + 82pp. *AR 1981-82*, p.63.

J. LUTHER THOMAS
Papers (donated by J. Luther Thomas) of John Roberts (d. 1827) and Samuel Roberts (1800-85) of Llanbryn-mair. Other papers of John and Samuel Roberts, from the same source, are NLW MSS 3265-8, 9511-98, 11891-3 and 14035-94. See **'S.R.' and 'J.R.'**.

AR 1942-43, p.25.

JOHN THOMAS
Music manuscripts of John Thomas ('Pencerdd Gwalia', 1826-1913), harpist and composer (*NLW MSS 19118-47*).

Schedule (1950 + suppl.), 21pp. *AR 1949-50*, p.34; *1965-66*, p.46.

JOHN THOMAS, MACHYNLLETH
Records of John Thomas, Machynlleth, grocer, draper and chemist, 1807-92, and other records of local interest.

AR 1957-58, pp.26-7.

OWEN THOMAS
Papers of Owen Thomas (1812-92), Calvinistic Methodist minister and author. See also NLW MSS 624-40.

AR 1963-64, pp.32-3.

WILLIAM THOMAS
Papers, mainly literary, of William Thomas ('Glanffrwd', 1843-90), clergyman and author (*NLW MSS 16698-703*).

Schedule (1955), 11pp. *AR 1955-56*, p.43.

THOMAS-STANFORD see STANFORD

THORNE
Deeds (deposited by B.L. Thorne) relating to north Wales, 1298-1837, notably to the manor of Gogarth, co. Caernarfon.

Schedule (1957), 101pp.

THOROWGOOD, TABOR & HARDCASTLE
Deeds (deposited by Messrs Thorowgood, Tabor & Hardcastle) relating to north Wales, 1455-1895, notably to the family of Poole of Cae Nest, co. Merioneth, with lands in cos Merioneth and Anglesey. Other papers in Gwynedd R O (Caernarfon).

Schedule [1934], 113pp. Also **Maps**. *AR 1933-34*, p.45.

TICEHURST, WYATT & CO.
Records from the office of Messrs Ticehurst, Wyatt & Co., Cheltenham, solicitors, mostly 19th cent., relating in part to the family of Lloyd-Williams of Gwernant, co. Cardigan, including correspondence of John Lloyd Williams, 1818-38.

AR 1967-68, p.53.

TILLEY
Deeds and documents (donated by Albert Tilley) relating to the manor of Llanfihangel Tal-y-llyn and other properties in co. Brecon, 1815-1931. See also **Albert Tilley**.

Schedule (1956), 9pp. *AR 1955-56*, p.43.

ALBERT TILLEY
Papers of Albert Tilley of Brecon, antiquary, relating to the history of the town and county of Brecon, including earlier antiquarian collections relating to the county.

AR 1964-65, p.54.

VISCOUNT TONYPANDY
Papers of George Thomas, Viscount Tonypandy (1909-   ) MP, 1945-83, Secretary of State for Wales, 1968-70, Speaker of the House of Commons, 1976-83. *Conditional access.*

AR 1985-86, p.57; *1987-88*, p.59; @. Working list available.

TOWYN, EGLWYS GYNULLEIDFAOL BETHESDA
Records of Bethesda Congregational Church, Tywyn, co. Merioneth, 1809-1957 (*Minor Deposits 428-65*).

Schedule (Welsh) [1958], 5pp. *AR 1958-59*, p.66.

TRECEFEL
Diaries of several members of the Jenkins family of Trecefel, Tregaron, 1839-1947. *Conditional access.*

AR 1949-50, p.24; *1960-61*, p.30; *1984-85*, p.35.

TREDEGAR
Records of the family of Morgan of Tredegar and Ruperra, later barons Tredegar, 14th-20th cent., a very large archive. The Tredegar and Ruperra estates lay in co. Monmouth and eastern Glamorgan; there were also estates in the borough of Brecon and co. Brecon (the Therrowe and Palleg estates) and property in co. Hereford and London. Much of the 19th-century growth of Newport and Cardiff is documented. The archive includes deeds, 14th-20th cent.; records of the lordship of Wentloog (Newport) and many Monmouthshire manors, mainly 17th-19th cent., some 14th-16th cent.; records of the manor of Brecon and others in co. Brecon, 17th-19th cent.; records of industrial interests, mainly coal and iron, 18th-20th cent.; records of the Tredegar Wharf Co., from 1807; papers relating to north America, 18th cent., notably to Nova Scotia and Canada, 1730-73. Other records in Gwent R O.

Schedules: *Manuscripts and documents...*, *vol. I* (1950), 171pp.; *Preliminary schedule of the Tredegar Park muniments* [1954-59], 3711pp. in nine vols (lists the contents of boxes 1-143 in detail but without archival order, and in vol. [X] under the heading 'bound volumes' it lists many of the early rentals and manorial court books); *Tredegar Park Muniments, vol. XI* (1986), ii + 114pp. (mainly manorial records); *Tredegar Park Muniments (BRA Group)* (1988), [ii] + 60pp.; *Letters from the Crimea 1854-5* (1950), 85pp. (transcripts of letters from the Crimea from Godfrey Charles Morgan and Frederick Courtenay Morgan, viz Tredegar 992-1024, briefly described in vol. I). A working list of the fine series of 19th and 20th-cent. estate rentals is available. Many of the post-1850 records remain uncatalogued (1994). Also **Maps**. *AR 1949-50*, pp.43-5; *1958-59*, pp.59-65 (these two reports cover the main archive); *1969-70*, p.58; *1970-71*, p.38; *1975-76*, p.47; *1981-82*, p.58; *1982-83*, p.53; *1985-86*, p.63; *1986-87*, p.66 (these covering the BRA group).

TRE-FAES
Records of the Phillips family of Tre-faes Uchaf, parish of Llanilar, co. Cardigan, 1664-1909, relating to properties in co. Cardigan and including documents associated with Augustus Brackenbury ('Y Sais Bach').

Schedule (1969 + suppl.), 23pp. *AR 1947-48*, p.25; *1969-70*, p.58; *1970-71*, p.71; *1971-72*, pp.43-4.

TREFECHAN SAWMILLS
Records of the Trefechan sawmills, latterly of the firm of J. D. Lloyd, Aberystwyth, 1865-1957.

AR 1958-59, p.34. Also **Maps**.

TREFEGLWYS AND LLANGURIG
Records of Trefeglwys School Board, 1871-97, and of Llangurig School Board, 1874-98; and Poor Law records, 1845-96, for the parish of Trefeglwys, co. Montgomery.

Schedule (1981), i + 7pp. *AR 1940-41*, p.17.

TRENEWYDD
Records (deposited by Mrs Johns and Mrs Brown of Trenewydd) of estates of the families of Thomas of Carmarthen, and of Posty and Cilciffeth, co. Pembroke, Gwynne of Cilciffeth and Court, and Mortimer of Trehowel and Penysgwarn, co. Pembroke, 1488-1926. Other records in Dyfed R O (Haverfordwest) *s.n.* Court.

Schedules [1955] and (1973), 146pp. in two vols. *AR 1943-44*, p.30; *1949-50*, p.41; *1951-52*, p.34; *1952-53*, p.50; *1961-62*, p.48; @. *NLWJ*, 9 (1955-6), pp.475-94.

TREWERN
Deeds and documents relating to the estate of Beynon of Trewern, Whitland, and elsewhere in cos Carmarthen and Cardigan, 1695-1897. Other records in Dyfed R O (Carmarthen) *s.n.* Protheroe-Beynon.

Schedule (1948), 69pp. Also **Maps**. *AR 1946-47*, p.29. See also *AR 1954-55*, p.56; *1958-59*, p.38; *1959-60*, p.35.

JOHN TRIPP
Papers of John Tripp (1927-86), poet.

John Tripp Papers (1991), 17pp. *AR 1987-88*, p.62.

TWEEDY
Deeds (donated by A. C. Tweedy) relating mainly to co. Monmouth, 1615-1900.

AR 1935-36, p.40.

TŶ CENEDL
Papers and ephemera collected by 'Tŷ Cenedl', Aberystwyth, relating to the Welsh Republicans, the National Patriotic Front, Cymru Coch, Cofiwn,

the Free Wales Army and other fringe nationalist and republican groups in Wales, 1950s-80s.

Tŷ Cenedl Papers (1994), ii + 30pp. *AR 1988-89*, p.67.

TŶ-GLYN
Records of the Davies family of Tŷ-glyn, co. Cardigan, 18th-20th cent. See also **Minor Lists 1983**.

Schedule [*c.* 1955], 26pp. *AR 1954-55*, p.24.

TŶ-LLWYD
Deeds relating to the Tŷ-Llwyd estate, parishes of Betws Ifan and Blaenporth, co. Cardigan, and other property in cos Cardigan, Carmarthen and Pembroke, 1590-1852. See also **Minor Lists 1987**.

Schedule (1926), 52pp. Also **Maps**. *AR 1925-26*, p.12.

KEMEYS-TYNTE
Estate and family records of Kemeys and Kemeys-Tynte of Keven Mably (Cefn Mabli), co. Monmouth, mainly 18th-19th cent., the correspondence mainly 17th-18th cent. The main Kemeys-Tynte archive is in Glamorgan R O; another group is in Gwent R O.

Kemeys-Tynte Papers (1991), 71pp. (vol. I); (1992), 157pp. (vol. II, correspondence). *AR 1948-49*, p.41.

UNDEB CYMRU FYDD
Archives of Undeb Cymru Fydd ('The New Wales Union'), from foundation to dissolution, 1941-70.

Schedule (Welsh) [*c.* 1946 + suppls], 40pp. Numerous accessions from 1946, references to *AR* not detailed here.

UNITED NATIONS ASSOCIATION
Records of the Welsh National Council of the League of Nations Union and of its successor, the Welsh National Council of the United Nations Association, 1922-56.

AR 1965-66, p.62. Working list available.

UNITED REFORMED CHURCH
A collection of records of the United Reformed Church (Province of Wales) comprising records of English Congregational Unions for several parts of Wales and records of individual Congregational churches, 1868-1973.

Schedule [1981 + suppl.], 9pp. *AR 1980-81*, p.81; @.

URDD GOBAITH CYMRU
Archives of Urdd Gobaith Cymru ('The Welsh League of Youth'), from 1927.

Archifau Urdd Gobaith Cymru (1989), iii + 43pp. Several accessions since 1957, references to *AR* not detailed here.

URDD GOBAITH CYMRU DEEDS
Deeds (donated by Urdd Gobaith Cymru) relating mostly to co. Merioneth, 1679-1900.

Schedule (1974 + suppl.), 8pp. AR 1973-74, p.48.

VALE OF NEATH BREWERY
Records of the Vale of Neath Brewery, Neath, 1844-1913.

Schedule [1936], 3pp. *AR 1935-36*, p.47.

LLOYD VERNEY
Deeds relating to the family of Lloyd, Youde and Verney of Clochfaen, Llangurig, co. Montgomery, of Lloyd of Plas Madog, Ruabon, and Youde of Ruthin, co. Denbigh, 15th-19th cent.

Schedule [pre-1928], 18pp.

VIVIAN
Records of the family of Vivian, later barons Swansea, of Cornwall and Swansea. Include records of the copper industry in Cornwall and Swansea (the Hafod works), 1792-1934, from 1720 for Cornwall; correspondence, 1807-1934, notably that of John Hussey Vivian (1785-1855), MP for Swansea, 1832-55, and Henry Hussey Vivian, 1st baron Swansea (1821-94), MP for Swansea, 1855-93. A major source for the 19th-cent. history of Swansea.

Schedule (1982), ix + 615pp. in three vols. *AR 1965-66*, pp.59-61.

VOELAS AND CEFNAMWLCH
Records of the family of Wynne and Wynne Finch and the estates of Voelas, co. Denbigh, and Cefnamwlch, co. Caernarfon, mainly 19th-20th cent. Rentals, 1808-1949. The uncommonly full estate correspondence, 1866-1948, is detailed in the schedule. Other records in Gwynedd R O (Caernarfon). See also **BRA 1956**.

Schedule (1983), v + 426pp. in two vols. *AR 1956-57*, pp.47-50; *1960-61*, p.54; *1970-71*, p.64. Some of the records remain uncatalogued (1994).

VORLEY
Deeds (purchased from H.H.G. Vorley) relating to the parishes of Llanbadarn Fawr, 1548-97, and Llangynfelyn, 1841-8, co. Cardigan.

Schedule [1967], 5pp. *AR 1967-68*, p.37.

WADDINGHAM
Papers (from the Estate of T.J. Waddingham) relating to the Hafod estate, co. Cardigan, 1794-1904, including records relating to lead-mining. (*Minor Deposits 574-85*).

Schedule [1939], 7pp. *AR 1938-39*, p.45.

W. RHYS WATKIN
Papers of W. Rhys Watkin, Llanelli (1875-1947), Baptist minister, including manuscripts, largely of Baptist interest, collected by him. (Some now *NLW MSS 17242-302*.)

Schedule [after 1948], 70pp. (only pp.1-5 relate to his papers). *AR 1948-49*, pp.36-7. See also *AR 1967-68*, p.35.

M. P. WATKINS
Records (donated or deposited by M.P.Watkins) from the office of Vizard & Son, Monmouth, solicitors (successors of Powles & Tyler), including office records, 18th-19th cent.; deeds, mainly co. Monmouth, 16th-19th cent.; manorial records, co. Monmouth, 16th-18th cent.; Monmouthshire Turnpike Trust records, 1755-1879; records relating to the town of Monmouth, 18th-19th cent. See also **Sir L. Twiston Davies**. Other records in Gwent R O.

AR 1942-3, p.26; *1949-50*, pp.48-9; *1951-52*, p.35; *1965-66*, p.61.

VERNON WATKINS
Papers of Vernon Watkins (1906-67), poet (*NLW MSS 20787, 21263-6, 22440-89, 22552-3, 22728-9, 22841*). Other papers are in the British Library and Hull University Library.

Vernon Watkins MSS (1979), i + 15pp.; *Vernon Watkins MSS: Group II* (1988 + suppls), 50pp. *AR 1970-71*, p.74; *1974-75*, p.47; *1982-83*, p.47; *1983-84*, p.52; *1985-86*, p.60.

WATKINS & DAVID
Deeds and documents from the office of Messrs Watkins & David, Newtown, solicitors, relating mostly to co. Montgomery, 1615-1910.

Preliminary schedule (1940), 8pp. *AR 1940-41*, p.29. See also *AR 1941-42*, p.28.

L. WATTERS
Deeds and documents (donated by L. Watters) relating to Amlwch, co. Anglesey, 1784-1920.

Schedule [1965], 7pp. *AR 1964-65*, p.40.

HARRI WEBB
Papers of Harri Webb (1920-   ), poet and nationalist. *Conditional access.*

AR 1989-90, p.65.

WELSH AGRICULTURAL ORGANISATION SOCIETY
Archives of the Welsh Agricultural Organisation Society, a co-operative society, from its foundation in 1922. Many of the pre-1945 records were destroyed. Records of local societies have been distributed to county record offices. *Conditional access.*

W.A.O.S. Archives (1985), iv + 16pp. *AR 1984-85*, p.38.

WELSH ARMY CORPS
Records of the Welsh Army Corps, 1914-25. Include correspondence with suppliers of clothing and equipment, 1914-16; applications for commissions, 1914-16; and general administrative records, 1914-25. Also include records relating to Local Employment Exchanges in Wales, 1914-22. These records were received with the personal papers of Owen William Owen (1863-1930), secretary of the Welsh Army Corps Committee.

Schedule (1993), iv + 128pp.

WELSH ARTS COUNCIL
Manuscripts of Welsh writers in English collected by the Welsh Arts Council in 1968-70 (*NLW MSS 20770-809*).

Welsh Arts Council Manuscripts [1974], 16pp. *AR 1967-68*, p.53; *1968-69*, p.53; *1969-70*, p.60; *1970-71*, p.74; *1971-72*, p.55.

WELSH ARTS COUNCIL ARCHIVES
Archives of the Welsh Arts Council, established in 1967, mostly from 1968, but including some earlier files relating to work of the Welsh Committee of the Arts Council of Great Britain. *Conditional access.*

Welsh Arts Council Archives (1984 + suppl.), 15pp. *AR 1984-85*, p.44; *1987-88*, p.63; *1990-91*, p.64. @.

WELSH ARTS COUNCIL: AUTOBIOGRAPHICAL WRITING COMPETITION

Writing submitted in the Welsh Arts Council's competition in 1987-88 for autobiographical writing by Welsh women or women living in Wales.

WAC: Autobiographical Writing Competition 1987-88 (1989), 35pp. *AR 1988-89*, p.63.

WELSH FOLK MUSEUM DEEDS

Deeds relating to several Welsh counties, 1496-1667, deposited by the Welsh Folk Museum.

Schedule [1967], 7pp. *AR 1966-67*, p.60.

WELSH HOUSING AND DEVELOPMENT ASSOCIATION

Archives of the Welsh Housing and Development Association, 1916-30, and its precursor, the South Wales Garden Cities and Town Planning Association, 1912-16.

AR 1938-39, p.33.

WELSH LAND SETTLEMENT SOCIETY

Deeds relating to the Boverton estate, mostly in co. Glamorgan, 1714-1928, deposited by the Welsh Land Settlement Society. *Transferred to Glamorgan R O (Cardiff)*.

Schedule [1936], 28pp. *AR 1935-36*, pp.54-5.

WELSH LIBERAL PARTY

Archives of the Welsh Liberal Party, 1963-85. *Conditional access*.

Welsh Liberal Party Papers (1994), i + 21pp. *AR 1987-88*, p.59.

WELSH NATIONAL OPERA CO.

Archives of the Welsh National Opera Company, preserved from the beginning, 1943-83; also the archives of the Welsh Drama Company, 1971-9.

AR 1986-87, p.66. Working list available.

WELSH PLANT BREEDING STATION

Archives of the Welsh Plant Breeding Station, Gogerddan (now incorporated in the Institute of Grassland and Environmental Research), 1928-79.

Schedule (1994), ii + 172pp. *AR 1992-93*, p.59.

WELSH SCHOOL, ASHFORD
Records of the British Charity School, established in London in 1718, later the Welsh Charity School, moved to Ashford, Middlesex, in 1857, 1718-1921, including records of its property. Include minute books of the Society of Antient Britons, 1823-56, and of the Cymmrodorion, 1828-49.

Schedule [1950], 142pp. *AR 1938-39*, p.44. *NLWJ*, 1 (1939-40), pp.107-8.

WELSH WOOLLEN MANUFACTURERS
Records of the Welsh Woollen Manufacturers Association from foundation in 1954 to dissolution in 1961.

AR 1961-62, p.47.

WELSHPOOL BOROUGH
Records of the borough of Welshpool, 1406-1971, mostly 19th-20th cent.

List of Welshpool Borough Records (1975), 49pp. *AR 1974-75*, p.72.

WENNIAR
Deeds and documents relating mainly to the Wenniar estate, Llansanffraid Glynceiriog, co. Denbigh, 1557-1825.

Schedule [1934], 7 + 7pp. *AR 1933-34*, pp.30 and 36.

WIGFAIR
Estate and family records of Lloyd of Hafodunos, co. Denbigh, and Wigfair, co. Flint, 1229-1898, mostly 16th - 18th cent. The associated manuscripts are NLW MSS 12401-513. Other records in Clwyd R O (Hawarden).

Schedule (1973), 1055pp. in three vols (the pagination is erratic, omitting pp.509, 538-57 and 737-936). *AR 1925-26*, pp.21-3; *1926-27*, pp.46-7.

DAFYDD WIGLEY
Papers of Dafydd Wigley (1943-), MP for Caernarfon from 1974, president of Plaid Cymru, 1981-4, and from 1991. *Conditional access.*

AR 1987-88, p.63. Working list available.

WILLANS
Deeds (deposited by J.B. Willans) relating to the estates of Herbert of Dolforgan, and Owen of Llynlleoedd, Machynlleth, co. Montgomery, 1590-1898; also manorial records of the lordship of Powis, 1579-1745. See also **Powis** and **Minor Lists 1987**.

Schedule (1987), iv + 143pp., superseding two earlier schedules of 100pp. and 37pp. *AR 1920-21*, p.12; *1932-33*, p.45.

A. J. WILLIAMS
Papers of Arthur John Williams (1830-1911), Liberal MP for Glamorgan, 1885-95, and founder of the National Liberal Club.

A.J. Williams Papers (1989), iv + 79pp. *AR 1986-87*, p.64.

D. GETHIN WILLIAMS
Deeds (donated by D. Gethin Williams) relating to cos Carmarthen and Glamorgan, 1687-1889.

Schedule (1956), 7pp. *AR 1955-56*, p.43.

D. J. WILLIAMS (ABERGWAUN)
Papers of David John Williams, Abergwaun (1885-1970), writer, including records of his ancestors in co. Carmarthen, 1793-1882.

Schedule [after 1970], 8pp. (family records only). A working list of D.J. Williams's own papers is available. *AR 1970-71*, pp.36-7.

D. J. WILLIAMS (BETHESDA)
Manuscripts and papers of David James Williams (1870-1951), headmaster of Bethesda County School, including material relating to the history of Bala-Bangor College and correspondence, 1891-1916. See also NLW MSS 15508-9.

Rhestr o Bapurau D.J. Williams (1870-1951) (1979), i + 81pp.

D. J. WILLIAMS (LLANBEDR)
Papers of David John Williams of Llanbedr (1886-1950), local historian and author of children's books.

Schedule [1950 + suppls], 13pp. *AR 1950-51*, pp.29-30; @.

D. PRYSE WILLIAMS
Papers of David Pryse Williams ('Brythonydd', 1878-1952), Baptist minister and local historian, with papers of others collected by him. Contain material on the history of the lower Teifi valley and the Rhondda. Include the papers of Benjamin Williams ('Gwynionydd', 1821-91), author, grandfather of D. Pryse Williams, and the papers of several poets and ministers, mostly Baptist, among them David Jones ('Defynnog', d. 1928), Benjamin Thomas ('Myfyr Emlyn', 1836-93) and Thomas Cynfelyn Benjamin ('Cynfelyn', d. 1925) (*NLW MSS 15622-963, 15985-16039*).

Schedule (1955), [i] + 99pp. *AR 1953-54*, pp.33-4; *1954-55*, pp.36-9.

185

D. R. I. WILLIAMS
Deeds (purchased from or deposited by D.R.I. Williams) relating to the parish of Llandeglau, and to other property in co. Radnor, 1585-1885. *Partly withdrawn.*

Schedule [1957], 15pp. *AR 1956-57*, pp.35 and 46.

DAVID WILLIAMS
Papers of David Williams (1900-78), historian.

AR 1980-81, p.58.

E. WILLIAMS (HOVE)
Deeds (purchased from E. Williams, Hove) relating to all Welsh counties, 1437-1823.

Schedule [1926 and earlier], 91pp. (continuous pagination of several short schedules).

ELIOT CRAWSHAY-WILLIAMS
Papers of Eliot Crawshay-Williams (1879-1962), MP and author; include letters from Morfydd Llwyn Owen (1891-1918), composer, 1911-18.

Eliot Crawshay-Williams (1989), iv + 115pp. *AR 1986-87* p.64

EMLYN WILLIAMS
Papers of George Emlyn Williams (1905-87), actor and playwright.

AR 1993-94.

GORONWY WILLIAMS
Deeds (purchased from Goronwy Williams) relating to cos Anglesey, Denbigh and Flint and to Oswestry, 1507-1839.

Schedule (1973), 15pp. *AR 1933-34*, p.36; *1934-35*, p.40.

GRIFFITH JOHN WILLIAMS
Papers of Griffith John Williams (1892-1963), Welsh scholar.

AR 1978-79, pp.40-1.

HARRI WILLIAMS
Deeds and documents (deposited by Harri Williams) relating mainly to the parish of Aberdaron, co. Caernarfon, and to ships, 1757-1841; letters from America, 1863-77.

Schedule [1957], 13pp.

HENRY WILLIAMS

Deeds (donated by the Ven. Henry Williams) relating to Bylchau Peniarth, parish of Llangelynnin, and to Barmouth, co. Merioneth, 1731-1893.

Schedule (1955), 6pp.

HENRY RUMSEY WILLIAMS

Papers deriving from the legal practice of Henry Rumsey Williams (1774-1841), 'the most influential Tory attorney in Caernarfon', including papers relating to the estate of Wynn of Glynllifon and many others, mainly in cos Caernarfon and Anglesey, 18th cent. - 1841 and a few later; also records of his own family, in cos Brecon, Monmouth and Caernarfon, 18th cent. - 1841 and a few later.

Schedule (1984), v + 672pp. in two vols. *AR 1941-42*, p.23.

I. MOSTYN WILLIAMS

Papers (donated by I. Mostyn Williams) of Edward Jones Williams (*c.* 1858-1932) relating to the Welsh settlement in Patagonia in the late 19th and early 20th cent. and to his connection with the Chubut Mercantile Company (*NLW MSS 19715-24*).

Schedule [1967 + suppl.], 13pp. *AR 1966-67*, pp.38-9; *1971-72*, pp.42 and 45.

IEUAN WILLIAMS

Manuscripts collected by and papers of Evan Williams of Rhyd, parish of Llanfrothen, co. Merioneth, relating mainly to local history, 1865-1909 (donated by Ieuan Williams).

Schedule [1958], 4pp. *AR 1958-59*, p.40.

J. JONES-WILLIAMS

Deeds (deposited by J. Jones-Williams) relating mainly to co. Merioneth, 1597-1896.

Schedule [*c.* 1933], 7 + 48pp., the second part superseded by a slightly revised schedule [?1950s], 56pp. *AR 1932-33*, p.45.

J. LLOYD WILLIAMS

Music manuscripts collected by and papers of John Lloyd Williams (1854-1945), professor of botany and foremost collector of Welsh folksongs.

Schedule [1949], 32pp. See also *AR 1986-87*, p.61

J. O. WILLIAMS
Papers of John Owen Williams (1892-1973), author.

AR 1974-75, p.76; *1975-76*, p.82.

JAC L. WILLIAMS
Papers of Jac Lewis Williams (1918-77), educationalist.

AR 1980-81, p.58.

SIR JOHN WILLIAMS
Papers of Sir John Williams (1840-1926), first president of the National Library (see above, pp.5, 6); also deeds and a few letters which formed part of his collection. The deeds, 1324-1896, relate mainly to co. Carmarthen, 16th-19th cent., and include groups centred on the families of Vaughan of Llanelli and Jones of Ystrad; also a group relating to Wynn of Gwydir, co. Denbigh, 1352-1797.

Sir John Williams Deeds and Papers (1980), xv + 304pp.

JOHN WILLIAMS (AB ITHEL)
Papers of John Williams ('Ab Ithel', 1811-62), clergyman and antiquary (*NLW MSS 17163-90*). See also NLW MS 23104.

Schedule (1952), 30pp. *AR 1951-52*, p.25.

JOHN ELLIS WILLIAMS
Papers of John Ellis Williams (1901-75), author and playwright.

AR 1975-76, p.35.

JOHN G. WILLIAMS
Account rolls of the manors of Ewyas Lacy and Ewyas Harold, co. Hereford, 1377-1505, and deeds, mainly co. Monmouth, 1473-1822 (deposited by John G. Williams). *Withdrawn.*

Schedule [1950], 16pp. *AR 1949-50*, p.49.

L. EIRLYS WILLIAMS
Papers of Mrs L. Eirlys Williams relating to work for the Baptist Union of Wales and other Baptist causes, 1924-78. See also **Minor Lists 1989**.

Schedule [1978], 12pp. *AR 1978-79*, p.58.

MARY WILLIAMS
Papers of Mary Williams (1883-1977), French scholar.

Mary Williams Papers (1983), iii + 39pp. *AR 1968-69*, p.35; *1974-75*, p.45; *1977-78*, p.50.

PETER WILLIAMS

Papers of Peter Williams ('Pedr Hir', 1847-1922), Baptist minister and author.

AR 1952-53, p.32; *1963-64*, p.40; *1965-66*, pp.41-2.

R. BRYN WILLIAMS

Papers of Richard Bryn Williams (1902-81), poet and historian of Patagonia. Include a collection of manuscripts relating to the history of the Welsh settlement in Patagonia from 1865. (*NLW MSS 18175-246*). See also NLW MSS 19010-37 and 19356-7.

Schedule (Welsh) [1963], 17pp. *AR 1962-63*, pp.35-6. See also *AR 1965-66*, p.42, *AR 1978-79*, p.58, and *1979-80*, p.64 (corresponding to the NLW MSS given above).

RAYMOND WILLIAMS

Papers of Raymond Williams (1921-88), writer. *Conditional access.*

AR 1991-92, p.58.

RICHARD ELLIS WILLIAMS

Papers of Richard Ellis Williams (1862-1926), Baptist minister in Cwmavon, London and Pembrey.

Schedule (Welsh) (1981), iv + 16pp. *AR 1981-82*, p.61.

SIR T. H. PARRY-WILLIAMS

Papers of Sir Thomas Herbert Parry-Williams (1887-1975), poet and scholar, and Lady Amy Parry-Williams (1910-88).

AR 1987-88, p.57. Working list available.

W. ISAAC WILLIAMS

Deeds and documents (purchased from or donated by W. Isaac Williams) relating to cos Cardigan and Montgomery and to the Hughes family of Gogarth, parish of Tywyn, co. Merioneth, 1517-1910.

Schedule [after 1958], 38pp. *AR 1934-35*, p.40; *1958-59*, p.41; @.

MICHAEL WILSON

Deeds (deposited by Michael Wilson) relating to cos Brecon, Carmarthen, Glamorgan and Monmouth, 1542-1797, and a memorandum book relating to the borough of Brecon, 1679-1768.

Schedule [1972], 11pp. *AR 1972-73*, pp.74-75.

F. C. WINCHESTER (HOVE)
Deeds (purchased from F.C. Winchester, Hove) relating to properties in cos Cardigan and Carmarthen, 1668-1757.

Schedule [1922], 7pp.

CORBETT-WINDER
Estate and family records, 1601-1935, of Lyon, Winder and Corbett-Winder of Vaynor Park, Berriew, co. Montgomery.

Schedules (1971, 1976), 179pp. in two vols; (1980), vii + 165pp. *AR 1962-63*, pp.52-3; *1976-77*, p.66; *1977-78*, p.67.

WREXHAM, CHESTER STREET BAPTIST CHURCH
Records of Chester Street Baptist Church, Wrexham, 1708-1922, and Holt Baptist Church, 1828-1943.

Schedule [1961], 7pp. *AR 1960-61*, p.62.

E. G. WRIGHT
Deeds (purchased from Archdeacon E. G. Wright), mostly relating to cos Anglesey and Merioneth, including the family of Lloyd of Dduallt, Ffestiniog, co. Merioneth, mainly 17th-19th cent. Acquired with **J. E. Griffith**, *q.v.*

E. G. Wright Deeds (1984), [i] + 10pp. *AR 1971-72*, p.60.

S. WRIGHT
Deeds and documents (deposited by Miss S. Wright) relating mostly to co. Radnor, 1587-1897.

AR 1975-76, p.83.

WYNN (OF GWYDIR)
Correspondence and papers of the Wynn family of Gwydir, 1515-1690. These are mostly bound in NLW MSS 407, 463-70 and 9051-69; a few are located elsewhere. See also **Gwydir (B.R.A.), Panton** and **Sir John Williams**.

Calendar of Wynn (of Gwydir) Papers, 1515-1690 (Aberystwyth, 1926), xx + 511pp. The main body of papers came to NLW partly with the Sir John Williams collection in 1909 and partly with the Panton collection, see *AR 1919 (Oct.)*, pp.9-12.

WYNNSTAY
Family and estate records of Wynn and Williams-Wynn of Wynnstay, 12th-20th cent. By marriage and purchase the Wynnstay estate brought

together in the 17th and 18th centuries earlier estates of Williams of Llanforda, Thelwall of Plas-y-ward, Kyffin of Glasgoed, Lloyd of Rhiwgoch and Vaughan of Llwydiarth, Llangedwyn and Glanllyn, and extended into all the counties of north Wales. The archive includes a few medieval manuscripts (most of the famous library was lost in the fire of 1858) and many legal manuscripts of 16th-17th century; a group of early charters of Strata Marcella abbey; correspondence, 1615-1852, including part of that of Sir William Williams (1634-1700); account rolls of Sir Richard Wynn, Treasurer to Queen Henrietta Maria, 1627-49; election papers, 1621-1861. Manorial records include, in co. Montgomery, those of Arwystli Uchgoed and Isgoed, 1609-1895, Cyfeiliog, 1635-1895, Machynlleth (town), 1630-1895, and Talerddig, 1583-1874; and in co. Denbigh, Ruthin, 1487-8, Bromfield and Yale, 1657-1879 and a few earlier, and Holt, 1719-1879 and a few earlier. Further records in Clwyd R O (Ruthin). See also **Percival Bevan, Coedymaen, Longueville, Trevor Owen**.

Wynnstay Manuscripts and Documents [1940], 269pp. (lists the manuscripts, much of the correspondence and the manorial records); *Wynnstay 1945 Deposit* (1978), [ii] + 26pp. (describes the Strata Marcella charters, incorporating J. Conway Davies, 'Strata Marcella Documents', *Montgomeryshire Collections*, 51 (1949-50), pp.164-87, see also 3-22); *The Wynnstay MSS. and Documents deposited in 1952* (1955, a preliminary schedule), 225pp.; *Wynnstay Archives*, vol. I: *Rentals and Accounts* (1980), xv + 216pp.; (supersedes part of the 1955 preliminary schedule). Recataloguing of the remainder of the contents of the 1955 schedule is well advanced. Also **Maps** (schedule). *AR 1933-34*, pp.46-7; *1940-41*, p.29; *1944-45*, pp.32-3; *1951-52*, pp.35-7. *NLWJ*, 2 (1941-2), pp.26-32. On the Montgomeryshire manorial records see *Montgomeryshire Collections*, 48 (1943-4), pp.70-5.

YALE

Papers (deposited by Mrs Yale) relating mainly to the family of Jones-Parry of Madryn, co. Caernarfon, 19th-20th cent., and to Roger Edwards, Mold (1811-86), Calvinistic Methodist minister and author; with a few deeds. Other papers in UW, Bangor, *s.n.* Yale and also Belmont.

Schedule [1934], 14pp. *AR 1933-34*, p.48. See also *AR 1947-48*, p.43; *1948-49*, p.61.

YNYSFOR

Records of the families of Jones of Ynysfor, Llanfrothen, co. Merioneth, 1607-1871, and Roche of Tregunter, Talgarth, co. Brecon, 1746-1896. Other records in Gwynedd R O (Dolgellau).

AR 1948-49, pp.55 and 61; *1949-50*, p.51; @.

YNYSGAIN
Records of the family of Jones and Pughe Jones of Ynysgain, Cricieth, co. Caernarfon, including deeds, mostly relating to the Cricieth area and to co. Merioneth, 1501-1890. The manuscripts in the group are now *NLW MSS 16135-8*.

Schedule [1957], 24pp.

LORD YSTWYTH
Papers of Matthew Lewis Vaughan-Davies, later 1st Baron Ystwyth (1840-1935), MP for Cardiganshire, 1895-1920.

AR 1936-37, p.33.

APPENDIX II

SPECIAL AND SUBJECT LISTS

During the 1930s the Department produced a series of typescript subject guides, together with a series of county lists, listing records county by county. The latter were not maintained, becoming for all practical purposes superseded by indexes, and have been withdrawn from use; some of the former have for the same reason also been withdrawn. Those which have some residual value, some of them updated, are listed below, together with later lists, drawn up for a variety of purposes, varying in quality and degree of comprehensiveness. The lists are typescript except where place of publication is given. The titles given below are mostly shortened from that which appears on the lists; the words 'in the National Library of Wales' are here omitted except when the list is a published one. Reference to many relevant published surveys will be found in Royal Commission on Historical Manuscripts, *Surveys of Historical Manuscripts in the United Kingdom : a Select Bibliography* (London, 1989). Many of these surveys will be found on open shelves in the manuscript reading room.

Agricultural manuscripts (1935), 14pp.

Australian Joint Copying Project [List of materials in NLW] (1983), iii + 39pp.

Manuscripts relating to Brittany (1988), 15pp.

Business archives (1935), [21]pp.

Cornish manuscripts in the National Library of Wales, ed. W.Ll. Davies (Aberystwyth, 1939), 18pp. With additions.

Awduron Cymraeg yr Ugeinfed Ganrif (1985), 38pp.

Manuscripts of Twentieth Century Writers in English (1979), ii + 23pp. (largely superseded by *Location Register to Twentieth Century English Manuscripts and Letters* (1988), see above, p.13).

French manuscripts (1937), 6 + 4pp.

Material relating to German history and Anglo-German relations in manuscript [c. 1972], 31pp. See W. Lenz, *Archivalische Quellen zur deutschen Gesichte seit 1500 in Grossbritannien* (Boppard am Rhein, 1975).

Manuscripts and documents of Indian interest [c.1960], 7pp.

Italian material in manuscript (1971), 21pp. With additions.

Medieval MSS (1985), 58pp. With additions. Lists all Western medieval manuscripts other than the Welsh manuscripts described in *RMWL*.

Music MSS (1934), 551pp.

Music by named composers in MSS before 1800 (1977), ii + 63pp. With additions.

The National Library of Wales: Catalogue of Oriental Manuscripts, Persian, Arabic and Hindustani, ed. H. Ethé (Aberystwyth, 1916), 30pp.

Documents relating to Parliamentary elections (1952), 30pp. With additions. Partly superseded by *Poll books and electoral registers* (1988), see below.

Phillipps MSS (1977), [9]pp. With additions. Manuscripts from the collection of Sir Thomas Phillipps in NLW.

Poll books and electoral registers (1988), 18pp.

Manuscripts and documents relating to railways (1935), 6pp.

Manuscripts relating to Russia [c. 1985], 9pp. See J. M. Hartley, *Guide to Documents and Manuscripts in the United Kingdom relating to Russia and the Soviet Union* (London, 1987).

Manuscript material relating to the Temperance Movement in Wales [c. 1980], 7pp.

Tours in the British Isles (1935), 6pp. With additions. Partly superseded by *Tours in Wales* (1981), see below.

Tours in Wales: a handlist of manuscript journals (1981), 15pp. With additions.

APPENDIX III

MEDIEVAL MANUSCRIPTS

The National Library holds some three hundred medieval manuscripts, about a hundred of them in Welsh, over forty in French (mostly in the Bourdillon collection), nearly forty in English, one in Cornish, one in German, one in Italian, three in Netherlandish (all three Books of Hours), and the remainder in Latin. A full catalogue is in preparation. Meanwhile, the following remarks will offer some guidance. Similar guidance, to the holdings as they were in 1974, excluding small collections, will be found in N.R. Ker, *Medieval Manuscripts in British Libraries* (Oxford, 1969-   ), vol. II, pp. 21-3.

All but seven of the manuscripts in Welsh are described in *RMWL* (see above, p. 4). The exceptions are NLW MS 1, see J.H. Davies, *Catalogue* (above, p. 6), NLW MSS 5266, 5267, 6680 and 7006, see the *Handlist* (above, p. 4), NLW MS 20143, see *AR 1968-69*, p. 36, and Wynnstay MS 36, see below.

A number of manuscripts not in Welsh are included in *RMWL*, viz
Peniarth 28. Welsh law in Latin. s.xiii.
Peniarth 42. G. Monemutensis, Historia Regum Britanniae. s.xiii.
Peniarth 43. G. Monemutensis, Historia Regum Britanniae. s.xiv.
Peniarth 105. Ordinale de vita S. Mereadoci, a play in Cornish. 1504.
Peniarth 119 (pp. 504-735). Epistolae Roberti Joseph Eveshamiae monachi. 1527-32.
Peniarth 162i. Constitutiones P. Quivil. From Honiton. s.xv.
Llanstephan 175. Historia Brittonum, etc. s.xiii.
Llanstephan 176. Glanville, G. Monemutensis, etc. From Hyde Abbey. s.xiii.
Llanstephan 196. G. Monemutensis, Historia Regum Britanniae. s.xv.
Llanstephan 199. Abbo Floriacensis, Vita S. Edmundi, etc. s.xiii
The medieval manuscripts included in J. H. Davies, *Catalogue*, are NLW 1, 76, 423 (written 1480s, described in David Thomson, *A Descriptive Catalogue of Middle English Grammatical Texts* (New York/London, 1979)), and 442-6.

A further thirty five Peniarth medieval manuscripts in Latin and English are listed in the *Handlist*, vol. I, pp. 1-18. To these must be added Peniarth 540 (Beda, De natura rerum, s.xii, fragm., 4ff.) and 541 (fragmenta). See above, pp. 4-5.

Medieval manuscripts among NLW MSS which have been listed in the *Handlist* are: MSS 492-9, 572 (Agnus Castus *c*. 1473, fragments of Guy of Warwick, s.xiv[1]), 733, 735 (see *NLWJ*, 18, 197-216), 1222, 1478, 1609iv (Comment. in Metaphysica Aristotelis, fragm., 6ff.), 1610i (Petrus Pictaviensis, Chronicon, fragm., 4ff.), 1611, 2050, 3020, 3024, 3074, 3090,

4874, 4920, 4997, 5001-5, 5008-18, 5020-33, 5035-41, 5043-4 (5001-44 are all in the Bourdillon collection), 5266-7, 5667, 6133-6, 6680, 6985, 7006, 7851, 7855, 8431, 9852, 11330, 11611, 12389, 13052 and 13210. The following NLW MSS have yet to appear in the *Handlist*.

14025A.	Voie de Paradis, prose, fragm., 2ff. s.xiv[1].
14650D.	Beda, In cantica canticorum, etc, fragm., 2ff. s.xii.
15536E.	Missale (Sherbrooke Missal, Yates Thompson 94). s.xiv.
15537C.	Horae (De Grey Hours, Yates Thompson 27). s.xv.
16147A.	Breviarium (Sarum). s.xv.
16338C.	Missale, fragm., 2ff. s.xi/xii.
16347A.	Compilationes fratris Petri de Moguntia. 1510-11.
16983B.	Sermones. s.xiii.
16986A.	Statuta Angliae. s.xiv.
17110E.	Liber Landavensis. s.xii. See *NLWJ*, 25, 133-60.
17430B.	R. Higden, Polychronicon (excerpta). s.xv.
17520A.	Horae (Llanbeblig Hours, Dyson Perrins 15), s.xiv[2].
18951C.	Gesta Romanorum. s.xv. *AR 1964-65*, 28-9.
18952C.	W. Brito, Vocabularium Bibliae (abbrev.). s.xiv. *AR 1964-65*, 40-1.
20143A.	Welsh law in Welsh ('Y'). s.xiv[2]. *AR 1968-69*, 36.
20541E.	Antiphonale (Penpont Antiphonal). s.xiv. *AR 1969-70*, 40-1.
21241E	(Mostyn 71). Lucas glosatus. s.xii/xiii.
21242C	(Mostyn 85). Lydgate, Life of Our Lady. s.xv.
21245D	(Mostyn 181). Beda, Historia Ecclesiastica, etc. s.xiii[2].
21247E	(Mostyn 274). Chroniques de France. *c.* 1500.

For these four MSS see *Mostyn MSS* (1975), above p. 141.

21552B.	G. Monemutensis, Historia Regum Britanniae. s.xiii[2]. *AR 1975-76*, 52.
21553C.	Donatus, Ars maior. s.ix. See *Scriptorium*, 30, 225-31.
21586A.	Cicero, De amicitia, etc. s.xv. *AR 1976-77*, 50.
21587D.	Caesar, De Bello Gallico, s.xv. *AR 1976-77*, 49.
21588C.	Frontinus, Stratagemata. s.xv. *AR 1976-77*, 49.
21589C.	Claudianus, Carmina maiora. s.xiii. *AR 1976-77*, 49.
21604A.	Breviarium (Sarum). From Ireland. s.xiv/xv. *AR 1977-78*, 51.
21608D.	Brut, in English, *c.* 1470. *AR 1978-79*, 60. *NLWJ*, 27, 373-6.
21612A.	H. Augustodunensis, Imago mundi, etc. (formerly in University College, London). s.xiv. *AR 1978-79*, 59. *MMBL*, I, 357-8.
21613E.	Leviticus et Numeri glosatus. s.xii[2]. *AR 1978-79*, 59.
21614C.	Boccaccio, De mulieribus claris, etc. s.xv[1]. *AR 1978-79*, 59.
21623C.	Dictionarium juris canonici, fragm., 14ff. s.xiv/xv.
21664C.	Hugo Floriacensis, Historia ecclesiastica. s.xii. *AR 1979-80*, 61.
21665A.	Sermones de tempore. s.xiii. *AR 1979-80*, 61.
21667D.	L'image du monde. s.xiii/xiv. *AR 1979-80*, 61-2.
21668A.	Psalterium. Written at Bamberg in humanist script, 1450. *AR 1979-80*, 62.
21679B.	W. de Pagula, Oculis sacerdotis. s.xv[1]. *AR 1980-81*, 61.
21680B.	G. Peraldus, Summa de vitiis. s.xiii[2]. *AR 1980-81*, 62.

21693B	(Mostyn 215). Distinctiones. s.xiii[1]. *AR 1980-81*, 61.
21703B.	N. Salernitanus, Antidotarium, etc. s.xiv. *AR 1980-81*, 61.
21875A.	Jeronimus, De viribus illustribus. Written by Milo de Carraria. s.xiv/xv. *AR 1982-83*, 46.
21876A.	Vita S. Katerinae, etc. s.xii. *AR 1982-83*, 46.
21877B.	Psalterium, s.xiii. *AR 1982-83*, 46.
21878E.	Biblia. From Norwich Cathedral. s.xiii. *AR 1982-83*, 46.
21879C.	Officium Hebdomadae Sanctae. s.xv[1]. *AR 1982-83*, 46.
21953D.	Psalterium glosatum. s.xii[2]. *AR 1983-84*, 48.
21972D.	Chaucer (The Merthyr Fragment). s.xiv[1]. *AR 1983-84*, 48. See *NLWJ*, 25, 114-21.
22050A.	Biblia. s.xiii[2]. *AR 1984-85*, 40.
22051A.	Horae. Of London origin. s.xiv[2]. *AR 1984-85*, 40
22080E.	Livius, fragm., 2ff. s.xv.
22081D.	Missale, fragm., 2ff. s.xii.
22251B.	Processionale (Sarum). s.xv.
22252A.	Officium mortuorum (Sarum). s.xv.
22253A.	Breviarium (Sarum). From Lanteglos by Fowey. s.xv.
22423A.	Breviarium (Sarum). s.xiv/xv.
22631C.	Biblia. From Tintern Abbey. s.xiii. See *The Monmouthshire Antiquary*, 6, 47-54.
22688B.	T. de Wygenhale, Speculum juratoris. s.xv.
22857E.	Fragmenta (incl. motets, s.xiii, missale, from Evesham Abbey, s.xv).
22872C.	Aegidius Columna, Liber de regimine principium. s.xiv[1].
22873C.	Rules of the Third Order of St Francis, in English. *c*.1500. See *EETS*, OS, 148.
23205D.	Jean de Rovroy, Les Stratagèmes. s.xv[2].

The following medieval manuscripts are in other archives and collections.
Bettisfield (see above, p. 53)
18. Verse, in French, fragm., 2ff. s.xiii.
19. Vie de S. Melor. s.xiv. See *NLWJ*, 15, 167-76.
Brogyntyn (see above, p.59)
I.8. Brut, in English. See *NLWJ*, 27, 376-7.
I.17 (Porkington 17). G. Monemutensis, Historia Regum Britanniae. s.xiii.
I.25. Legal precedents, in Norman-French. s.xv[2].
II.1 (Porkington 10). Sir Gawain and the Carl of Carlisle, etc. *c*.1470. See *Neuphilologische Mitteilungen*, 54, 33-67.
II.2 (Porkington 15). De legibus, etc. s.xiv.
II.3 (Porkington 16). Explanatio in psalmos [*PL* 116.193]. s.xii.
II.4 (Porkington 18). Biblia. s.xiii.
II.5 (Porkington 19). The Seven Points of True Love. s.xv.
II.6 (Porkington 20). The Prick of Conscience. s.xv.
II.7 (Porkington 21). R. de Bury, Liber Epistolaris. *c*.1325. Edited by N. Denholm-Young (1950).
II.9 (Porkington 23). Collectanea Thomae Edenham O.F.M. 1483.

II.24 (Porkington 40). R. Higden, Polychronicon. s.xv.
II.51 (Roll 1). Petrus Pictaviensis, Chronicon. s.xiii[2].
II.52 (Roll 2). Pedigree-chronicle, *c.* 1465.

Bronwydd (see above, p. 60)
1. G. de Columnis, Historia destructionis Troiae. s.xv.

Chirk Castle (see above, p. 67)
F 11549. Chronicon, etc (a roll). s.xiii-xvi.

Cwrtmawr (see above, p. 73)
MS 671. Horae (?Rheims). s.xv[1].

Dillwyn
MS 1. Horae (Flemish production, English calendar). s.xv[2].
MS 2. Horae (Rouen). s.xv[2].

Minor Deposits (see above, p. 17)
683. Missale (Italian origin). s.xv.

NLW Rolls (see above, p.9)
22 (Ridgeway 1). Pedigree-chronicle. *c.*1470.
39 (Ridgeway 18). Pedigree-chronicle. *c.*1430.
42 (Ridgeway 21). Pedigree-chronicle. *c.*1460-70.
55 (Madryn Roll). Pedigree-chronicle. *c.*1450

Powis Castle (see above, p. 158)
1965 Deposit (unnumbered). Armorial, etc, of Sir Thomas Wriothesley (d.1534).

Wynnstay (see above, pp.190-1).
MS 14. G. Monemutensis, Historia Regum Britanniae, fragm., 20ff. s.xv[2].
MS 36. Welsh law, in Welsh ('Q'). s.xv.

INDEX

This index has value as an index to the names of persons, families, estates and institutions. Those named in the Guide are comprehensively indexed. In this regard the index offers a fair reflection of the Department's archival holdings. But as a topographical index to these holdings it is only of small value: we need only to consider the fact that a small group of a dozen documents may contribute the names of three parishes to the index while the great estate archives contribute none at all. The value as a subject index is also limited, if less so, for similar reasons. Names of Welsh counties where used to identify or locate places have not been indexed, nor, in general, other place-names where used to identify persons. In other respects, also, practicality has prevailed over consistency: artists' and musicians' archives, for instance, have subject entries, but not the innumerable archives of churchmen, politicians, scholars and writers.

205

206

Trehale, 124
Treharne, Reginald Francis, 132
Trehowel, 178
Treleck, manor, 51
Trelewelyn, 84
Tremadog, 119
Trenewydd, 178
Tretower, lordship, 51
Trevecka, Methodist records, 37
Trewern, co. Pemb., 84
Trewern, co. Carm., 178
Trewern Hall, Buttington, 132
Trinsaran Coal, Iron & Steel Co., 52
Tripp, John, 155, 178
Troed-yr-aur, 150
Trofarth, 70
True Ivorites, 136
Trygarn, estate, 64
Trygarn, family, 64
Tuberculosis, 131
Tucker, family, of Sealyham, 169
Turbeville, family, of Cilybebyll, 68
Turnpike trusts, 63, 77, 139, 159, 181
Tweedy, A C, 178
Tŷ Cenedl, 178
Tŷ Mawr, co. Card., 104
Tŷ-glyn, co. Card., 179
Tŷ-llwyd, co. Card., 179
Tyler, family, of Gernos, 166
Tynrhos, co. Card., 138
Tynte, Kemeys-, family, 179
Tywyn, co. Mer., 162, 176, 189

Undeb Cymru Fydd, 179
Unitarianism, 38-9, 89
United Nations Association, 179
United Reformed Church, 179. *See also*
    Congregationalist records
United States of America, 84, 133, 177, 186
United Westminster and Wrexham
    Collieries, 144
University of Wales:
    dissertations, 39
    Estates Committee, 35
    University College of North Wales,
    Bangor, 10
    University College of Wales,
    Aberystwyth, 48, 120, 136
Upton, co. Pemb., 84
Urdd Gobaith Cymru, 180
Usk, lordship, 51

Vale of Neath Brewery, 180
Valentine, Lewis E, 132
Van, estate, co. Glam., 158
Van, lead mines, co. Mont., 156
Vaughan, family, of Bredwardine, 50
    of Bronheulog, 142
    of Corsygedol, 59
    of Courtfield, 71, 78
    of Crosswood, 72, 156
    of Gelli, Ffestiniog, 155
    of Glanllyn, 191
    of Golden Grove, 80
    of Hengwrt, 82
    of Llanelli, 80, 188
    of Llangedwyn, 191
    of Llwydiarth, 191
    of Nannau, 82
    of Plas Llangoedmor, 156, 166
    of Pontfaen, 160
    of Porthamal, 50
    of Rheola, 164
    of Ruardean, 71
    of Rhug, 82, 168
    of Tanymanod, 155
Vaughan, Arthur Owen, 78, 164
Vaughan-Davies, Matthew L, 1st baron
    Ystwyth, 192
Vaughan-Thomas, Wynford, 136
Vaynor Park, 190
Venables, family, of Llysdinam, 124
    George Stovin, 124
    Richard, 124
    Richard Lister, 124
Verney, family, of Clochfaen, 180
Vivian, family, of Swansea, 12, 180
    Henry Hussey, 1st baron Swansea, 180
    John Hussey, 180
Vizard & Son, Monmouth, 181
Voelas, estate, 180
Vorley, H H G, 181

Waddingham, T J, Hafod, 181
Waddington, family, 61
    Georgina, 61
    Janet, 61
    Thomas, 61
Wade-Evans, Arthur Wade, 87, 91
Wales Gas Board, 134
Walsh, family, barons Ormathwaite, 145
    John, 145
    Sir John Benn, 1st baron Ormathwaite,
    145